IMAGES
of America

GEORGETOWN AND WINYAH BAY

To Linda and Bob

Fondly,
Mary Boyd
"Muff"

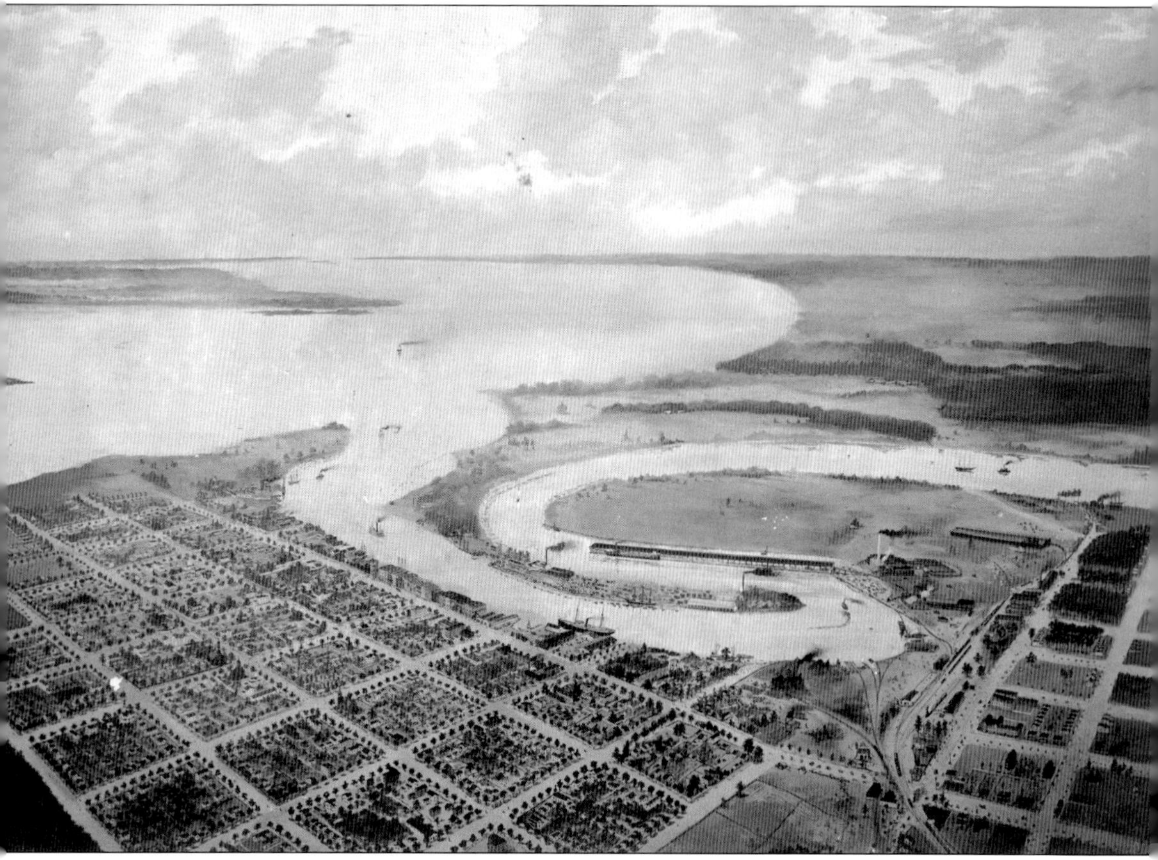

An amazing aerial view of Georgetown was presented in this oil painting of the city by Harper Bond in 1901 for display in the Georgetown booth at the Charleston Exposition of 1902. This large painting today hangs in the city hall. The painting was executed during the administration of Mayor W. D. Morgan and shows some of the 2,000 trees planted by the city during Morgan's time. The artist was reported to have individually measured each structure and block to paint what appears as an aerial view of the city around 1900. (Courtesy of the Georgetown County Digital Library.)

On the Cover: The four-masted schooner *Clara Davis* is docked in the Sampit River just west of Wood Street. The dock buildings of the Atlantic Coast Lumber Company are in the background on the left. Four-masted schooners were cargo vessels that frequently visited the Georgetown city docks in the early 1900s. (Courtesy of the Georgetown County Digital Library.)

IMAGES
of America

GEORGETOWN AND WINYAH BAY

Mary Boyd and James H. Clark
with the Georgetown County Historical Society

ARCADIA
PUBLISHING

ISBN 978-0-7385-8612-9

Published by Arcadia Publishing
Charleston, South Carolina

Printed in the United States of America

Library of Congress Control Number: 2010921330

For all general information, please contact Arcadia Publishing:
Telephone 843-853-2070
Fax 843-853-0044
E-mail sales@arcadiapublishing.com
For customer service and orders:
Toll-Free 1-888-313-2665

Visit us on the Internet at www.arcadiapublishing.com

This book is in memory of Alfred Trenholm and William Doyle Morgan, who had a great appreciation for their town and saw the value in preserving its everyday scenes for those of us who were to come later and see what is now long gone. The mariners and watermen who plied the waters in and around Georgetown for almost 300 years have left behind a heritage of industry and pleasure for modern-day man. To them we owe a debt of gratitude.

Contents

ACKNOWLEDGMENTS

The authors wish to thank Jill Santopietro of the Georgetown County Museum for her encouragement, support, and boundless enthusiasm for this project. Her suggestions and comments were invaluable. Julie Warren of the Georgetown County Digital Library spent much time working with the photographs from the collections housed in the Georgetown County Library to enhance them to publication quality and handled getting permission in using several photographs. We thank her for her patience in answering our many questions. Thanks also to Pat Doyle, Tom Davis, Jim Fitch, and L. C. Sloan for their monumental work in captioning each of the photographs from the Morgan-Trenholm Collection. Most of the photographs included here are from that body of work. Some of the captions used here are written by them or based on their original wording.

Additional information was found in George Roger's *History of Georgetown County*, Sarah Parker Lumpkin's *Heritage Passed On*, Bernard M. Baruch's autobiography *Baruch, My Own Story*, and Ronald Bridwell's *That We Should Have a Port*. Some information was taken from a study of old Georgetown newspapers from 1801 to 1857 by the author, Mary Boyd. Historic Georgetown County Leaflets Nos. 1, 4, and 10 published by the Rice Museum provided information.

A special thanks to Jimmy Elliott for his proofreading and editing. While already involved in other projects, he took the time to delve into this one. His expertise and suggestions are greatly appreciated.

Unless otherwise noted, all images appear courtesy of the Georgetown County Digital Library.

HERBERT
Muff Boyd — 843 527-4203
JULIE WARREN - GT Co DIGITAL LIB.
LIB - 843 545 3300
3316

Introduction

Georgetown, South Carolina, is a colonial city situated at the confluence of five rivers that flow into Winyah Bay on the Atlantic Ocean. Originally, several Native American tribes inhabited the area, and their names mark the rivers and landforms. The Waccamaw, Santee, Pee Dee, Sampit, and Winyah tribes were fairly docile and succumbed mostly to becoming slaves of other Native American groups.

It is believed that one of the earliest attempts to settle the New World happened near Georgetown when Lucas Vasquez de Allyon landed on the shores of Winyah Bay in 1527. The settlement failed in a short period due to heat, fever, and mutiny, and the Spanish sailed off the next year with what was left of their party.

Two hundred years later in 1729, the Reverend Elisha Screven, a Baptist minister, inherited from his mother 274.5 acres on the Sampit River. Lots were surveyed and sold for £7 at first, rising to £15 seven years later. A dispute was settled over ownership of the property between the Reverend Screven and John and Mary Perry Cleland, who claimed the right of an earlier land grant. The town soon became the center of population in this area, and lots were being sold steadily. Georgetown became an international port of entry in 1732, which relieved the citizens of duties and freightage to Charleston, a costly and hazardous journey. Chief exports were lumber, turpentine, and shipbuilding products. Cotton has always been a greatly sought after crop, and the American South has been the region where it grows best. Georgetown has grown its share of this important commodity, and its port handled its shipping through all of its existence. Cotton has been grown in Georgetown since its earliest days and shipped from Front Street docks domestically and abroad. Its production has endured those stormy times when other products have phased out over time and political changes.

By 1737, every lot in the town was taken. Lot owners were required in their contracts to build a house a minimum of 16 feet by 22 feet with a brick chimney. Failure to do this within 15 months resulted in forfeiture of the lot. Shipbuilding products and the growing of rice were initial backbones of Georgetown's economy. In 1740, the growing of indigo replaced these as the real moneymaker and made the gentlemen planters very wealthy. Indigo was a plant that produced a dark blue clothing dye, much sought after by the British, who paid a bounty for exclusive growing privileges. These gentlemen planters met regularly, usually in one of the local taverns, to discuss the cultivation of indigo and the market. They discussed world affairs reported in the British newspapers, usually less than three months old by the time they received them. By 1753, they organized themselves into the Winyah Indigo Society and received a royal charter. Dues were paid in the form of indigo, which was then sold on the open market. Seeking to do something benevolent with their surplus funds, they decided to open one of the first free schools in America. It was the only educational institution between Charleston and Wilmington, North Carolina, for many years. By 1790, the indigo industry was gone, through the turmoil of the war and the loss of the European market. Fortunately, the school continued in operation until the 1880s.

During the Revolutionary War, Marie-Joseph Paul Yves Roch Gilbert du Motier, better known as the Marquis de Lafayette, pledged his services to help lead Continental troops against the British. He arrived in the colonies on June 13, 1777, landing on North Island near Georgetown at Benjamin Huger's plantation. He stayed there for two weeks before being sent to Philadelphia. A friendship was forged, and Huger's son Francis attempted an unsuccessful rescue of the marquis from his prison at Olmutz, Austria, in 1794.

Georgetown was occupied by British troops from June 1780 to May 1781. Little action was seen locally, but one Georgetown citizen, Francis Marion, harassed the British army with his small band of fighters and disrupted their operations, to their great frustration. He was nicknamed "The Swamp Fox" by British general Banastre Tarleton as Marion escaped from one of his raids unscathed yet again into the wilderness of the swamps, which he knew intimately from his hunting and fishing expeditions. Finally, the British evacuated to Charleston, and later that evening, British sympathizers torched buildings along the Sampit River's business district, communicating the fire to other areas of the town.

With the loss in the Revolutionary War, Britain withdrew the lucrative bounty on indigo. The decline in demand and the attention of the planters distracted by war caused the indigo industry to cease. Planters turned once again to rice production and eventually surpassed the wealth brought by indigo. The banks of the Waccamaw, Black, Pee Dee, Sampit, and Santee Rivers were the perfect environment for growing rice. A labor force of slaves cultivated the crop, and by the 1850s, Georgetown County was one of the wealthiest counties in the entire United States. One grower, Joshua John Ward, produced 3.9 million pounds of rice in 1850. A total of 46,765,040 pounds of rice were exported that year. The census of 1860 revealed that Georgetown's population was 85 percent black, 15 percent white—the highest slave ratio anywhere in the United States.

Plantation owners enjoyed the luxury of having several residences for their use during different seasons of the year. Around 1808, families began leaving their plantations in late March or early April to go to their summer places in the mountains of North Carolina or in New England. Local beaches and Charleston were also popular resorts. They stayed there until late fall, when the first cold weather had come and was killing off mosquitoes. They returned to the plantations and stayed until January, when they moved to Charleston for the social season, residing in some of the most elegant and expensive homes Charleston had to offer. In late March, they returned to their plantations, but only to prepare to depart for their summer places. Overseers managed the workload on the plantations while the families were gone.

In 1861, the Civil War brought a harsh end to the rice-growing era in Georgetown. As in the Revolutionary War, only a few skirmishes were fought here. In May 1861, one plantation owner, Plowden C. J. Weston of Hagley, outfitted the Georgetown Rifle Guard with summer and winter uniforms and with English Enfield rifles. They had become Company A of the 10th Regiment of the South Carolina Volunteers. After a false alarm that called them to the beach, Weston provided a lavish full course dinner at Hagley upon their return that included wild turkey and rare wines. China and silver were provided for every place setting.

After the war, Union forces, ironically mostly black troops from Massachusetts, occupied the town from 1865 to 1868. They occupied the Winyah Indigo Society Hall as a hospital.

Without the labor force of the newly freed slaves, rice could not be cultivated. Never again was rice grown in Georgetown County in the quantities previously known, and an elegant Southern lifestyle enjoyed for so many years vanished. After the war, Georgetown limped along through Reconstruction in economic devastation. Finally, in 1889, a group of businessmen set up a forerunner of what was to become the Atlantic Coast Lumber Company (ACL) and began buying up pinelands. Within the next decade, lumber once again put Georgetown on the map. By 1913, the ACL was undisputedly the largest lumber mill on the East Coast and perhaps in the nation. Economic conditions were considerably better, but the ACL eventually began to feel the effects of the Depression, and in 1932 it succumbed to the pressures of the times. During this period, Georgetown supported at least three other lumber concerns.

In 1936, International Paper Company built its kraft paper mill in Georgetown, bringing some economic stability back. The mill is still going strong and is the county's largest employer. In 1969, a German American steel corporation opened a mill on the banks of the Sampit River, further enhancing the economic base. The steel mill closed in 2009. In modern times, development of recreation and tourism industries has brought much deserved attention to Georgetown County. Litchfield, Murrells Inlet, and Pawleys Island have become vacation meccas for hundreds of thousands. Once again, the heritage and beauty of the Grand Strand beaches are attracting people, just as they did almost 300 years ago when those first early immigrants were drawn to the ocean to escape the miasmic air of the plantations. Pawleys Island has been called America's first seaside resort, and it continues to offer a respite to fast-paced city life and an unforgettable experience that is handed down. Families come back year after year and bring their grandchildren. The history and heritage of Georgetown is a story unrivaled anywhere in America and continues to enfold people in its beauty and mystique.

One

Georgetown As It Was

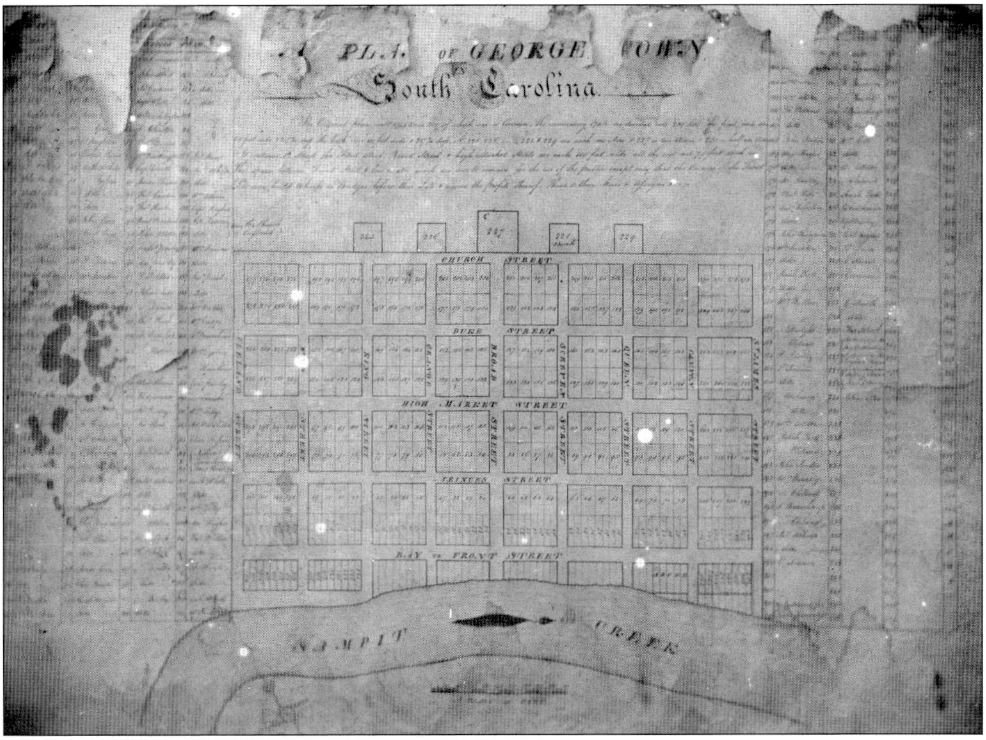

Georgetown was laid out in 1729. This early plan shows the new town was eight blocks by four blocks. Many of the streets were named with royal references, such as King, Queen, Princess (later changed to Prince), Duke, Orange, and St. James. In the original contracts, lot owners were required to construct a building a minimum of 22 feet by 16 feet with a brick chimney within 15 months, or the lot would be forfeited. The town common was located north of the city across Church Street, and each lot owner received the right to pasture one cow and one horse there. (Photograph by the author.)

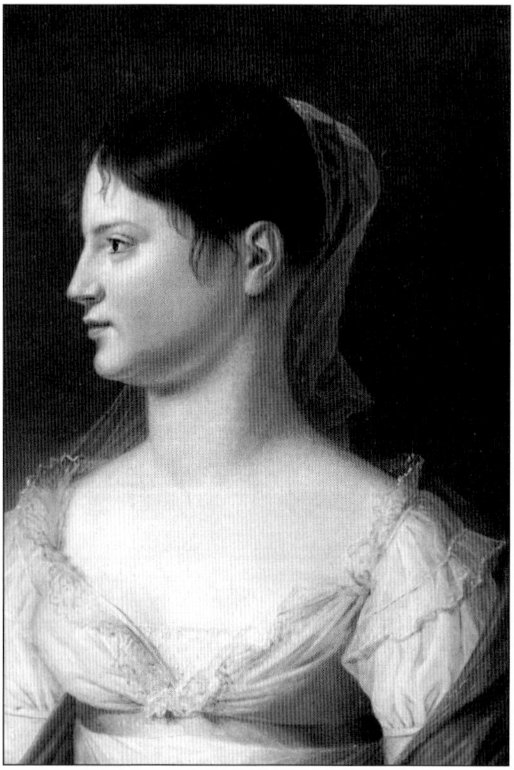

This photograph of John Vanderlyn's portrait of Theodosia Burr Alston, painted in 1802, depicts a young and stylish woman, newly married to Joseph Alston, a rich rice planter of Georgetown. Their home was The Oaks, located within what is now Brookgreen Gardens. Her father was Aaron Burr, vice president of the United States under Thomas Jefferson. A duel that resulted in the death of secretary of the treasury Alexander Hamilton took a toll on Theodosia. After the death of her young son in 1812, Theodosia embarked on a voyage to meet her beloved father but never arrived. It is supposed that she was lost at sea.

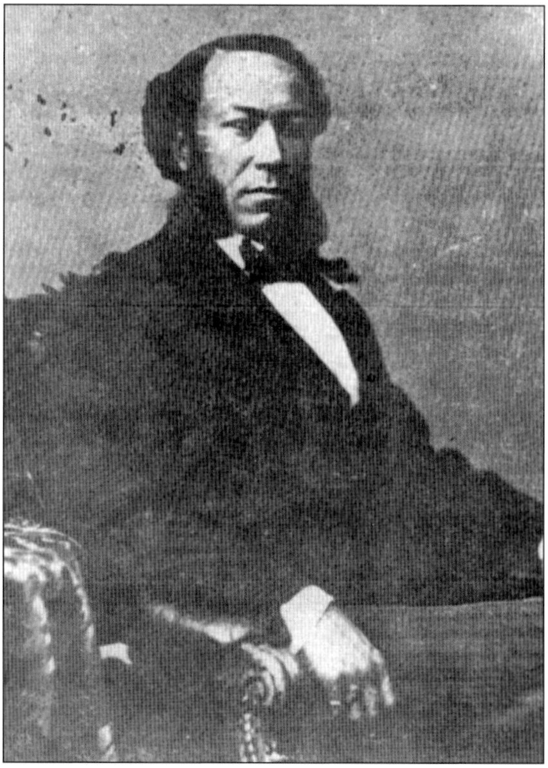

Joseph Hayne Rainey, born in 1832, was the son of a slave. His father was able to purchase freedom for the family through his work as a barber. In 1861, Joseph was working beside his father as a barber when the Civil War began. He knew he would be forced into the Confederate army and made his way to Bermuda. He returned to Georgetown after the Civil War ended. In 1870, he became the first African American in the United States to be appointed then elected to serve in Congress. He served in the House of Representatives from 1870 until 1878.

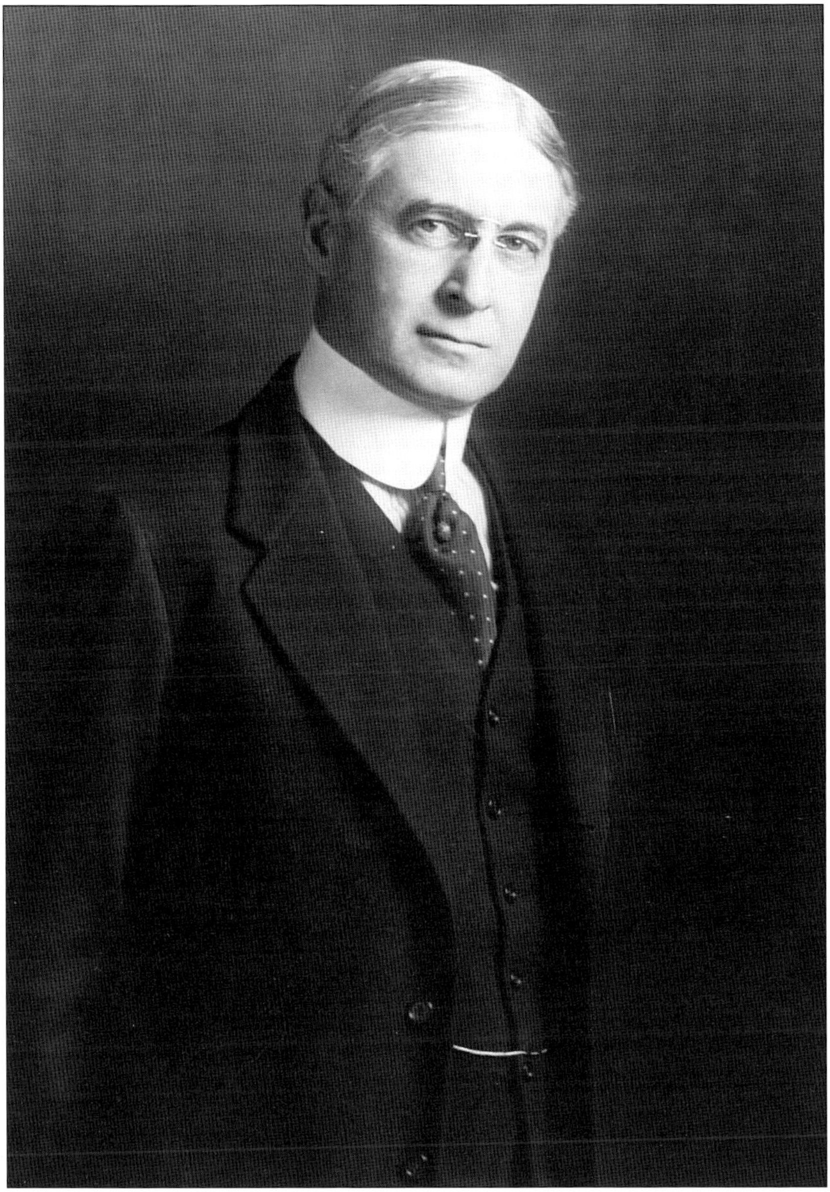

Bernard Baruch was born in Camden, South Carolina, in 1870. The family moved to New York, where he received an education that enabled him to become an influential Wall Street broker. He became very wealthy, and his financial advice was sought by Presidents Woodrow Wilson and Franklin Roosevelt. He purchased Hobcaw Barony near Georgetown and used it as his winter home between 1905 and 1910. There he entertained many dignitaries, including Sir Winston Churchill. Guests arrived from every area of society, including the political, medical, industrial and entertainment industries. Pres. Franklin D. Roosevelt spent a month at Hobcaw during World War II recuperating from polio. Baruch was one of many Jews who helped shape Georgetown. Jewish presence can be traced to the 1760s when Abraham and Solomon Cohen, along with Mordecai Myers, arrived. By 1800, there were 80 Jews, approximately 10 percent of the population. They became men of prominence, active participants in public affairs and social organizations through the 20th century. (Courtesy of the Belle W. Baruch Foundation.)

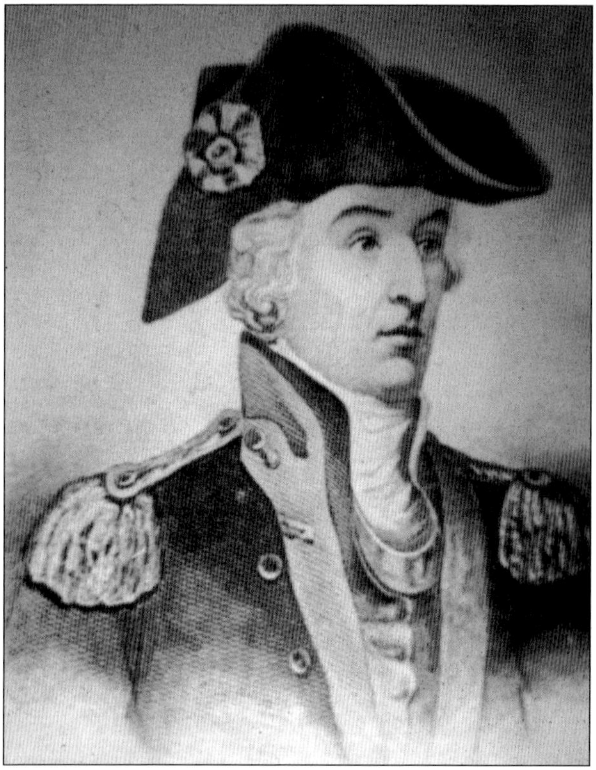

Francis Marion, better known as "The Swamp Fox," was born in Berkeley County in 1732. His family moved to the Georgetown area when he was quite young. Francis enjoyed hunting and fishing as he grew up and his knowledge of the backcountry and swamps in the area became useful to him as a general in the Continental Army. The swamps became his base of operations as he planned and carried out very effective surprise attacks against the British, acting on information from informants in Georgetown and Charleston. Upon another chase into the swamps, British general Banastre Tarleton called him "that wily old swamp fox," a nickname that followed him. Marion died on his estate in 1795 at the age of 62 and is buried in Berkeley County. (Courtesy of the G. Wayne King Slide Collection, Florence County Library.)

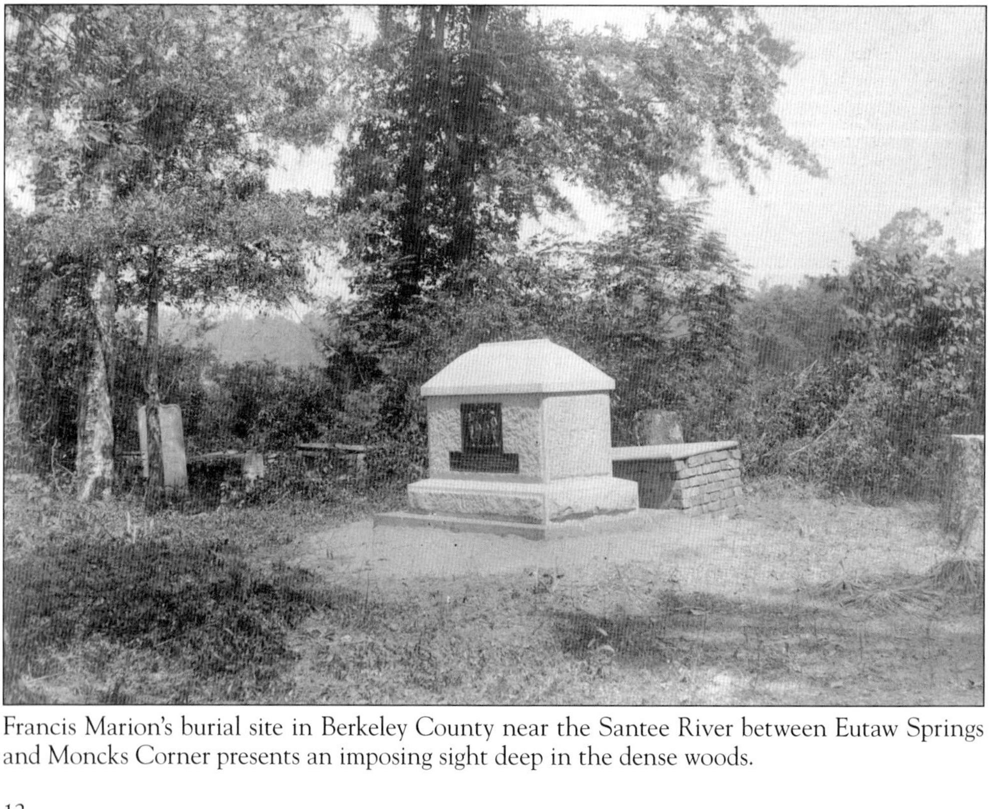

Francis Marion's burial site in Berkeley County near the Santee River between Eutaw Springs and Moncks Corner presents an imposing sight deep in the dense woods.

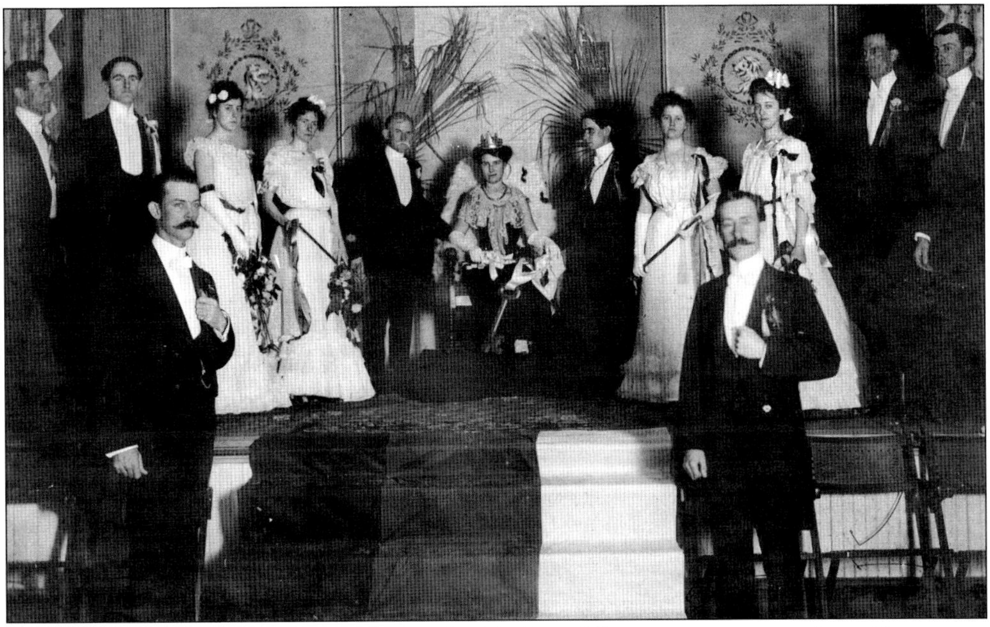

Social events, such as this carnival, were highlights of Georgetown society. Lena Young was crowned queen of the carnival of 1906 and given a key to the city in the ceremony pictured here. The two men in the foreground are Tom Forbes (left) and Fritz Young (right). From left to right on the stage are an unidentified man, A. I. Woodcock, Lee Burns, Kate Morgan, W. D. Morgan as the queen's escort, queen Lena Young, Herman Schenk, Annie Doar, Margaret Burns, Mayor Hugh Fraser, and an unidentified man. Splendid music was furnished by the carnival band and festivities lasted until a late hour.

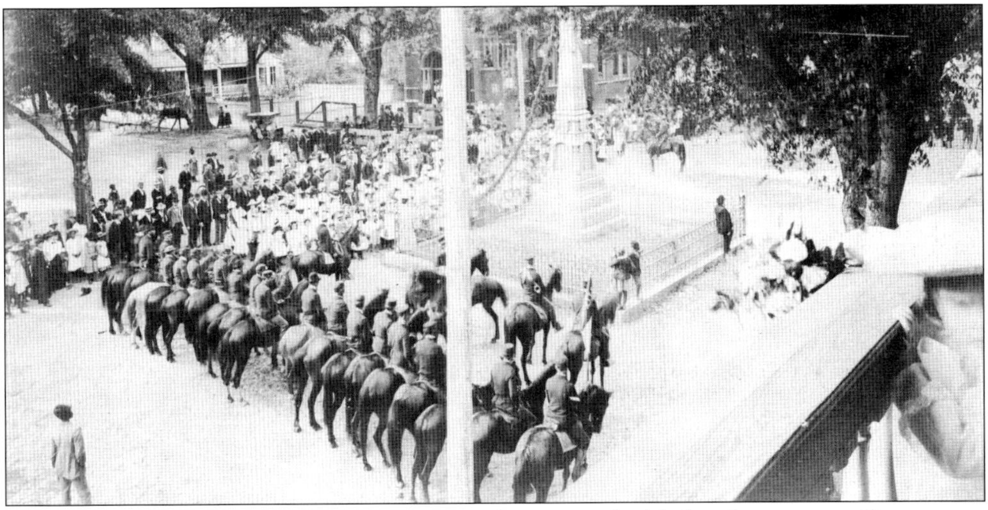

The annual celebration of Confederate Memorial Day was a highlight of activities in Georgetown for many years. One news account relates that all ships in the harbor displayed bunting and flags on Memorial Day, and at 9:00 a.m. all church bells tolled. Citizens gathered at the Winyah Indigo Society Hall at 4:00 p.m. for songs and speeches. Then a procession that included the Georgetown Rifle Guard, Marion's Men of Winyah, schoolchildren, the United Daughters of the Confederacy, and other citizens formed and marched to this Confederate monument at the corner of Broad and Highmarket Streets, where another ceremony was held.

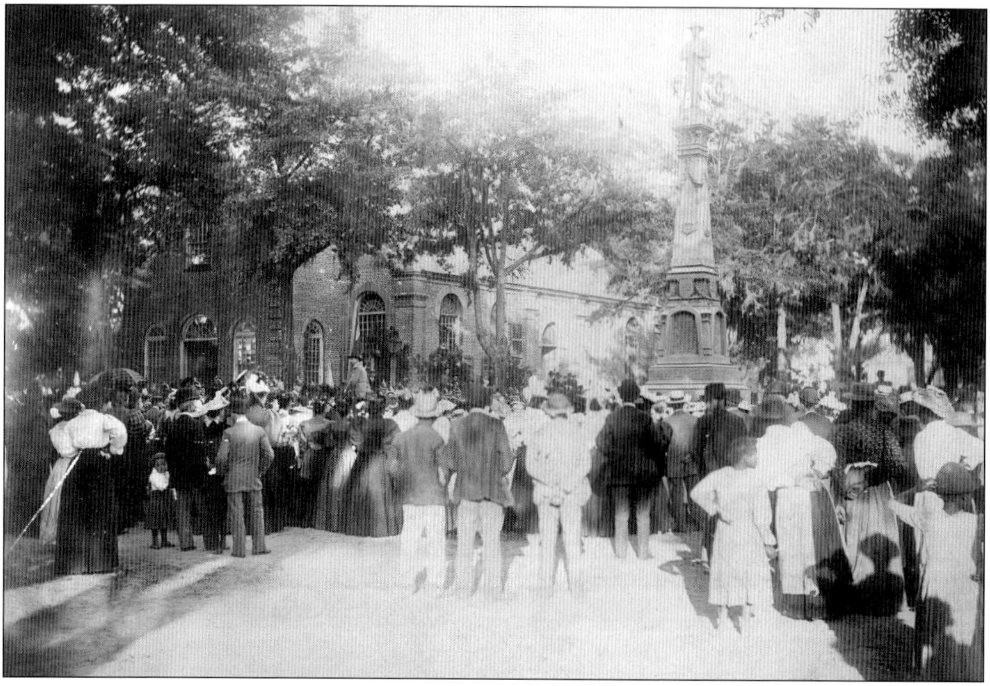

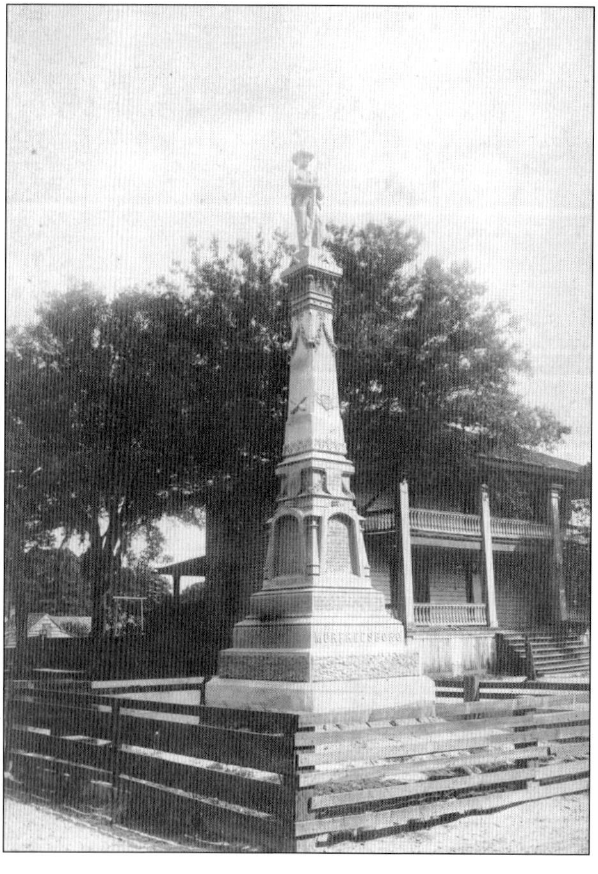

A typical Memorial Day event held in Georgetown is seen here. A high point of the celebration was the firing of a salute by the Georgetown Rifle Guard in tribute to the men of Company A of the South Carolina 10th Regiment, who were engaged in many of the battles of the Civil War. Historic Prince George Winyah Episcopal Church is in the background.

A monument to the men of Company A, 10th Regiment, was erected in 1891. This early photograph was taken before an iron fence was installed. On Confederate Memorial Day, there would be a parade down Front Street, speeches at the Winyah Indigo Society Hall, and then wreaths of flowers were placed at the foot of the monument. The celebration was continued well into the 20th century. The monument was later moved to the Baptist Cemetery on Church Street at the head of Screven Street.

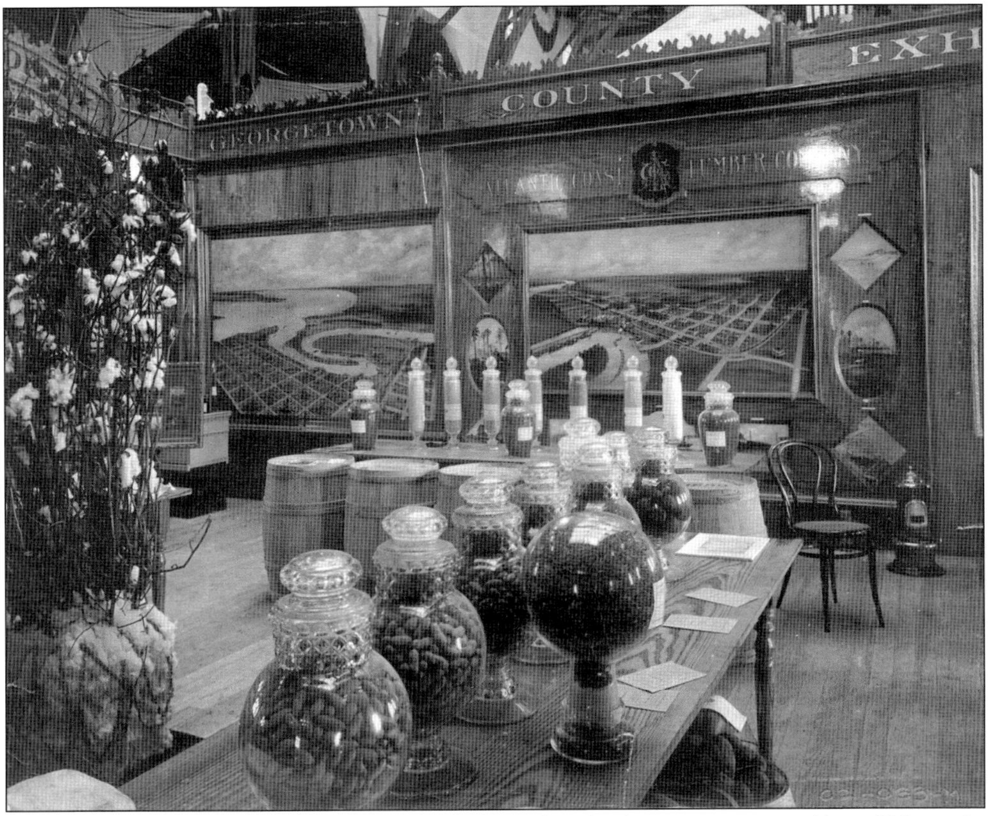

On April 17, 1902, Georgetown Day was celebrated at the Charleston Exposition. About 700 people, led by Mayor W. D. Morgan, arrived in Charleston on a train with 12 special cars. Georgetonians had reason to be proud of the exhibit pictured here, as it won third place. The two oil paintings show aerial views of the city before airplanes were invented. On left is the old city. The other is Atlantic Coast Lumber Company.

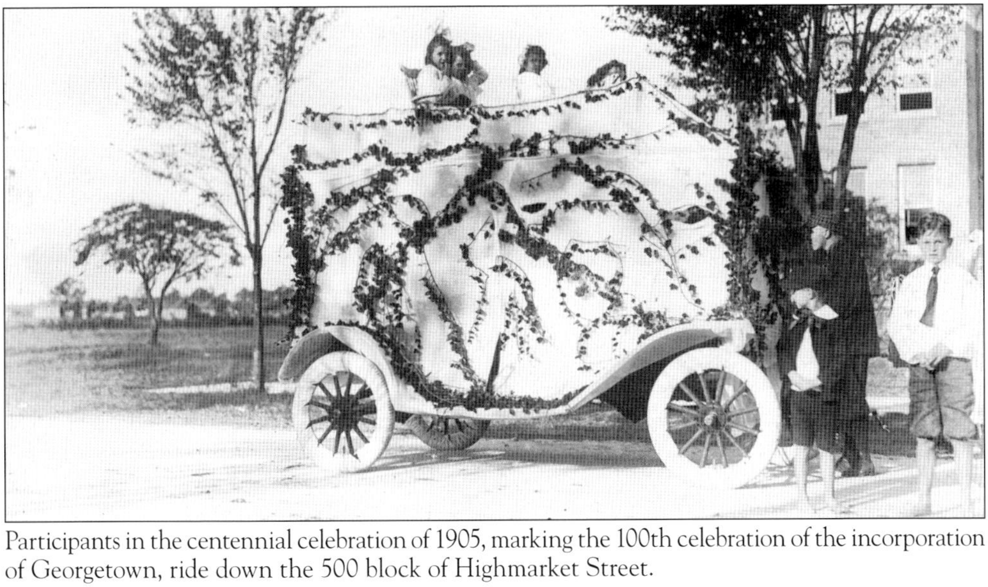

Participants in the centennial celebration of 1905, marking the 100th celebration of the incorporation of Georgetown, ride down the 500 block of Highmarket Street.

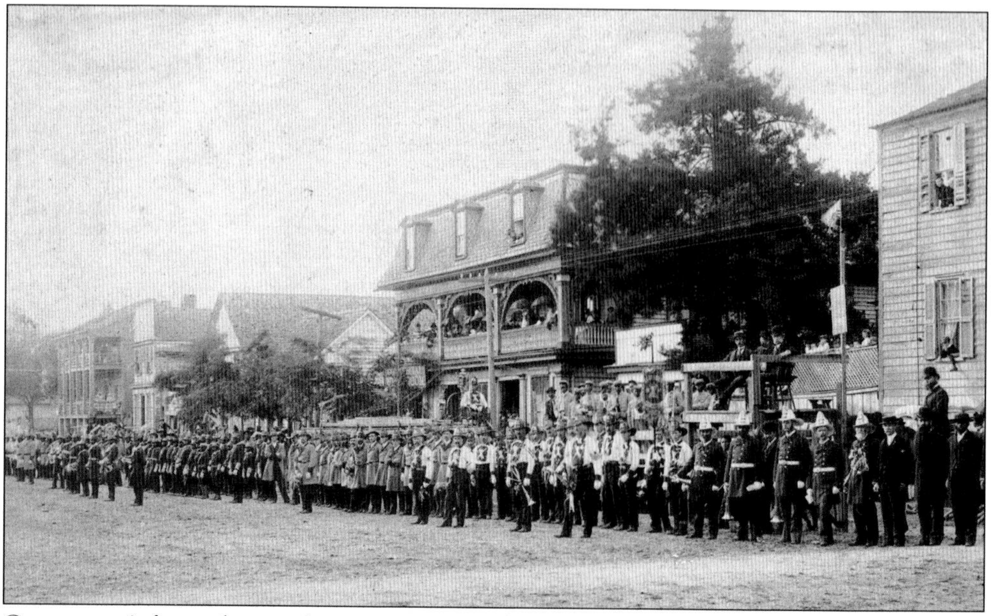

Georgetown's four volunteer fire companies are drawn up on the north side of the 700 block of Front Street for their annual inspection and races. The band is ready to strike up, and the spectators are, literally, coming out of the walls and over the fences. A newspaper clipping from one of W. D. Morgan's scrapbooks, dated 1888, tells of the 17th annual parade of the fire companies. There were four companies organized, two white (the Salamander Hook and Ladder Company and the Winyah Steam Fire Company) and two African American (the Heston Fire Engine Company and the Star Fire Engine Company). Each had its own fire engine and engine house located in various parts of town to give good protection. The Commercial Hotel is the large building with the three dormer windows. None of the buildings seen in the photograph remain.

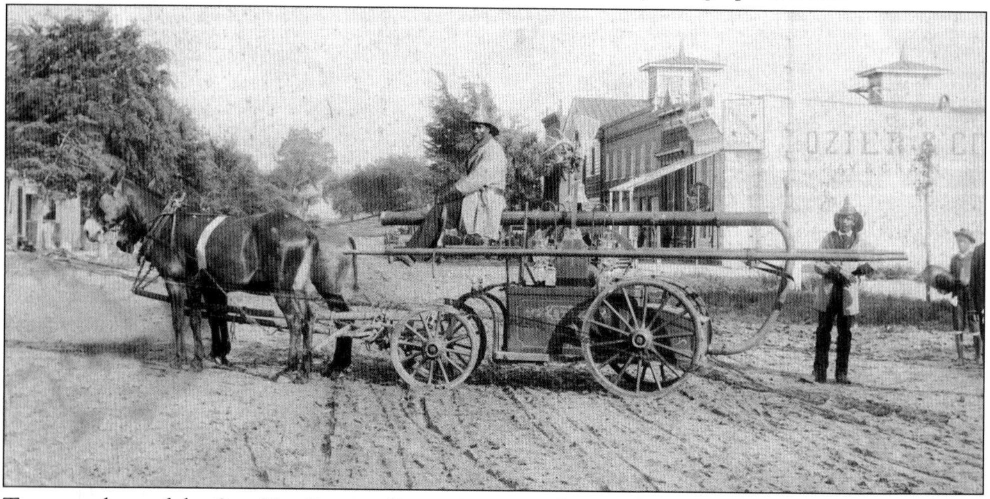

Two members of the Star Fire Engine Company, one of two African American groups (the other being the Heston Fire Engine Company), pose in readiness, with the pump engine harnessed to a pair of horses. One company was housed on King Street, but the men are seen here in the 600 block of Front Street. The building with the two cupolas is the Baltimore and Carolina Warehouse, and next to that is the Winyah Engine Hall. This photograph is looking eastward on Front Street.

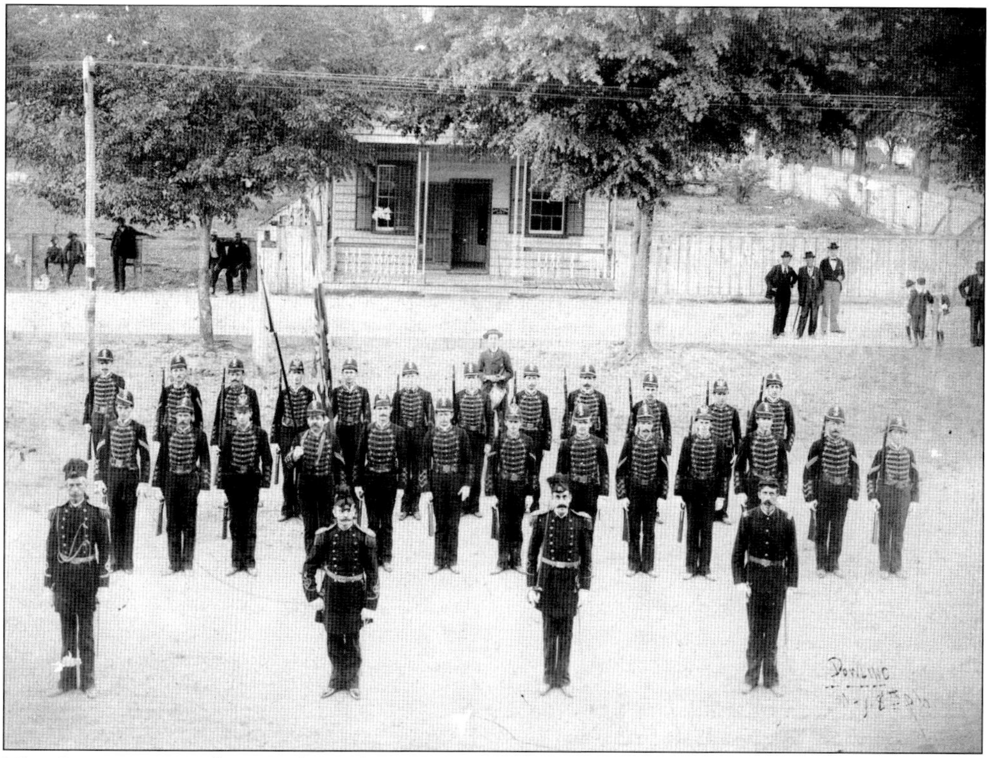

The Georgetown Rifle Guard parades in dress uniform on Front Street. The photograph is dated and signed May 8, 1906. The guard became Company A of the South Carolina 10th Regiment during the Civil War and fought in several important battles: the Battle of Atlanta, Chickamauga, Murfreesboro, Corinth, and Missionary Ridge.

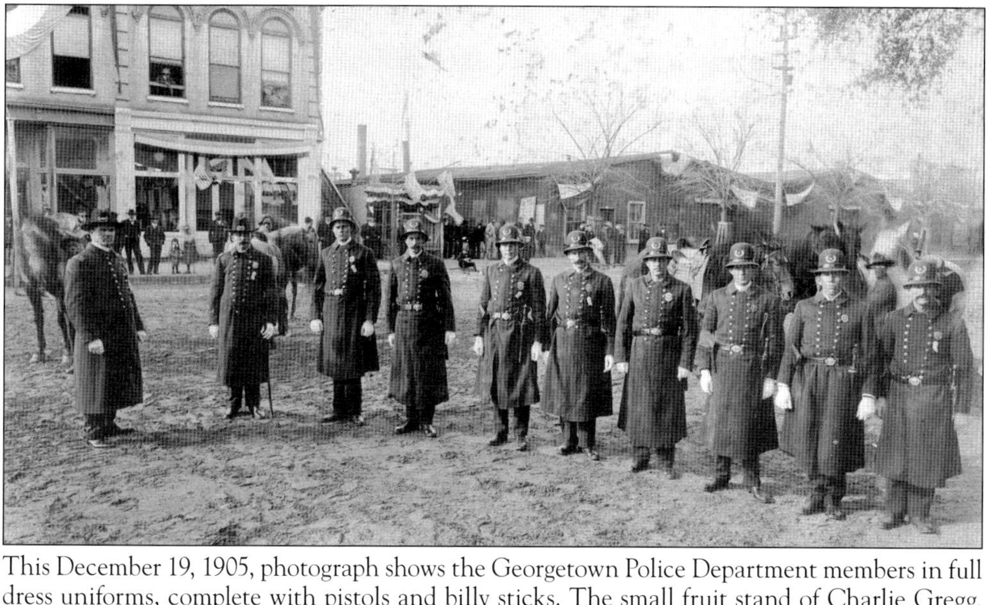

This December 19, 1905, photograph shows the Georgetown Police Department members in full dress uniforms, complete with pistols and billy sticks. The small fruit stand of Charlie Gregg, thoroughly decorated for the Centennial Parade, is seen between the Standard Opera House and the Georgetown Grocery warehouse in the 800 block of Front Street.

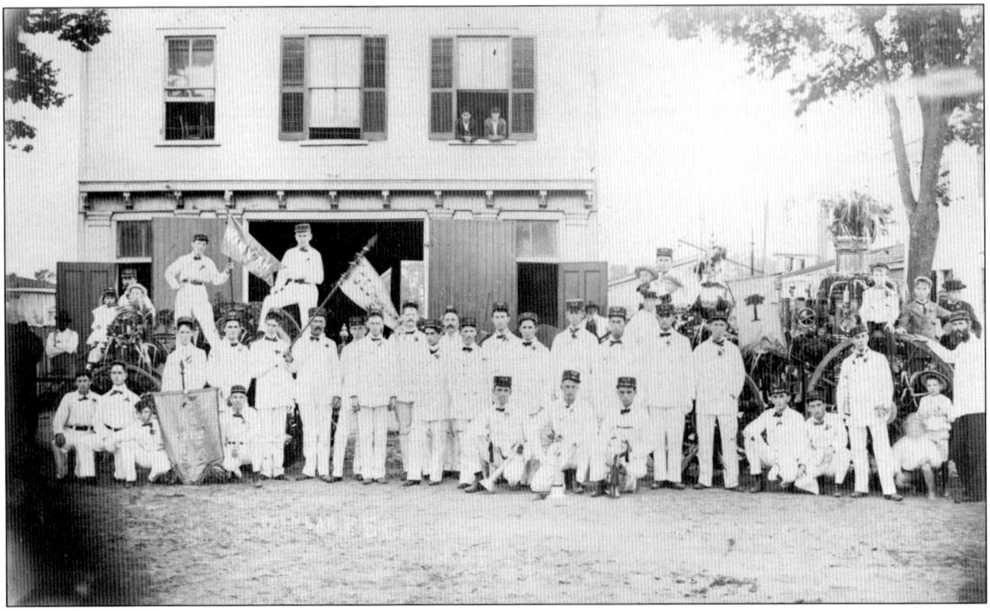

The Winyah Fire Engine Company is posed before its firehouse at the foot of Queen Street. The engine seen at the right is decorated, probably for the annual fire company inspection, competition, and parade. The ladies dressed the engine, and the gentlemen tried to win victory in the competitions. The upstairs hall was used for various entertainments, with the Palmetto Club meeting there regularly. Kate Morgan held dancing and deportment classes here also. The warehouses of Congdon and Hazard are to the right.

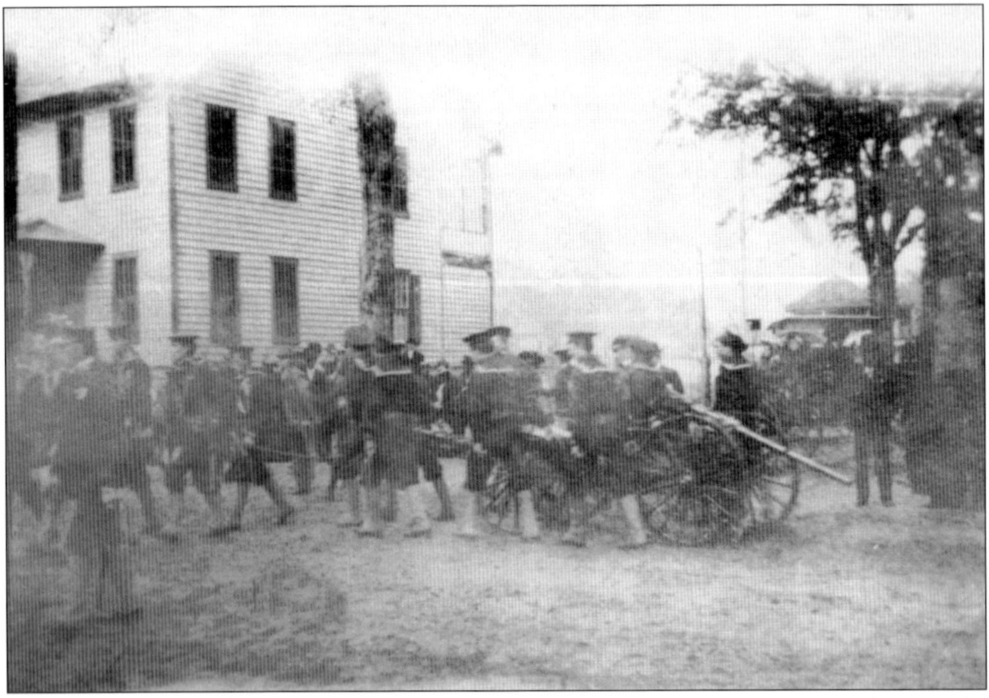

Sailors with the naval reserve pull cannons for the centennial celebration of 1905. They may be standing on the corner of Cannon and Prince Streets.

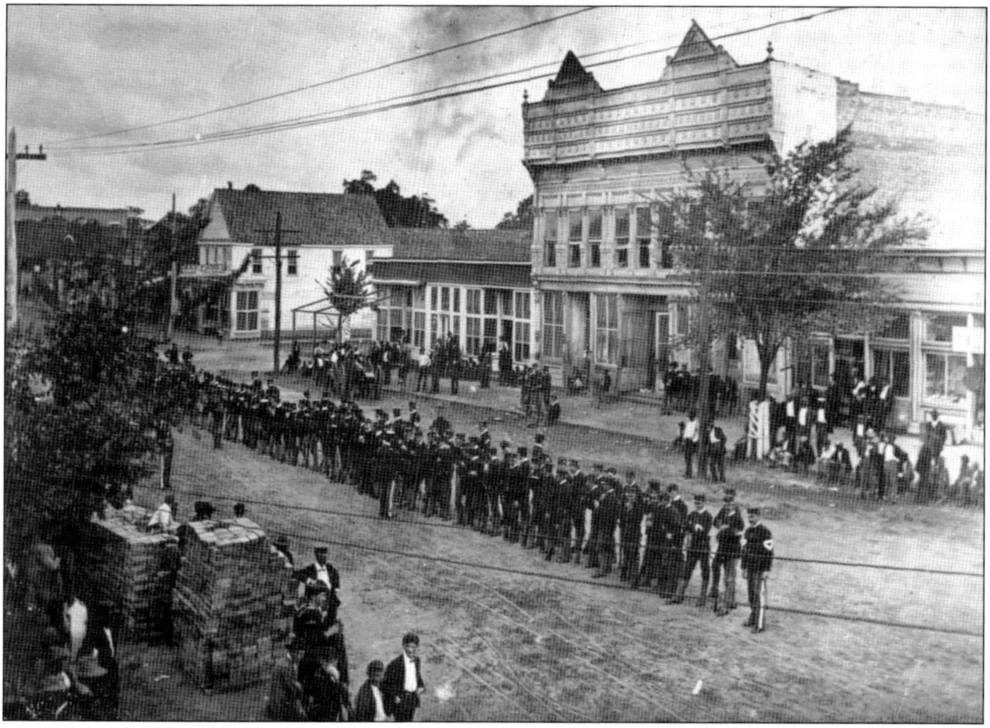

Georgetown Rifle Guard is seen here on parade on Front Street.

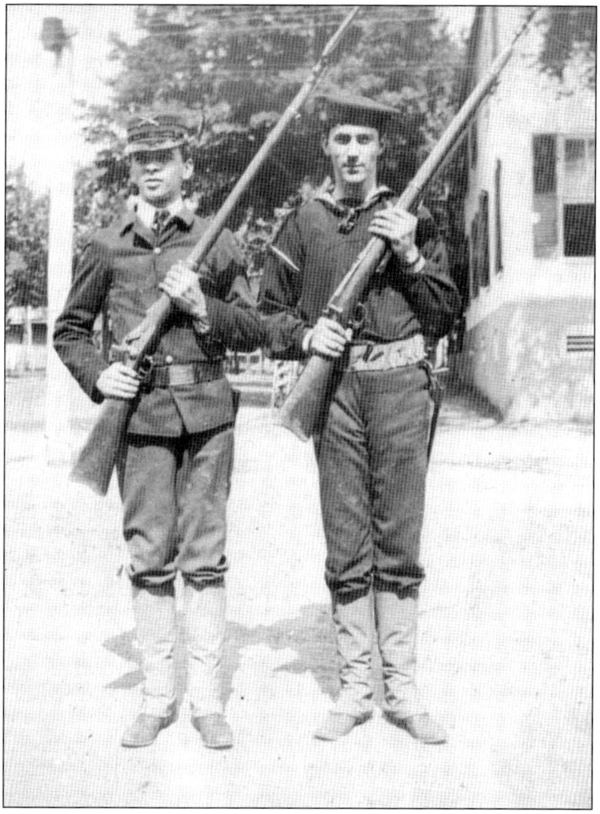

Two unidentified guards stand ready to act. They were from one of the four militia groups sent to Georgetown in 1900 during the trial of John Brownfield, a black man who was accused of shooting a white sheriff's deputy, creating a racially explosive situation.

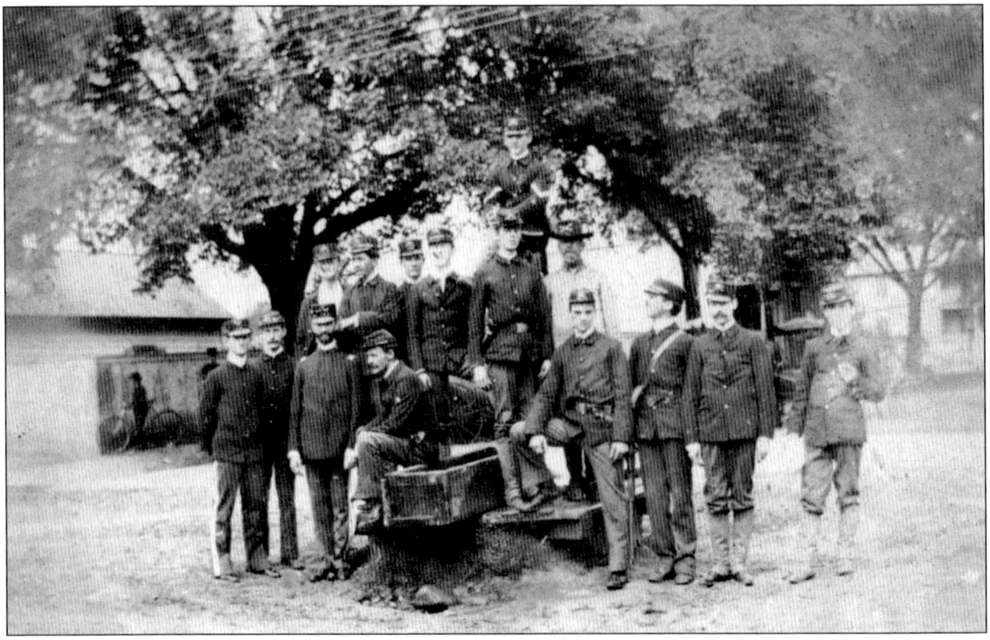

Members of the Washington Light Infantry stand in a Georgetown street. The WLI, sent in response to the Brownfield trial, was organized in 1907 after citizens of Charleston began to fear a second war with Britain. It was named in honor of George Washington.

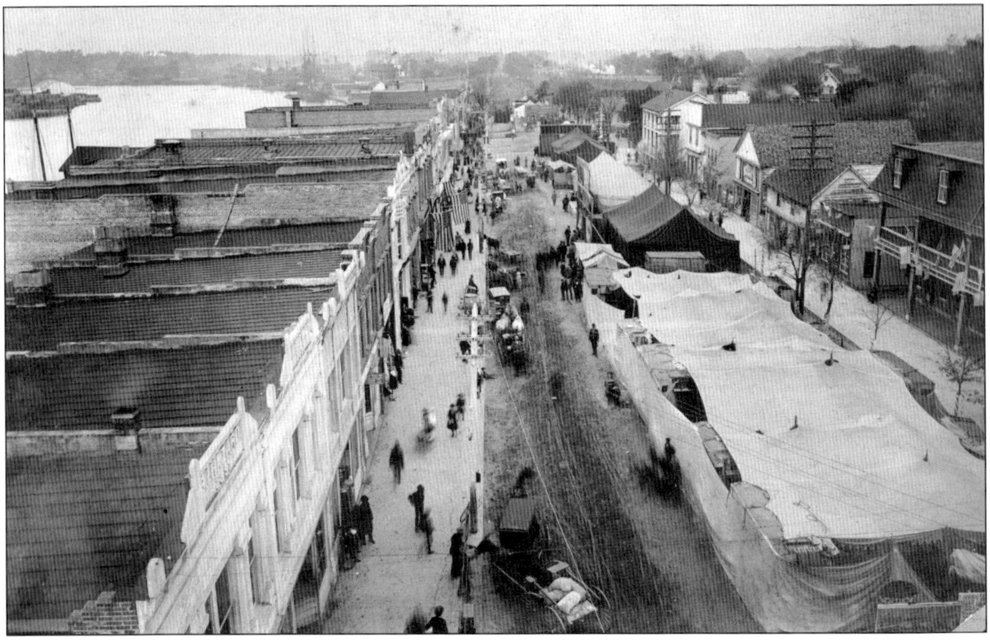

The circus came right to town in Georgetown around 1900, when it was set up in the middle of Front Street in the heart of the business district. Many of the buildings seen on the south side of Front Street (on the left) were built in the 1890s and were in use in the 1970s. All of the buildings on the north side of the street, including the two-story Gladstone Hotel (the white structure extending over the sidewalk), have been demolished. The large booth near the end of the row at Broad Street was called Gay Paris. The picture was taken from the town clock.

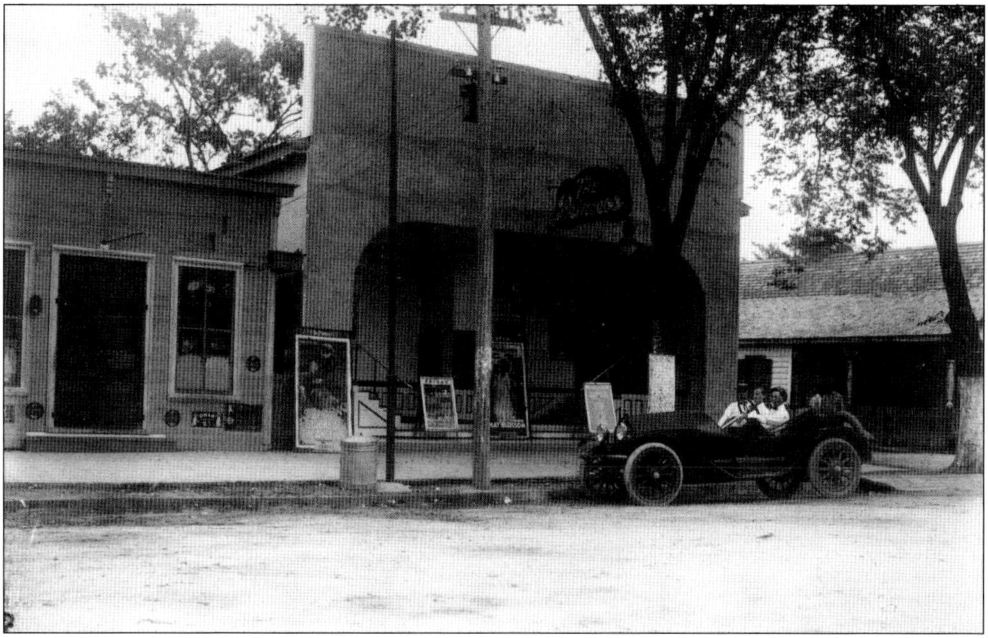

The Princess Theater was one of several theaters in Georgetown in the early 1900s. The Peerless, the Palace, and later the Strand provided an exciting diversion to everyday life. The Princess was located at 624 Front Street from 1914 to 1916.

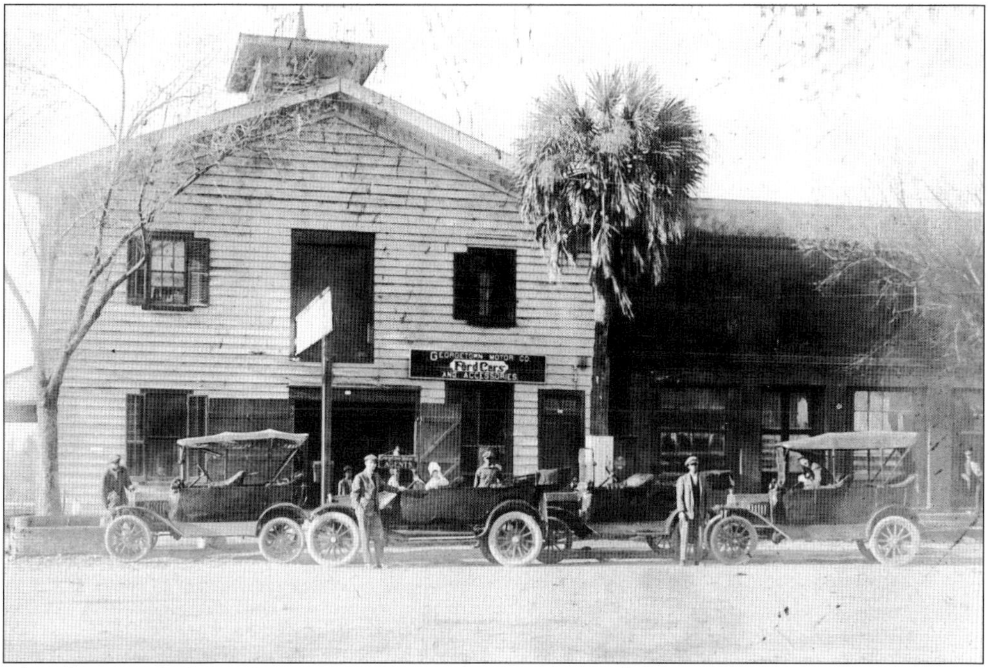

This photograph shows the Georgetown Motor Company and Accessories Store, which sold Ford automobiles. A September 15, 1915, advertisement from the *Georgetown Times* claimed, "Ford, the Universal Car." The Ford Motor Company was offering a Ford Runabout for $390, a Ford Touring Car for $440, and a Ford Town Car for $640. The advertisement also says that there was no speedometer included in that year's equipment, otherwise cars were fully equipped.

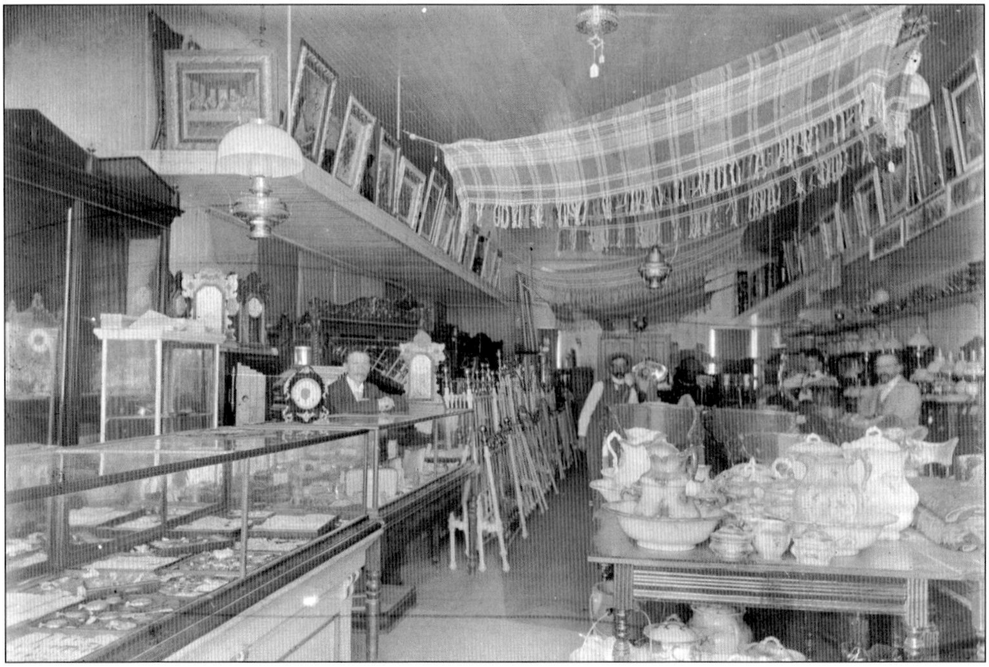

The interior and individuals shown in this photograph are unidentified, but it is typical of Georgetown business establishments in the 1890s. Most stores on Front Street were narrow and paneled, with narrow boards on walls and ceilings. There were several uses for this building, from dry goods to furniture.

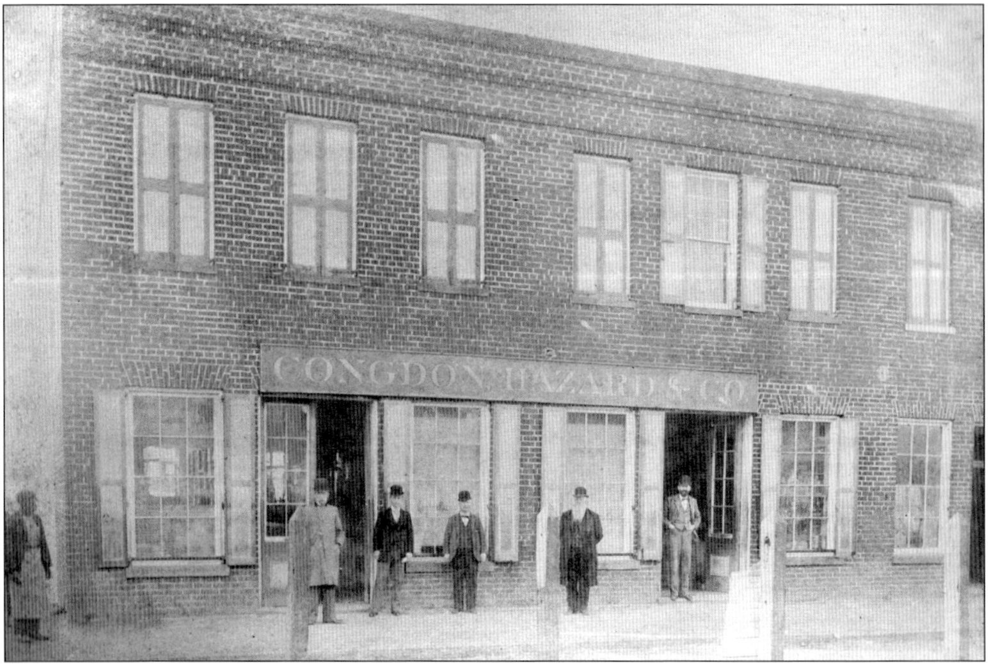

The Congdon, Hazard, and Company store was located at 701–703 Front Street. The six men posed in front are possibly owners and clerks. George R. Congdon and Benjamin I. Hazard operated a shipping and general merchandise business in Georgetown that they formed after the Civil War.

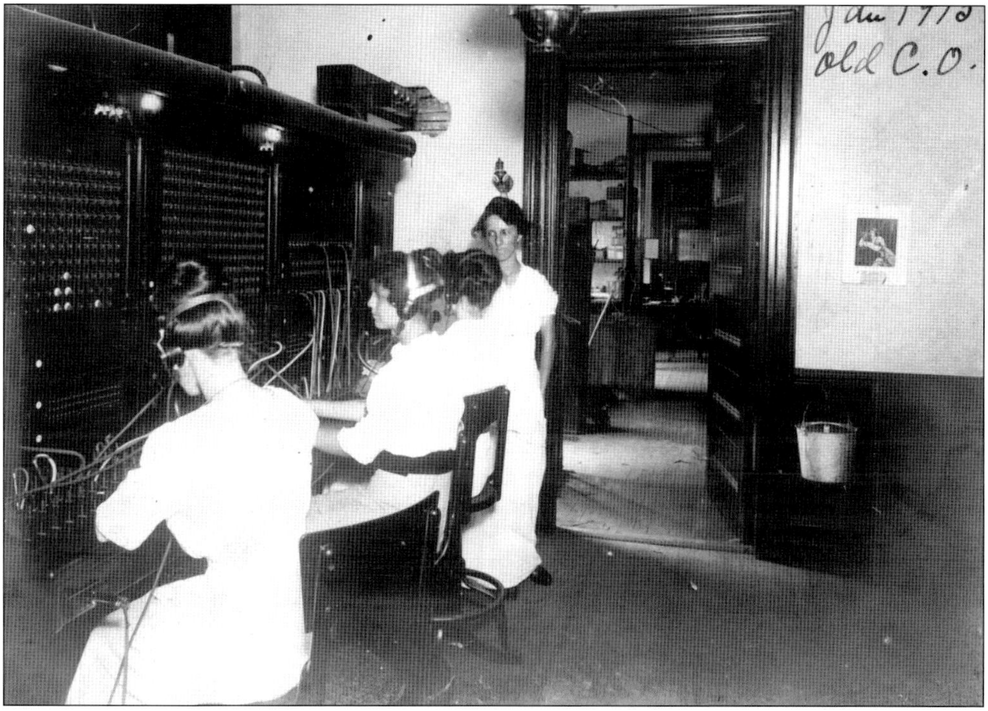

The telephone switchboard is described in a newspaper article of 1904 as the latest improvement. The telephone company spent $5,000 to install the switchboards. The user had simply to pick up the telephone and a button would light up, prompting the operator to ask what number the caller wished to reach. This photograph is dated January 1912 and shows three operators and a supervisor. The Home Telephone Company was located on the second floor of the Bank of Georgetown building.

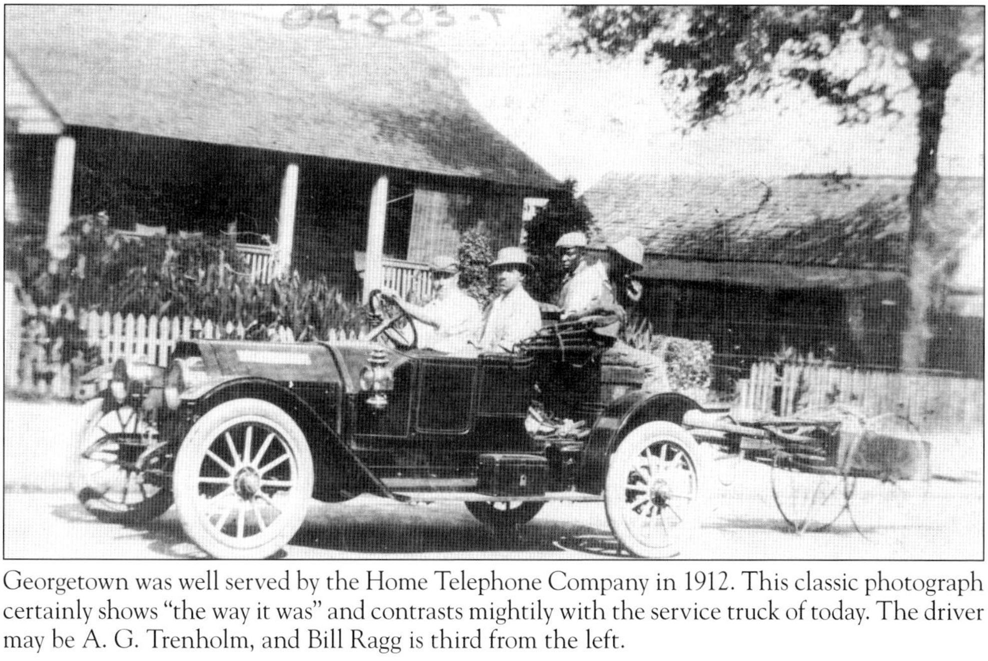

Georgetown was well served by the Home Telephone Company in 1912. This classic photograph certainly shows "the way it was" and contrasts mightily with the service truck of today. The driver may be A. G. Trenholm, and Bill Ragg is third from the left.

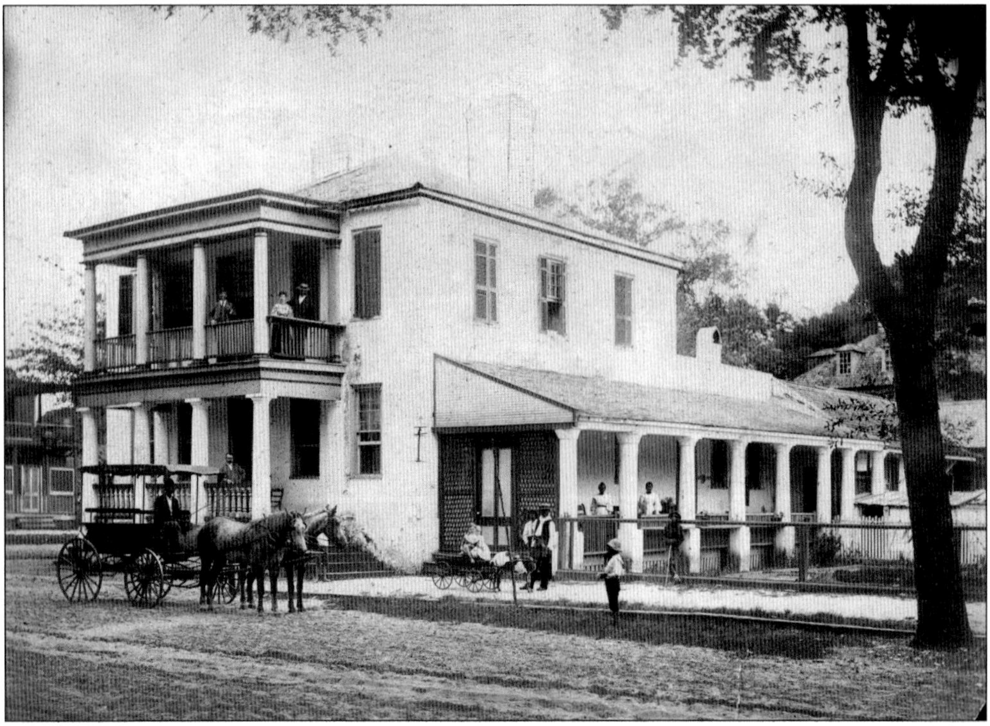

This building at the intersection of Prince and Screven Streets was built around 1735 and is said to be the first banking house in the colonies. It was a bank for more than 100 years. It has also been the Winyah Inn, an armory of the Georgetown Rifle Guards, and home to the Masonic Lodge in the 20th century. Today it is the Georgetown County Museum.

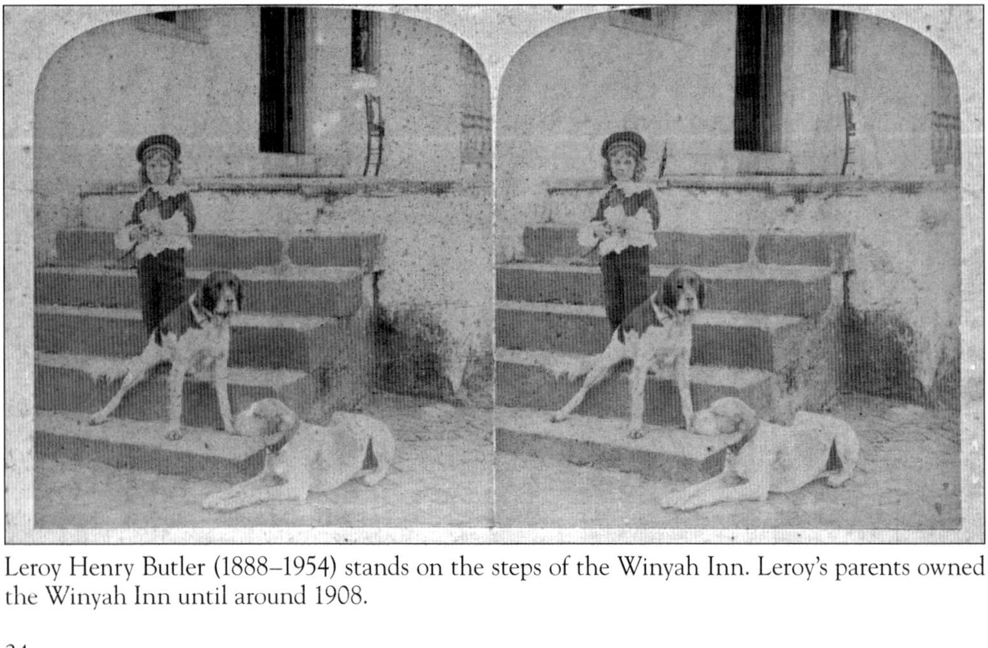

Leroy Henry Butler (1888–1954) stands on the steps of the Winyah Inn. Leroy's parents owned the Winyah Inn until around 1908.

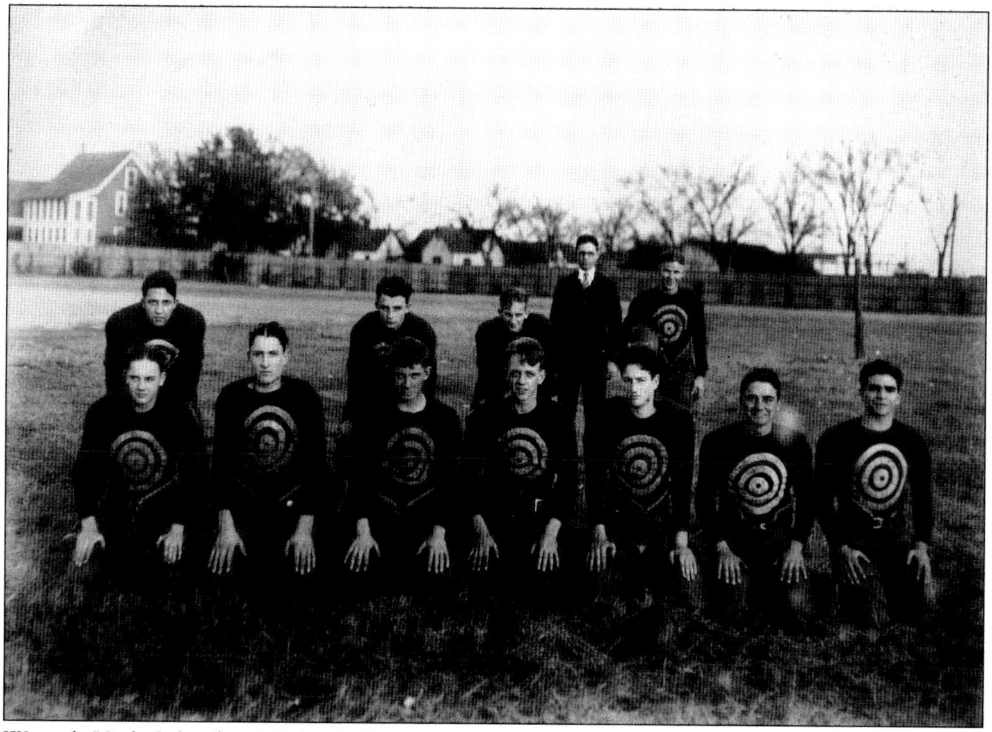

Winyah High School's 1927 football team commanded respect and enjoyed an enviable record. Shown from left to right are (first row) Beverly Sawyer, Bill Brown, Bill Higgins, Francis Siau, Sylvan Rosen, Lawrence LaBruce, and Joe Joseph; (second row) John Assey, Charles Barker, Herbert Hucks, and Basil Fore. Standing in the back is coach Tom Bailey.

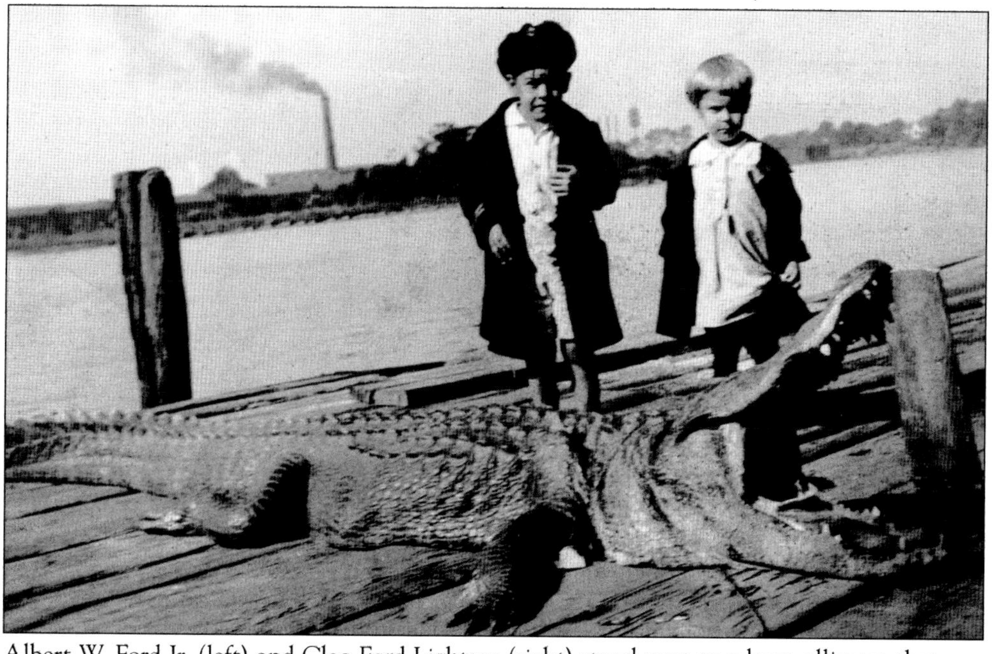

Albert W. Ford Jr. (left) and Cleo Ford Lightsey (right) stand next to a large alligator that was pulled out of the Sampit River in Georgetown.

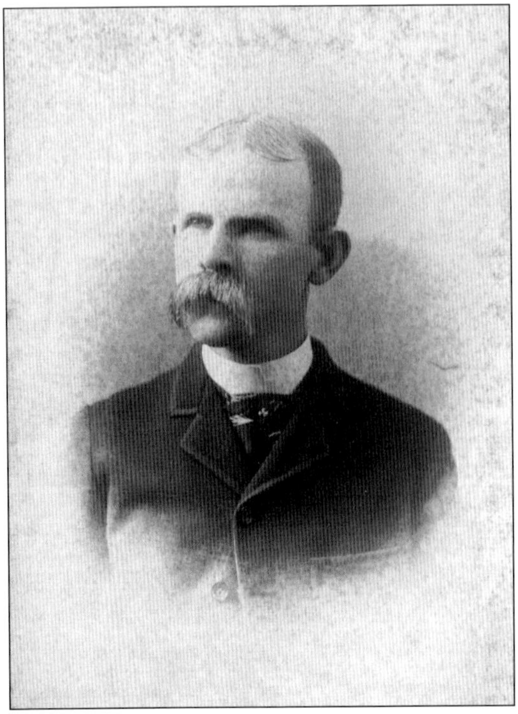

William Doyle Morgan is best known for the time he served as Georgetown's first mayor. Born in New York City, he moved to Georgetown with his family as a young child. His father died when he was 13, leaving William to care for his mother and three sisters. He worked as the assistant postmaster and was known for his careful bookkeeping, a skill he would later use in his job as the founder and president of the Bank of Georgetown.

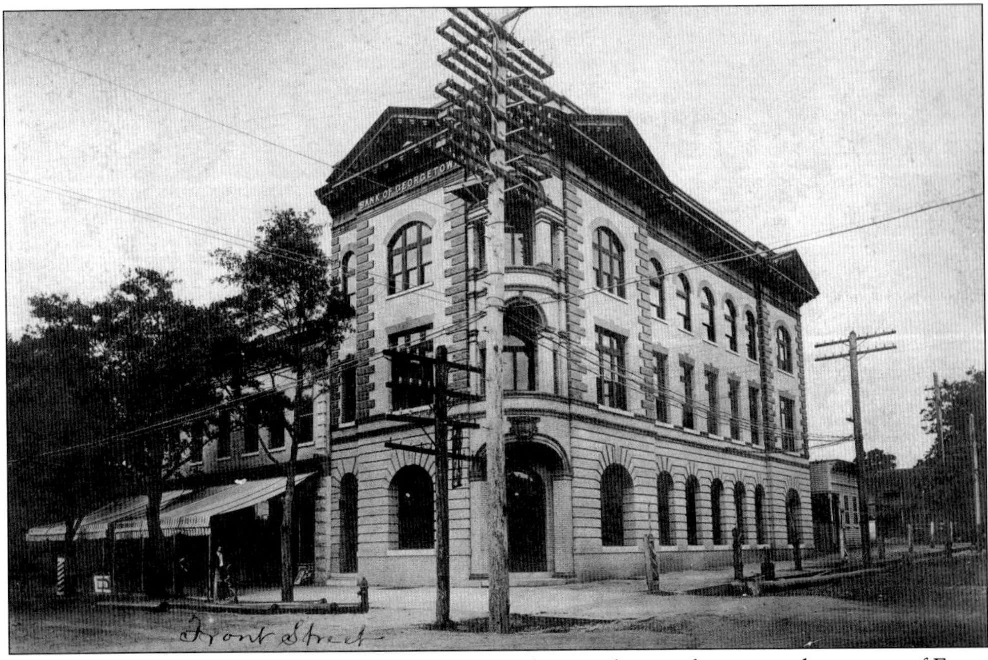

The Bank of Georgetown building was located at the very heart of town, at the corner of Front and Broad Streets. It was the tallest building in town. Morgan founded the bank in 1891 and was able to build this elaborate structure by April 1904, where it operated under his leadership until 1929. It was razed in 1959 because of structural weakness resulting from constant flooding of the basement. The small building behind the bank was the office of Dr. F. A. Bell, who practiced medicine in Georgetown for over 50 years.

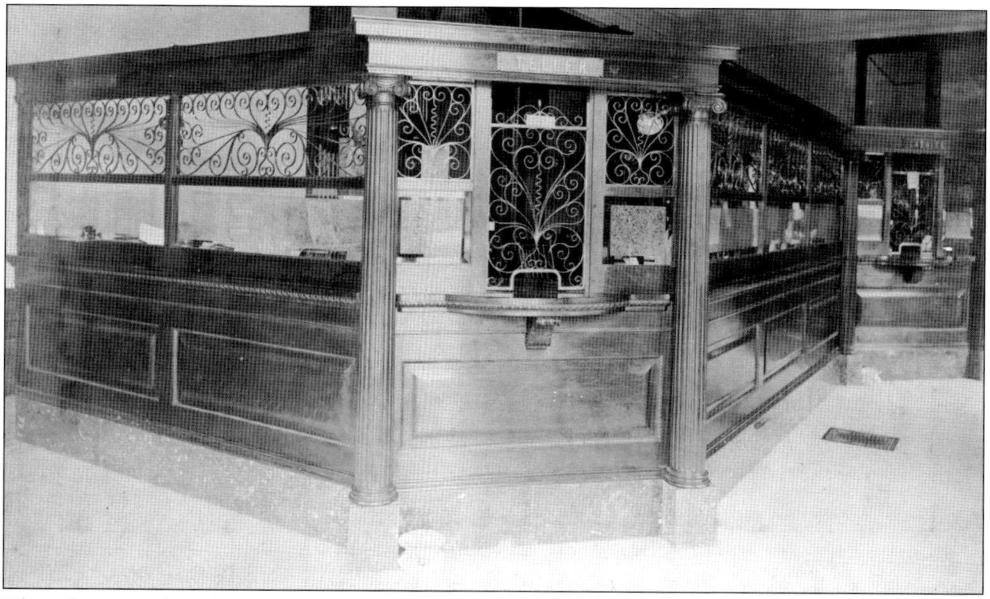

This photograph, taken in 1904 when the Bank of Georgetown moved into its new building, shows elaborate teller and cashier cages. The marble base, stained wainscoting with beaded trim, frosted glass the intricate ironwork, and the molding at the top are the epitome of refinement. The Ionic columns and decorative round counters are reminders of bygone elegance, not to mention the Ionic pilasters on the far wall. The spittoons placed strategically also attest to another time. The bank operated here until 1932 when it closed.

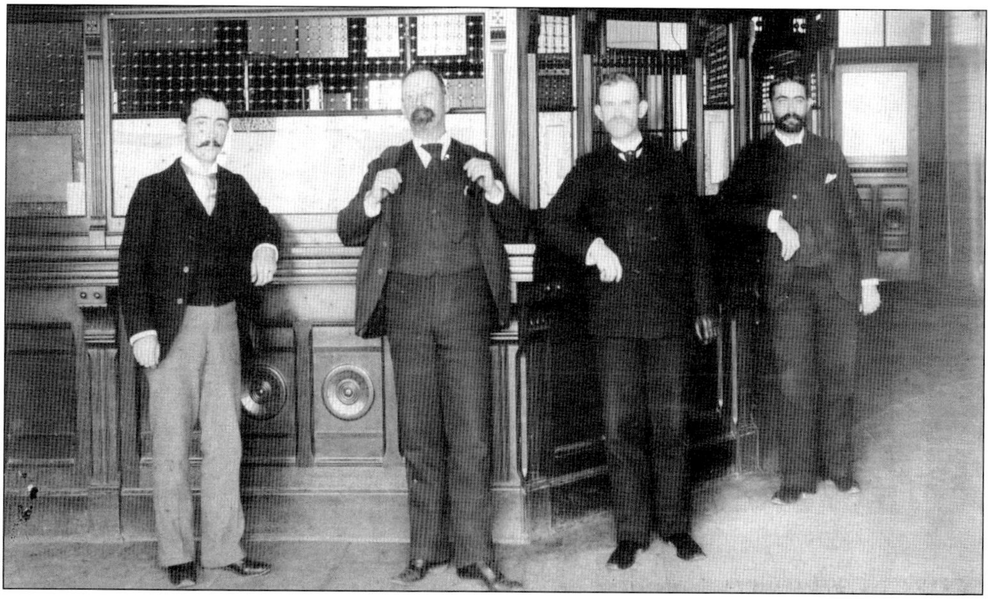

W. D. Morgan (second from right), president of the Bank of Georgetown, poses with cashier Jonathan I. Hazard (right) and two unidentified gentlemen in the new bank building at the corner of Broad and Front Streets. An item from the April 23, 1904, *Sunday Outlook* reads, "The Bank of Georgetown moved into its new building last Wednesday. Everything was brand new, even the money they used on that day. They have an elegant place, which would do credit to any city in the South. They gave away beautiful pocketbooks as souvenirs to all visitors."

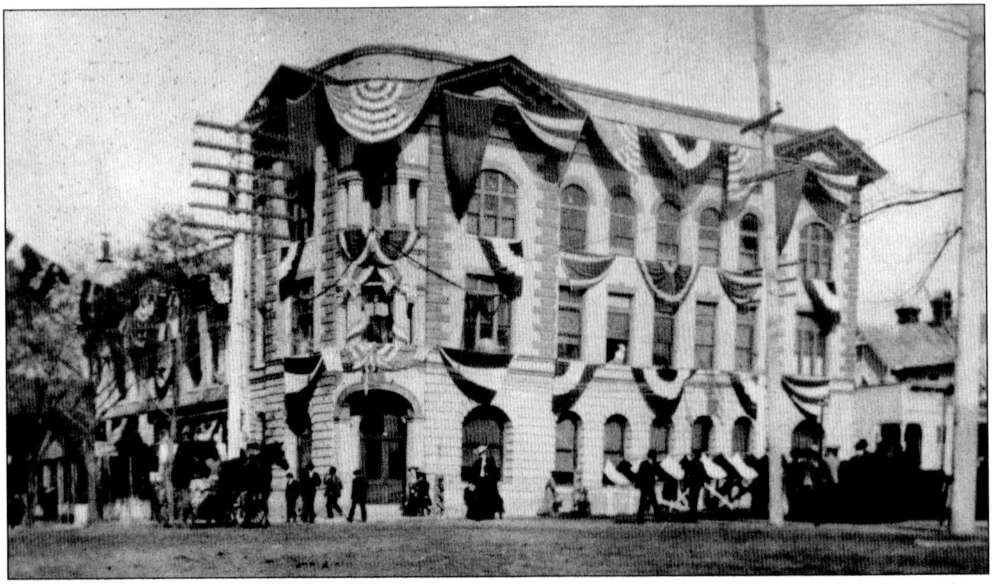

The Bank of Georgetown, on the northwest corner of Front and Broad Streets in the 800 block, is draped with flags for the centennial celebration of 1905. The building was torn down in 1959.

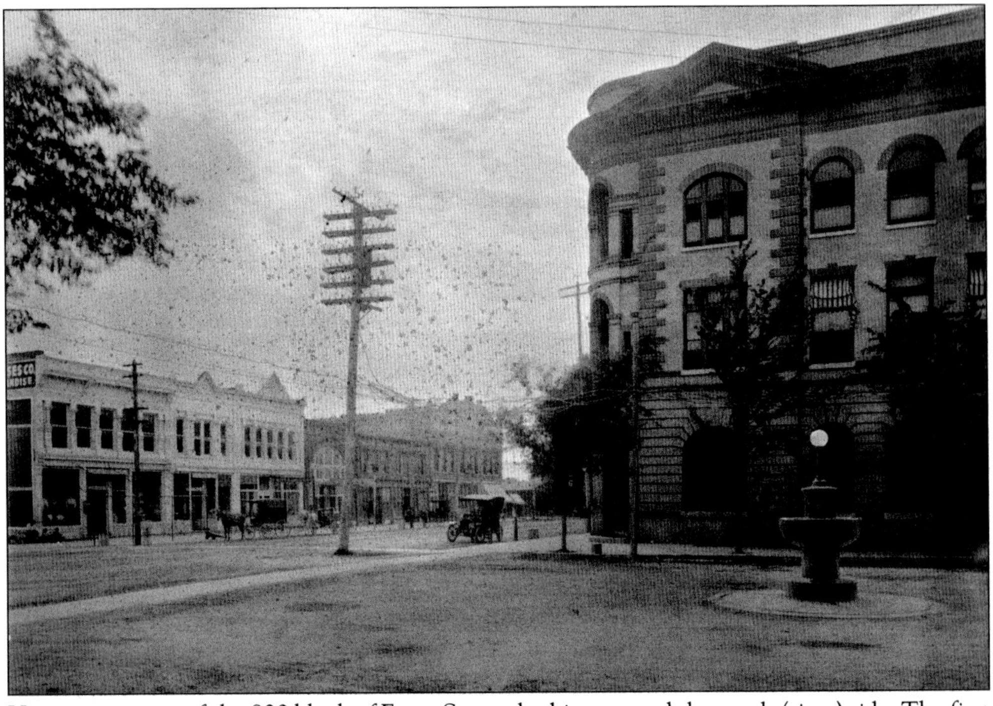

Here is a portion of the 800 block of Front Street, looking toward the south (river) side. The first two buildings on the left comprised the Steele-Moses Merchandise Company well into the 20th century. The next building was occupied by the Standard Opera House on the second floor, and various businesses set up in its three first-floor stores. The handsome Bank of Georgetown is seen on the right, with the fountain donated to the city in 1911 in the foreground. The horse-drawn delivery wagons hearken to a time when automobiles were not always such a big part of life. This is a good view of the sidewalks extending completely across the street.

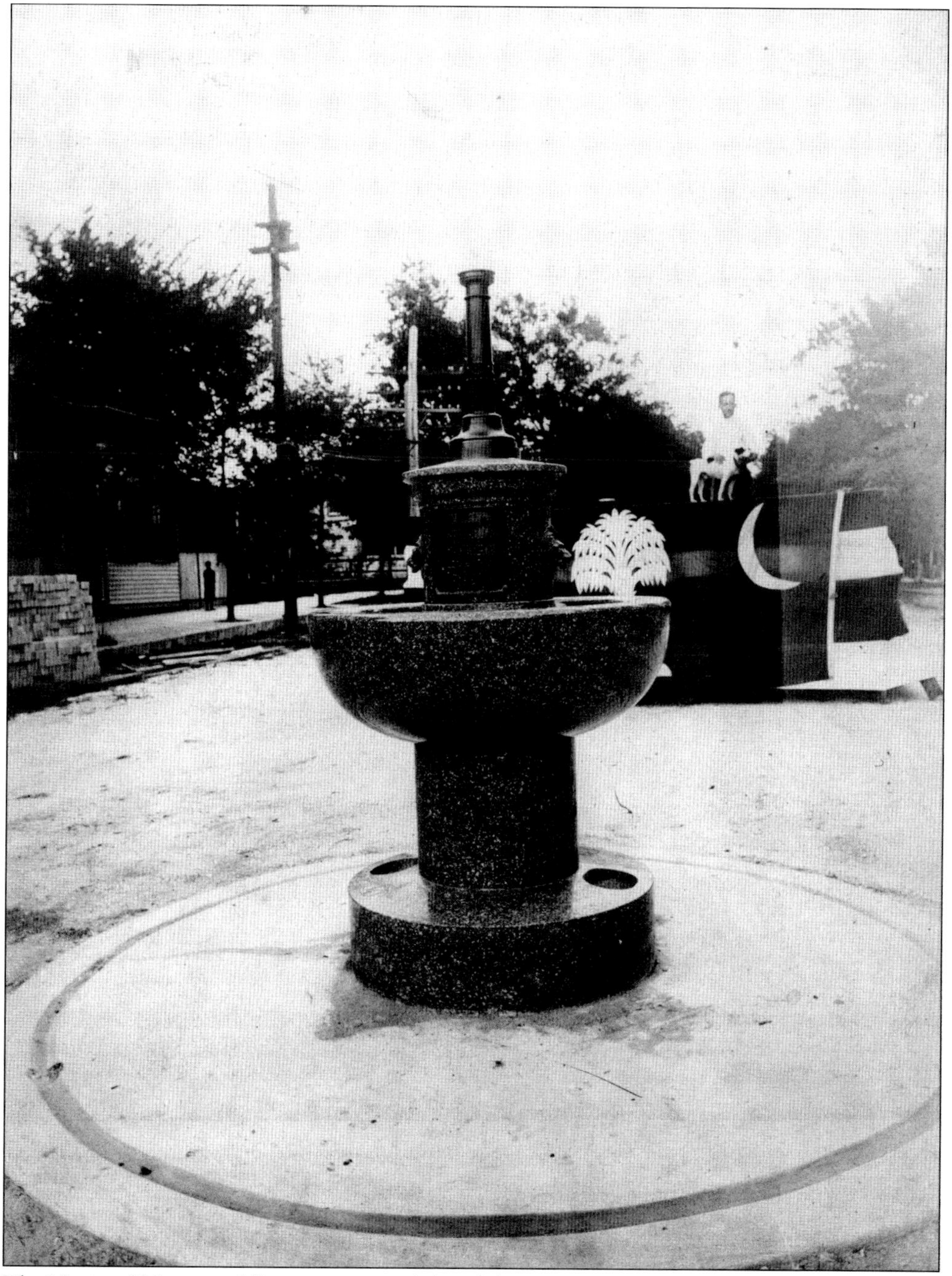

The National Humane Alliance presented this elaborate water trough to Georgetown in 1911. It was installed in the middle of Broad Street about 50 feet from the Front Street intersection. The top bowl held water for horses, while dogs could drink from the smaller bowls at the base. The post on top supported a lighted globe that matched the streetlights. When no longer needed, it became a traffic hazard and was moved to the garden behind the Rice Museum. In 1993, as part of the streetscape renovation, it became the focal point of a park at the corner of Front and Screven Streets.

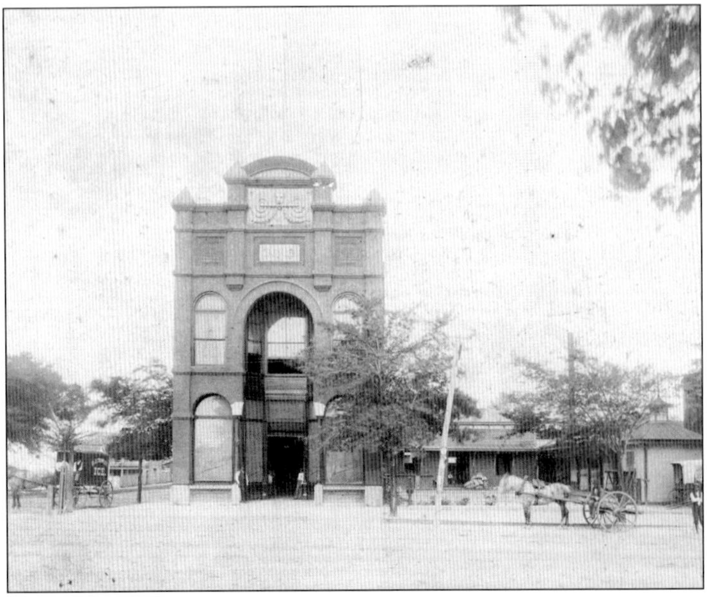

D. J. Crowley's grocery store and icehouse at Front and King Streets was a popular business in Georgetown around 1900. Youngsters were attracted by a large fishpond containing goldfish that was located behind the iron fence to the right of the building. A visit to see the fish was a highlight of many Sunday afternoon strolls. Seen in the background of this photograph is part of a long brick building, which was a livery stable operated by Crowley's.

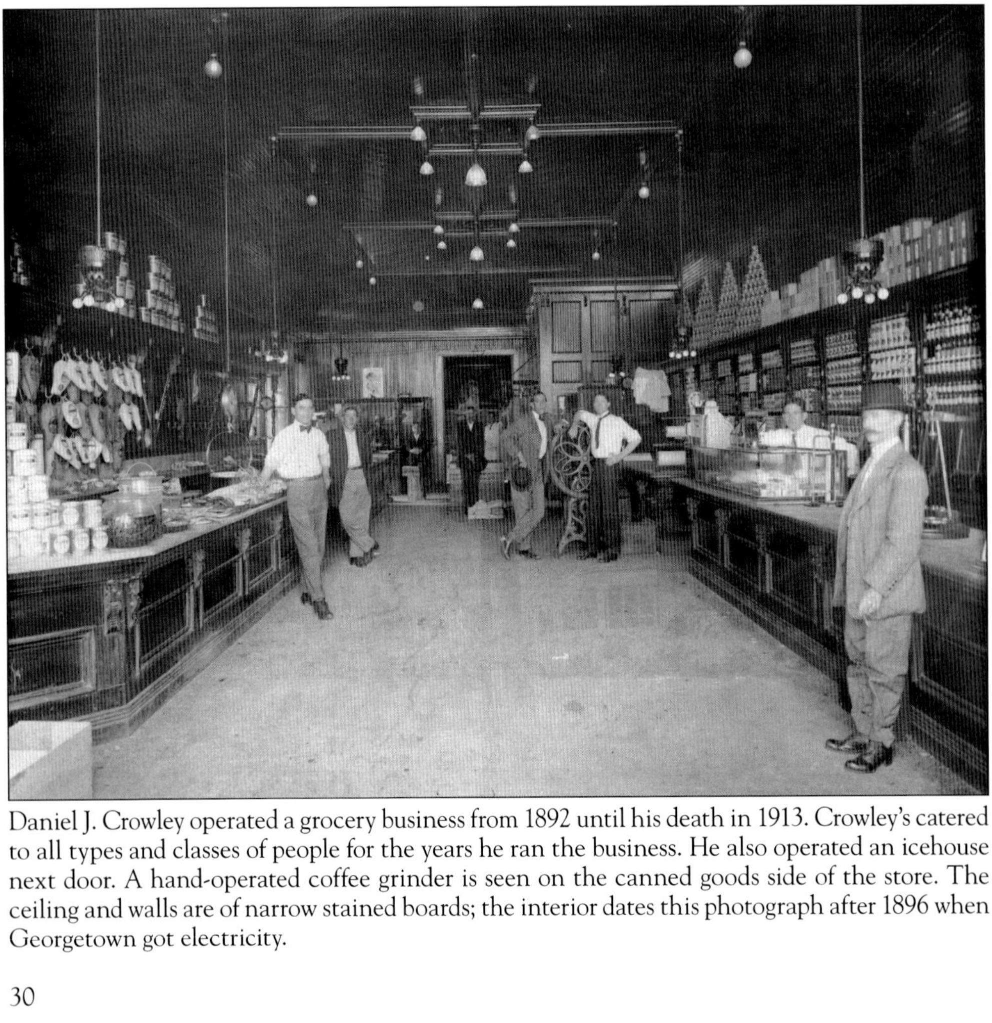

Daniel J. Crowley operated a grocery business from 1892 until his death in 1913. Crowley's catered to all types and classes of people for the years he ran the business. He also operated an icehouse next door. A hand-operated coffee grinder is seen on the canned goods side of the store. The ceiling and walls are of narrow stained boards; the interior dates this photograph after 1896 when Georgetown got electricity.

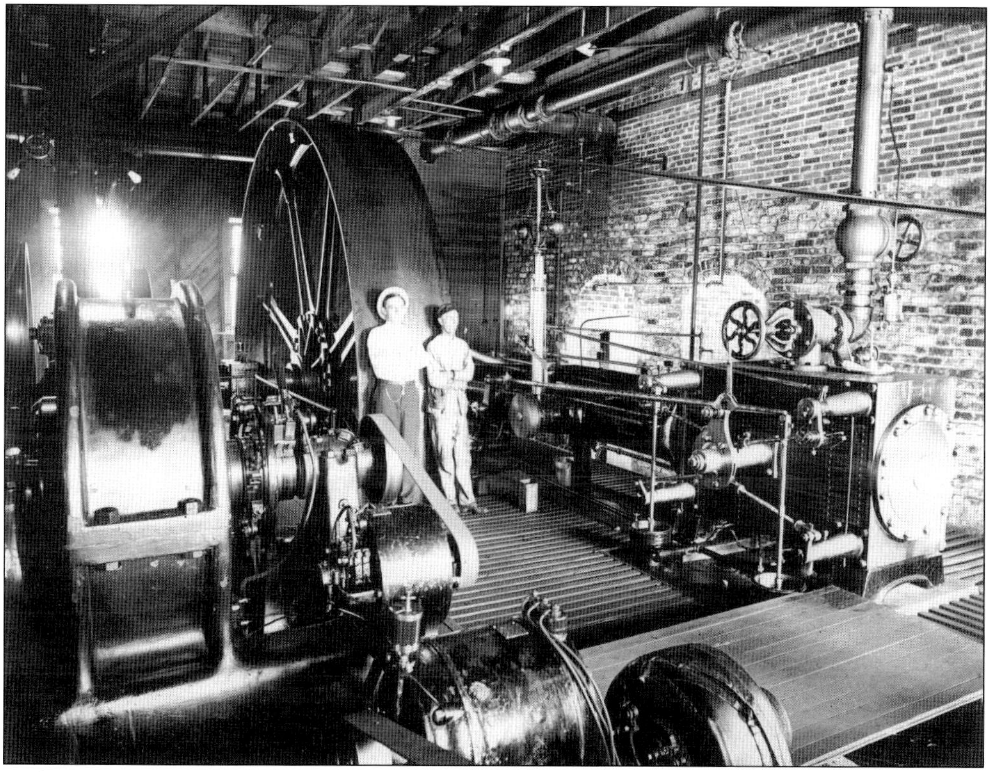

In the early years of the 20th century, Daniel J. Crowley operated an ice-making business next to his grocery store at 930–932 Front Street. The ice company was in operation in 1896. In 1903, he replaced his 5-ton per day ice machine with one that produced 25 tons per day. This photograph shows two men who probably operated the ice factory and the machinery for making ice.

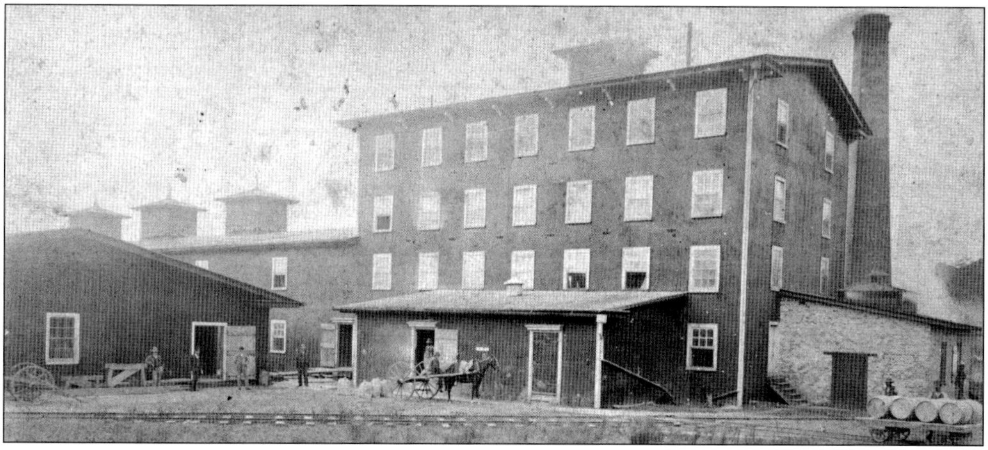

This massive, four-story structure housed the Georgetown Rice Milling Company, which stood near the foot of Wood Street in Georgetown until the 1940s when it was destroyed by fire. The company was established in 1879 as a joint stock company with an investment of $60,000. This mill and the Waverly Mill on Waccamaw Neck together pounded about 350,000 bushels of rice in 1902. It processed rice that was shipped to Charleston, Savannah, and New York in barrels like the ones seen on the right of the photograph. It processed 187,000 bushels of rough rice. However, by 1903, commercial rice production had almost disappeared in Georgetown County.

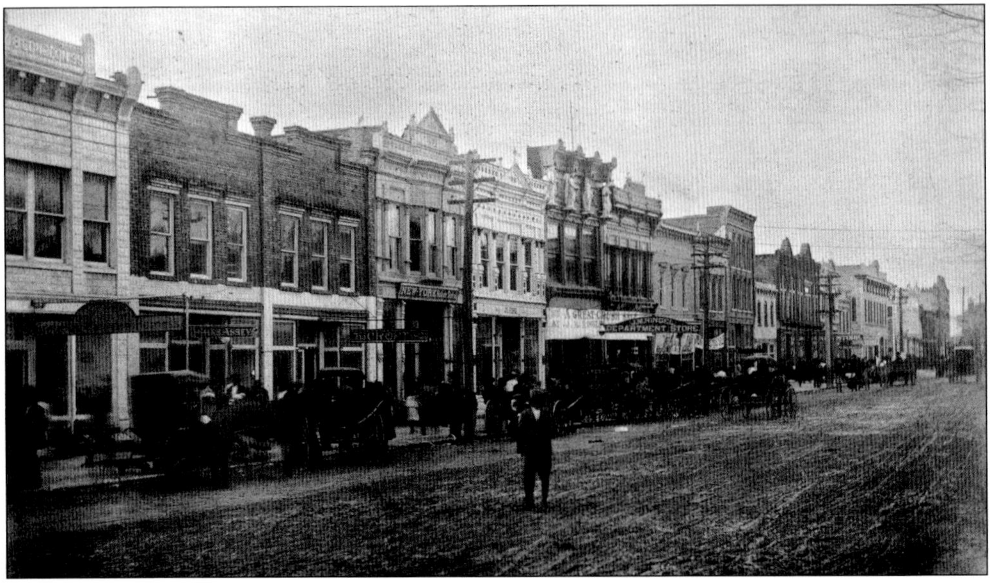

This remarkable photograph makes it possible to see the name of nearly every business on the south side of the 700 block of Front Street, *c.* 1911. Although many exterior changes have been made, some of the buildings are still recognizable.

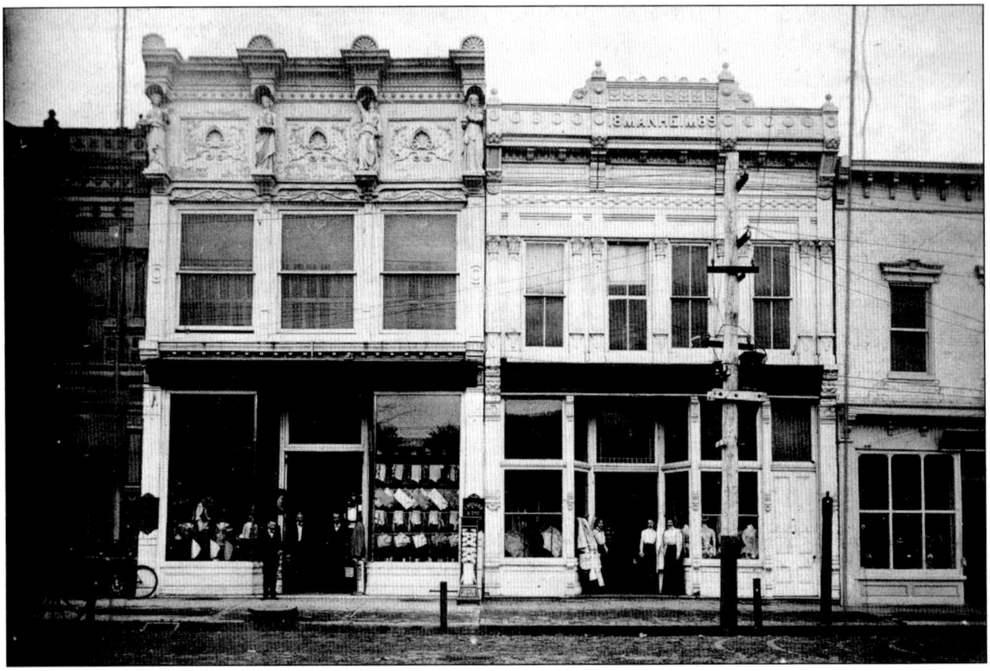

This building (at left) on the 700 block on Front Street featured large figures above the second floor which represent spring, summer, autumn, and winter. This was probably the most elaborate pediment on Front Street, but others were quite decorative. A favorite motif is represented by the other building, with the owner's name and the construction date inlaid in tile in the center of the top. Both buildings in the photograph were S. Brilles and Brothers stores. One was manned by salesmen while the other had only salesladies. The electrical wires date this photograph from 1896.

Heiman Kaminski (1839–1923) was a Prussian immigrant who came to the United States in 1854 and served with the Confederate army from 1861 to 1865. At the close of the war, he traveled to Georgetown. By 1867, he started his own hardware company and later expanded to dry goods and groceries. He would later diversify into the shipping business as well.

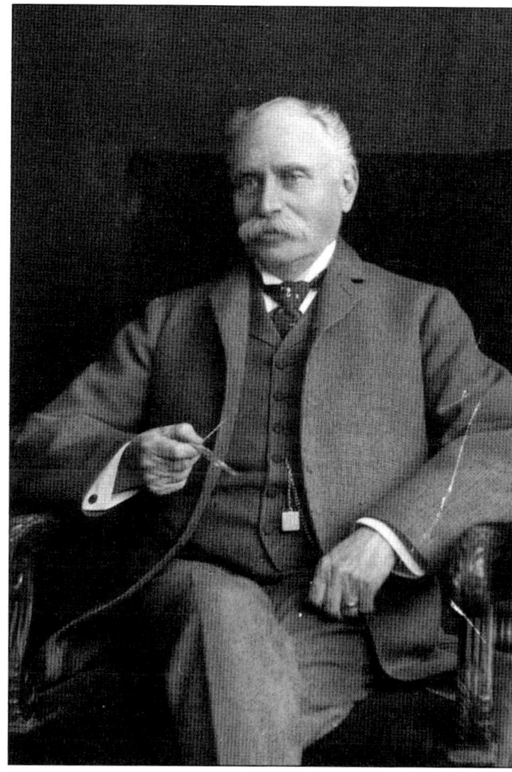

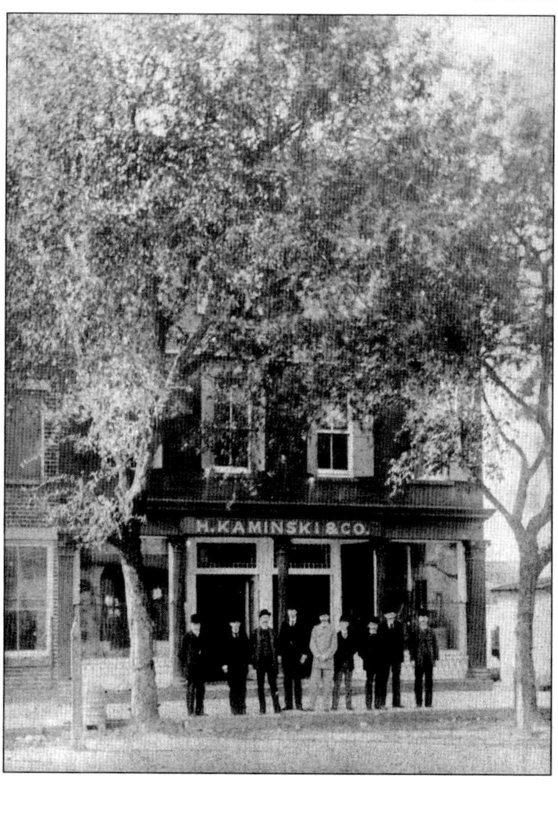

A Confederate mine, which sank the federal flagship USS *Harvest Moon* during the Civil War, was constructed in the Kaminski Hardware building. The three-story brick structure, which now is owned by the Georgetown County Museum of Arts and History, houses an extension of the Rice Museum. It was constructed in 1842. The cast iron front, including the fluted columns and an extension toward the Sampit River in the back, was added in 1878. Officials of H. Kaminski and Company stand in front of the building.

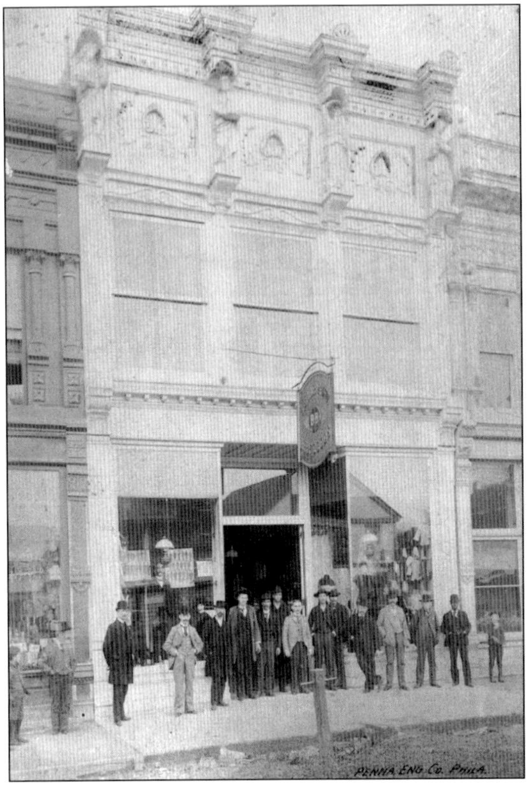

This unusual facade was a landmark on Front Street for many years. S. Brilles operated a dry goods store. J. M. Ringel acquired this building and the one to the right, both of which he remodeled in the 1930s. After Ringel's death, Belk-Scarboro operated in the buildings.

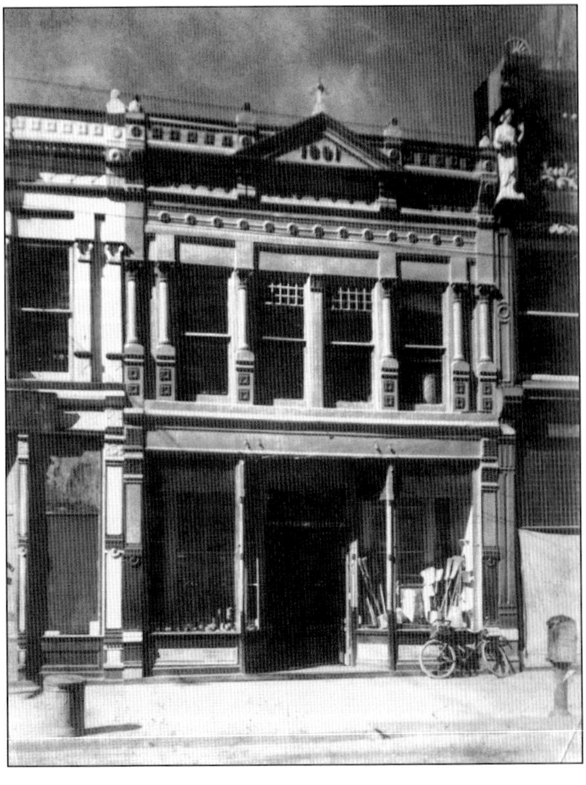

The building seen here is located in the 700 block of Front Street, on the river side. It and the store on the left were renovated in late 1930s or early 1940s by C. L. Ford and Sons. The left side was a hardware store and the right had groceries. The date of 1891 at the top of the structure probably denotes when the pressed tin front was put on to the already existing building.

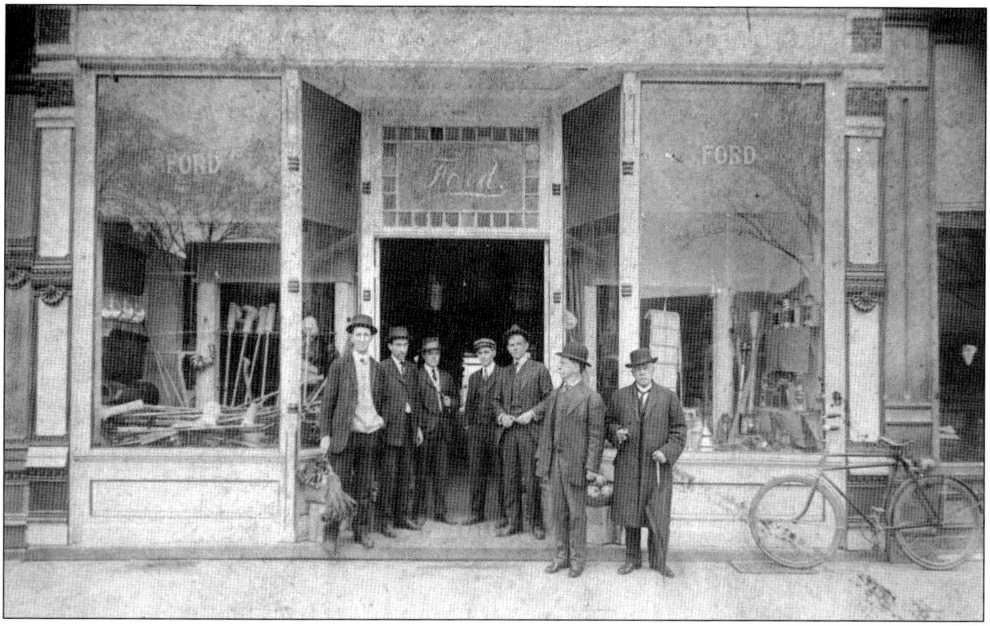

A group of seven men stand in front of the C. L. Ford store, which operated in Georgetown from 1894 to 1966. The store offered groceries, hardware, and other goods to area residents. From left to right are Mr. Kennedy, Mr. Harper, C. L. Ford Jr., A. W. Ford, R. M. Ford, and two unidentified men.

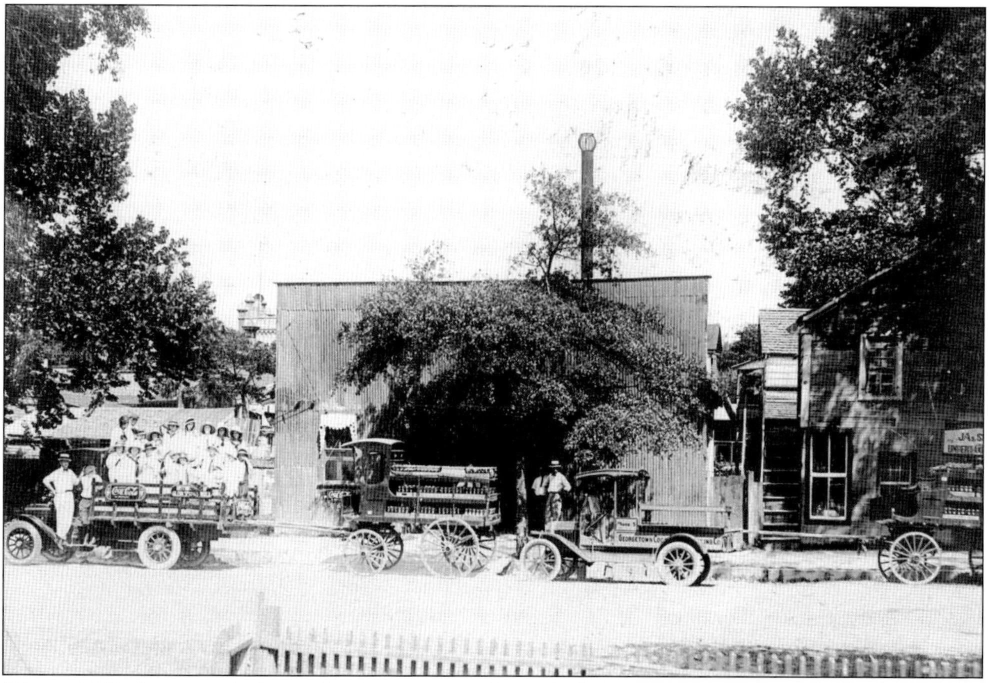

This *c.* 1915 photograph shows the Georgetown Coca-Cola Bottling Company, which was located on 115 Orange Street. A January 30, 1915, newspaper advertisement offered sarsaparilla, root beer, ginger ale, and soda water. None of the people in the photograph have been identified nor is the occasion known.

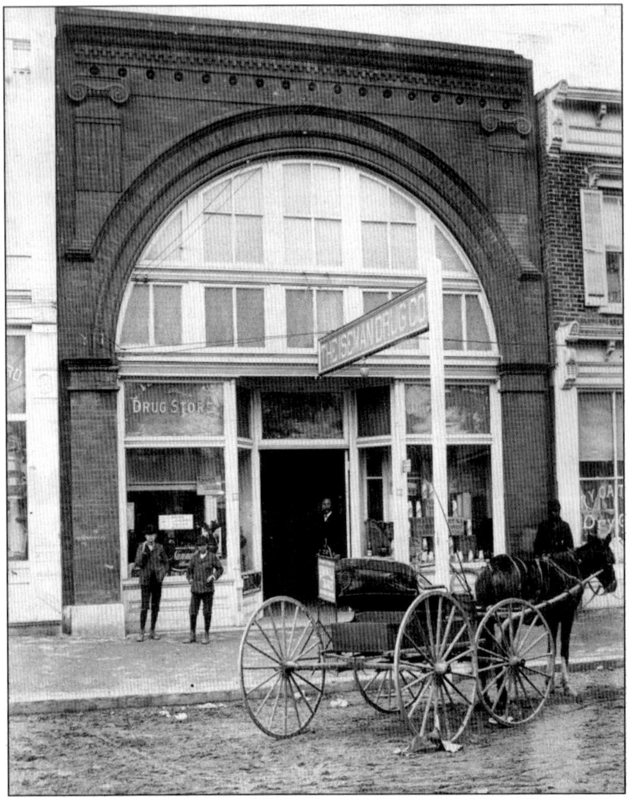

This building at 807 Front Street is the only one on the street to have the unusual brick arch on its facade and to be decorated with Ionic columns. By 1891, Dr. M. S. Iseman moved into this building. He later sold the business to Charles Weston Rosa, but the name Iseman remained until 1973 when the business closed.

The interior of Iseman Drug Company is seen in this photograph. Note the gallery over the first floor and the young man with the bicycle at the rear of the right counter.

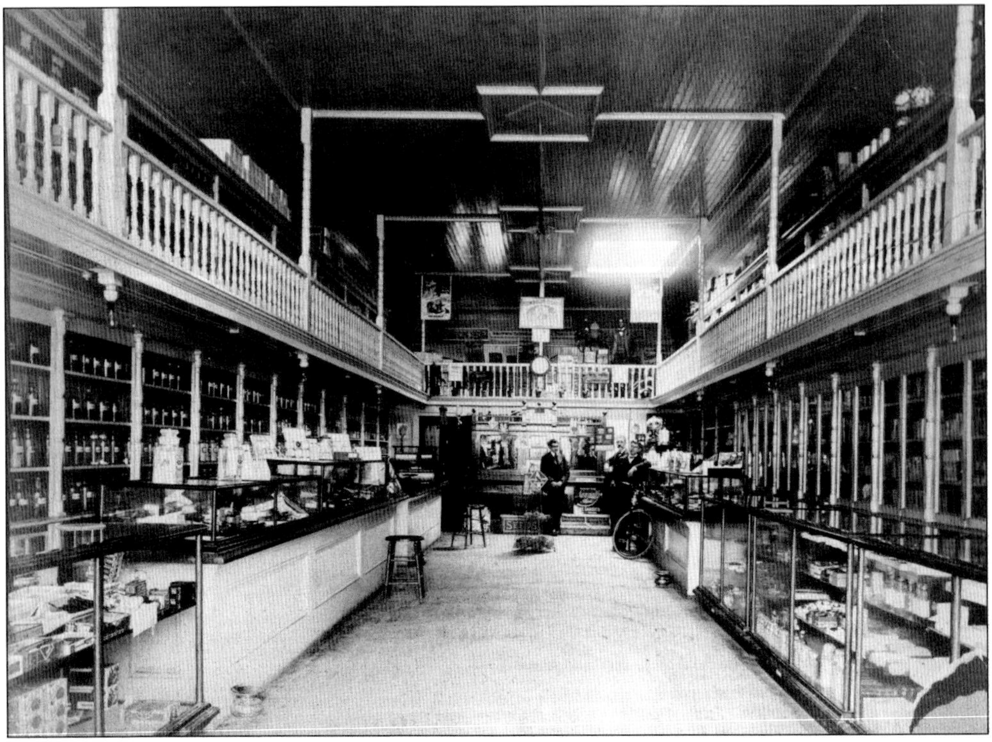

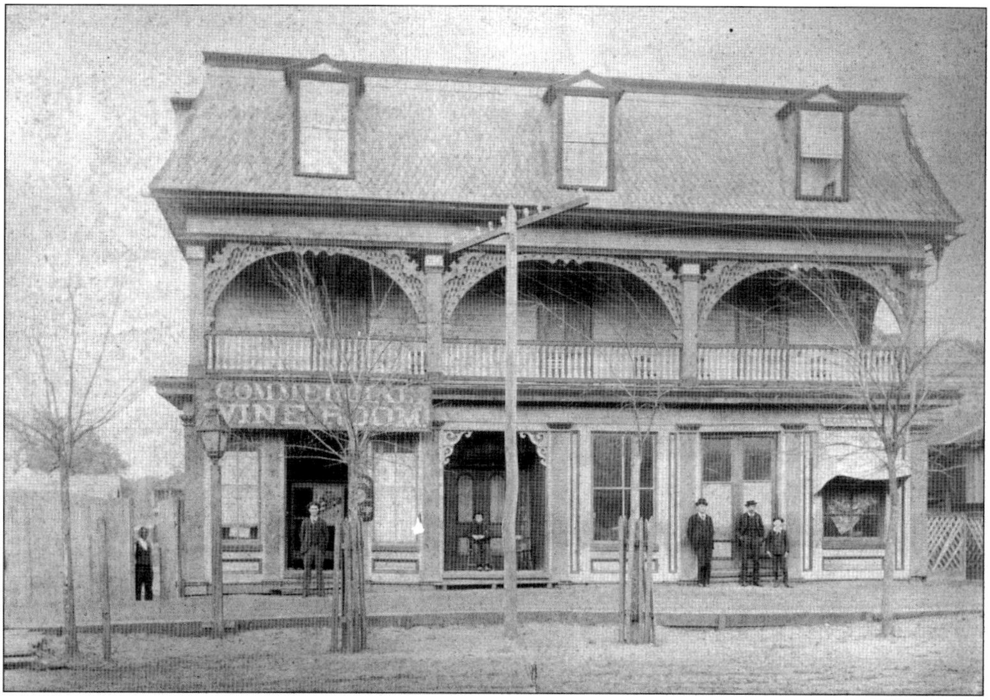

Although the sign only mentions the wine room, the remainder of this unusual building was the Commercial Hotel. It was located on the north side of Front Street in the 700 block where the Strand Theater currently stands. Other photographs in the Morgan Collection show this same establishment with a porch across the first floor and no gingerbread trim on the second floor.

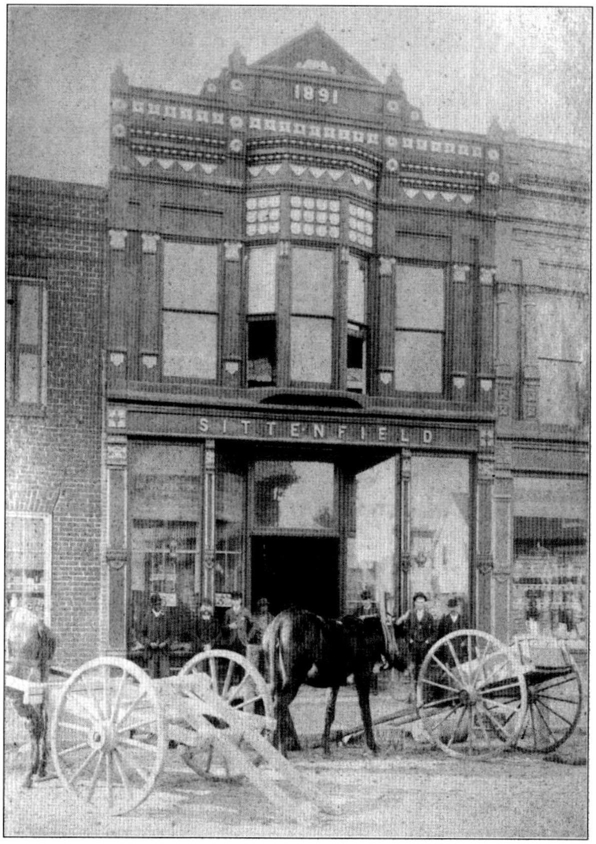

This decorative store front, dated 1891, is typical of the period. The pediment is one commonly seen, but the bay window on the second floor is unusual on Front Street. Sittenfield's was a dry goods and notions store at 711 Front Street. There are no electric wires, so the photograph would date before 1896.

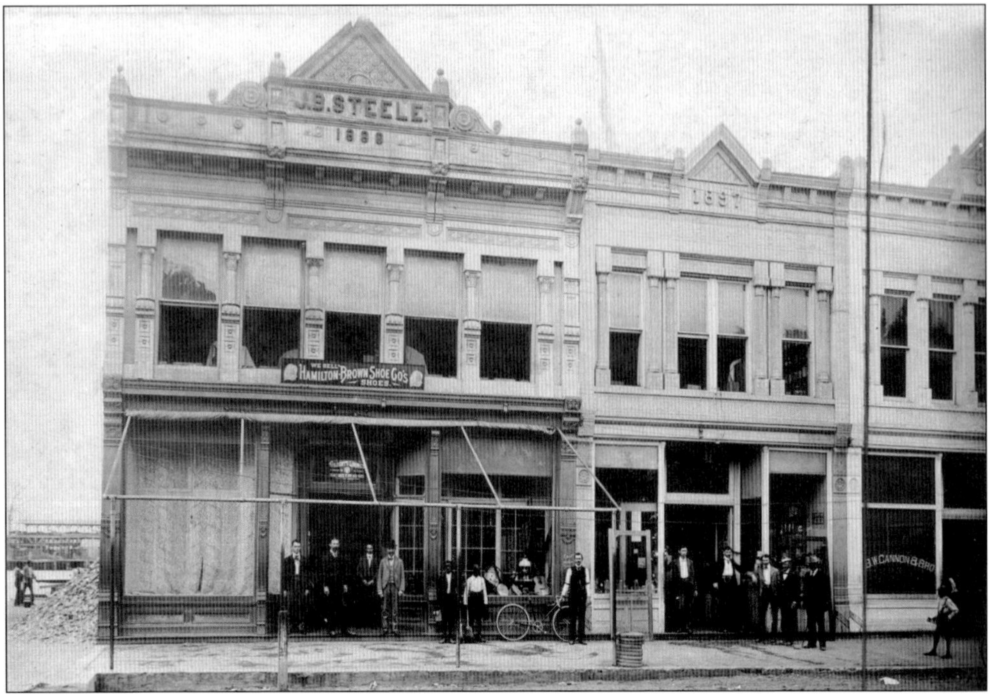

The Steele-Moses stores were popular business enterprises as the 19th century turned in 1900. Located on Front Street near the foot of Broad Street, Steele-Moses operated a dry goods store in the building on the left and a grocery in the store on the right, next to B. W. Cannon and Brothers. Hats were made on the second floor of the Steele building. Both buildings were later used for shoe stores. Clerks are shown standing in front of the stores.

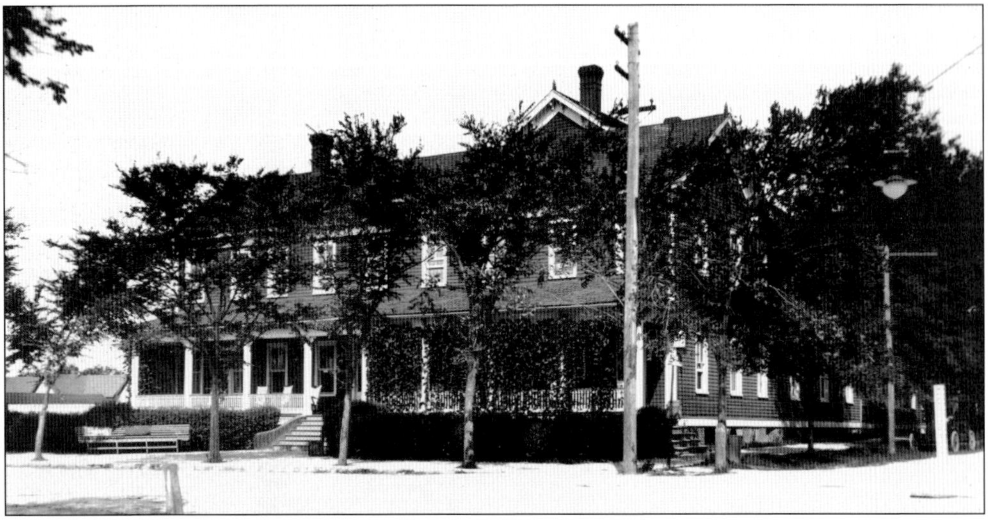

The Tourist Hotel occupied the southwest corner of Winyah Road and Fraser Street. It was built by the Atlantic Coast Lumber Company in 1904 to accommodate those arriving by the Georgetown and Western Railway (later Seaboard Airline Railroad) at the depot across the street. Before the hotel was opened, travelers had to get a horse-drawn taxi to the old part of town, to either the Commercial Hotel on Front Street or the Winyah Inn on Prince Street. This is a later photograph, judging from the size of the hedges and the trees.

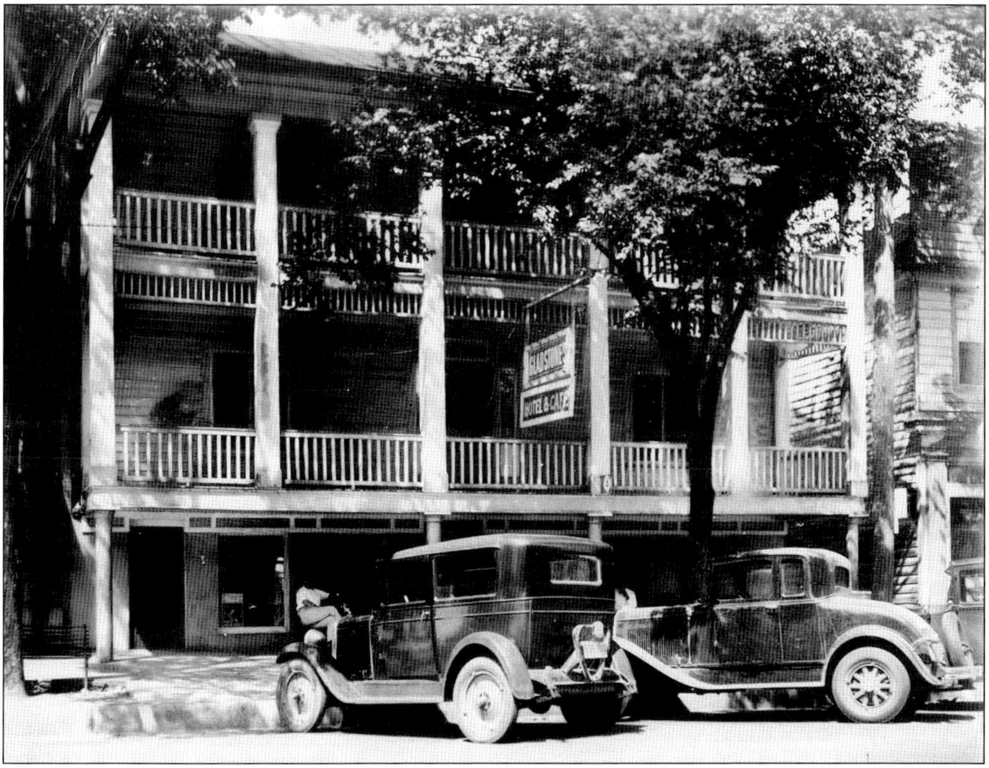

The Gladstone Hotel was torn down in 1967. The ground floor was the café where "Miss Nettie" Gladstone served red rice and duck every Saturday. The second and third floors, which were made of wood, housed the guests. The building to the right was an annex to take care of extra patrons. This annex was torn down in 1935 to make way for the Palace Theater.

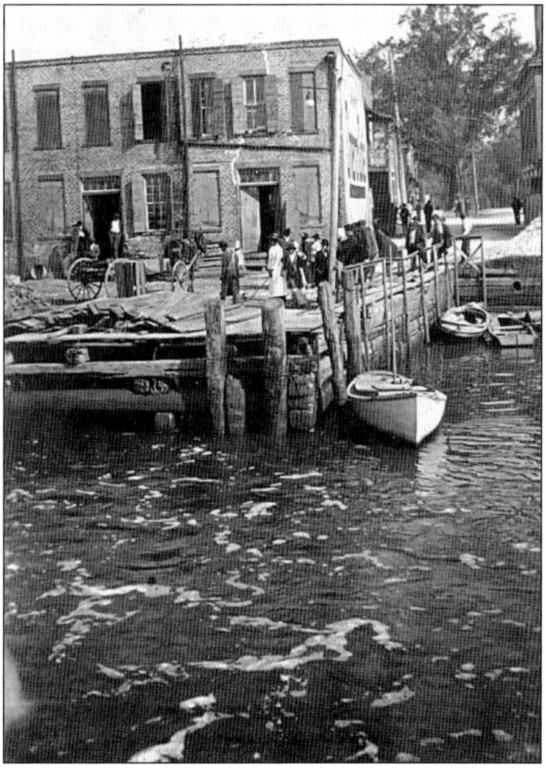

A group of African American men and women stand behind the clock tower in Georgetown near the 700 block of Front Street.

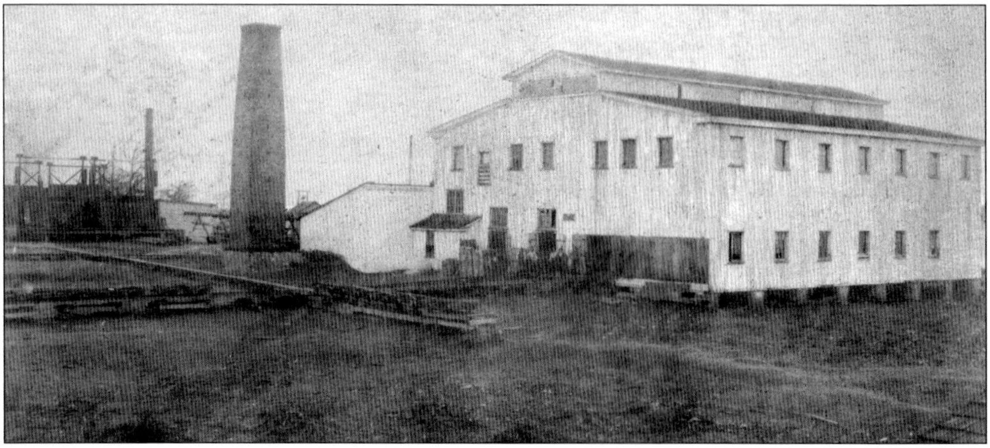

A vast industrial complex was operated by the Atlantic Coast Lumber Company in Georgetown and elsewhere in the Lowcountry in the early 1900s. Four sawmills in Georgetown, two of which were destroyed by fire in 1913, were the center of the complex, which included a planing mill with a capacity of 200,000 feet per day; immense storage sheds and stackers; a machine shop; foundry; a pattern and woodworking shop; a dry kiln; a power plant that generated electricity for ACL, its electric railroad, and the city of Georgetown; a large docking area and loading shed for ships; a turpentine still; and an alcohol plant. The ACL complex covered 56 acres bordering the Sampit River.

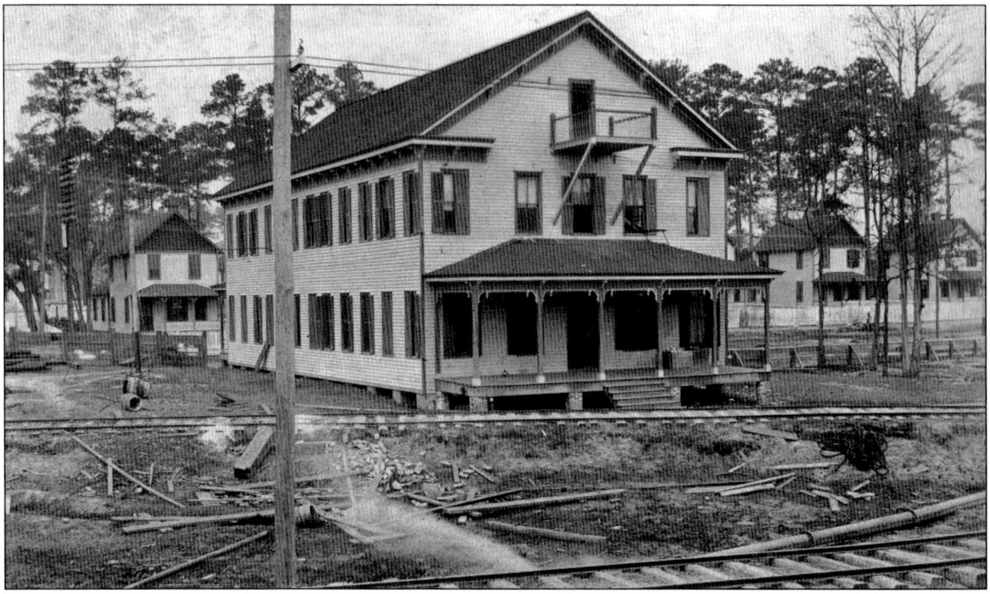

This is a back view of the Atlantic Coast Lumber Company office building. Directly in front ran Fraser Street. Across the street is a row of houses the company built for its employees. The ACL was a giant corporation in its time. When it came to Georgetown in the 1890s, it created "New Town," which consisted of the mill and all the houses for workers in the Fraser Street area. Numerous rows of homes were built. All on a row were alike, but the rows were different. There were single-family dwellings, such as these pictured with a fenced-in yard; multiple duplexes; some one-story units; and some two-story, single-family houses smaller than these and with less yard. The executives had very large single accommodations on Winyah Road nearby. Although many of these places have been torn down, there are still examples of each type in existence.

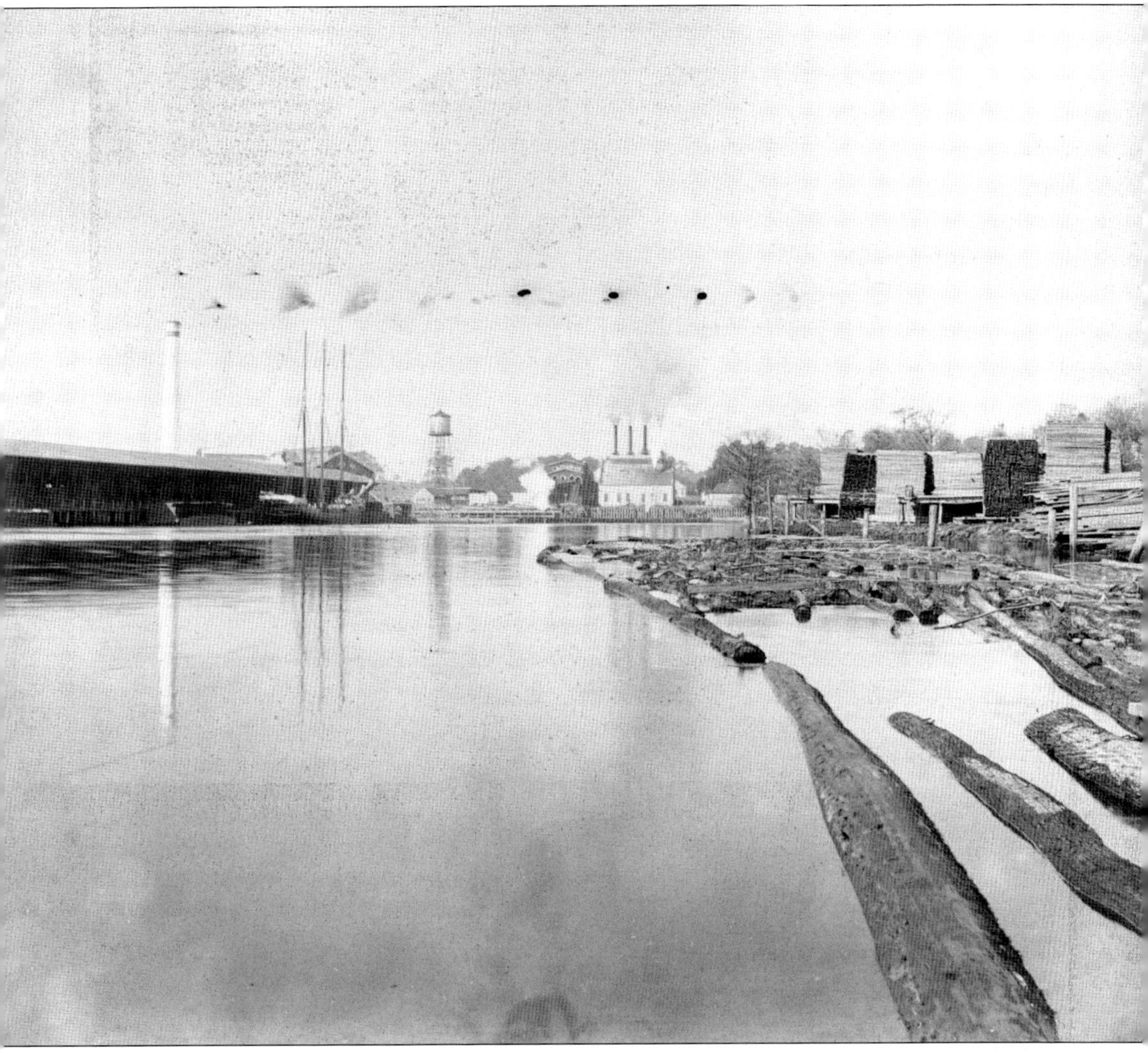

This photograph shows Atlantic Coast Lumber Company in a bend of the Sampit River looking from the south side of Goat Island in the center of photograph. To the right is the Gardner and Lacey Lumber Company on Goat Island and on the left of photograph is the ACL Company loading pier.

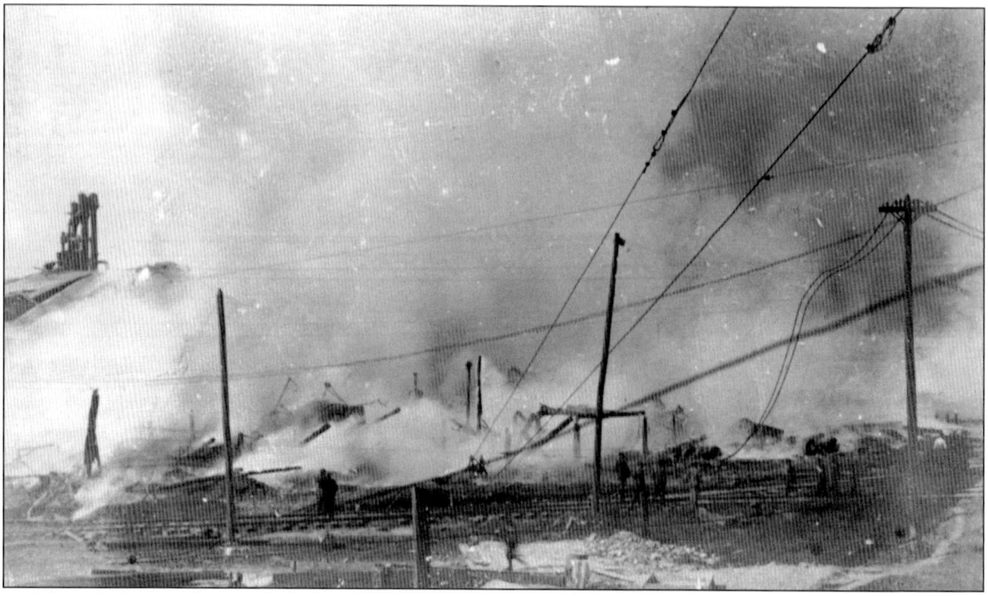

Two of Atlantic Coast Lumber Company's four sawmills burned to the ground on April 21, 1913. The two mills that escaped the raging inferno were not in the path of the fire fanned by winds out of the north. They later were replaced by a steel and concrete plant, which was erected and placed in operation by July 5, 1914. The new facility, one of the largest and most modern in the United States, cost $750,000. This remarkable recovery helped invigorate the Georgetown economy, which had suffered during the year's period when ACL production was curtailed.

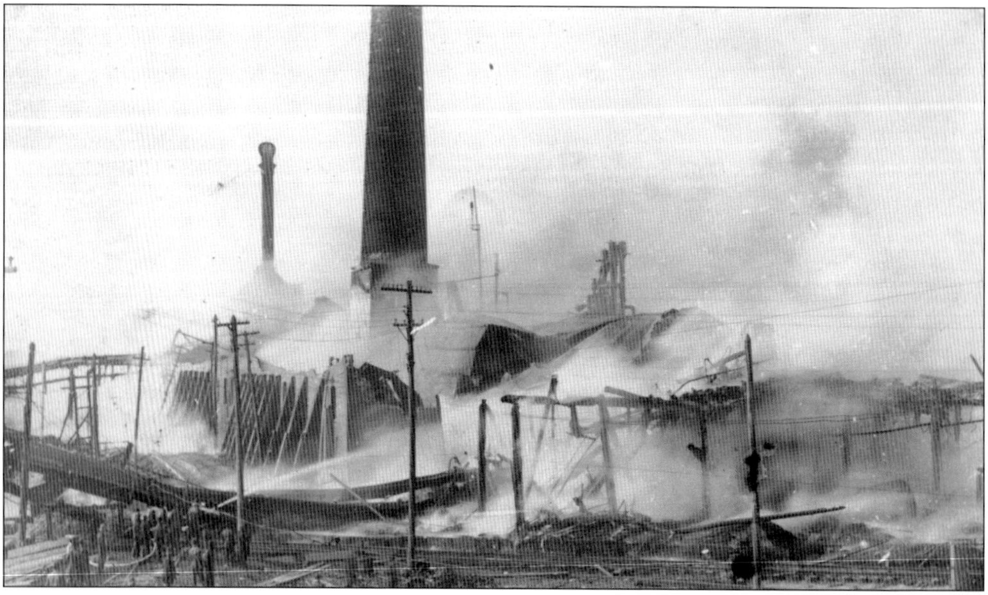

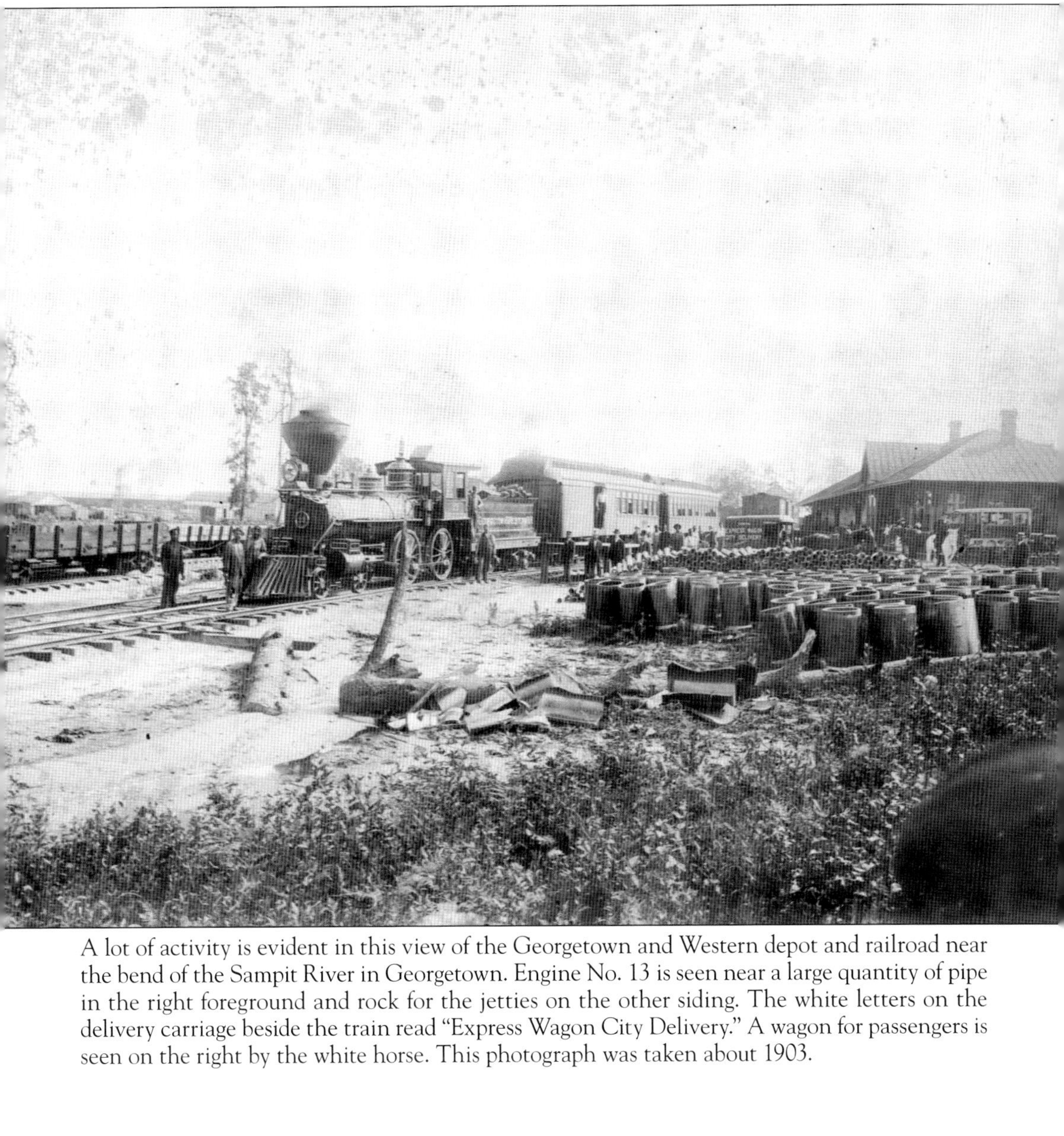

A lot of activity is evident in this view of the Georgetown and Western depot and railroad near the bend of the Sampit River in Georgetown. Engine No. 13 is seen near a large quantity of pipe in the right foreground and rock for the jetties on the other siding. The white letters on the delivery carriage beside the train read "Express Wagon City Delivery." A wagon for passengers is seen on the right by the white horse. This photograph was taken about 1903.

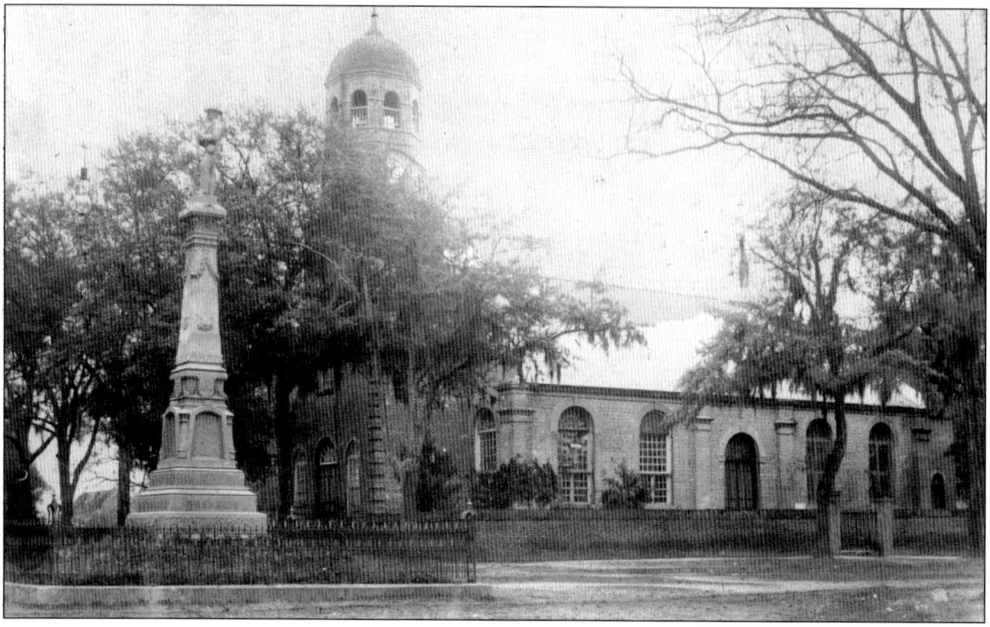

Prince George Winyah Episcopal Church, formerly Prince George Winyah Church of England, stands at the corner of Broad and Highmarket Streets. The parish was established in 1721, but the cornerstone was not laid until 1745 with the first service in August 1747. The brick was English brick used as ballast in ships. The bell tower was added in 1824. The parish and the town are named for George, Prince of Wales, later King George II. A beautiful English stained-glass window behind the altar was given to the church in 1873 from St. Mary's Chapel for slaves on Hagley Plantation. It is said that the British stabled their horses here during their occupation in 1780–1781 as did the Union army after the Civil War. Prince George has never closed its doors to worship.

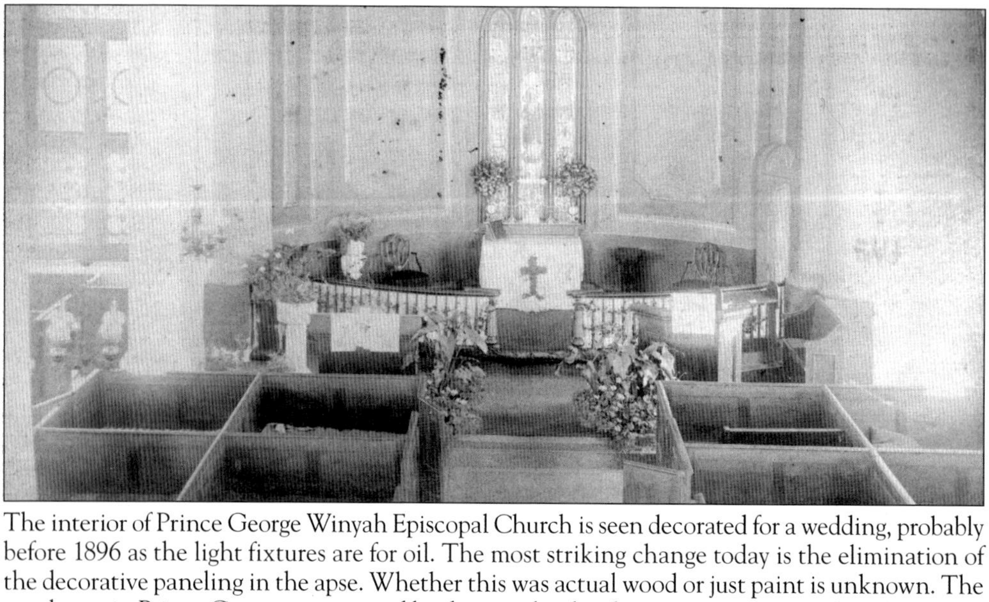

The interior of Prince George Winyah Episcopal Church is seen decorated for a wedding, probably before 1896 as the light fixtures are for oil. The most striking change today is the elimination of the decorative paneling in the apse. Whether this was actual wood or just paint is unknown. The pew boxes in Prince George were rented by the year, but hard times sometimes made it difficult to meet the minister's salary and make necessary repairs to the building, so lotteries were occasionally announced to sell the pews of those in arrears. Usually the rents were paid up quickly.

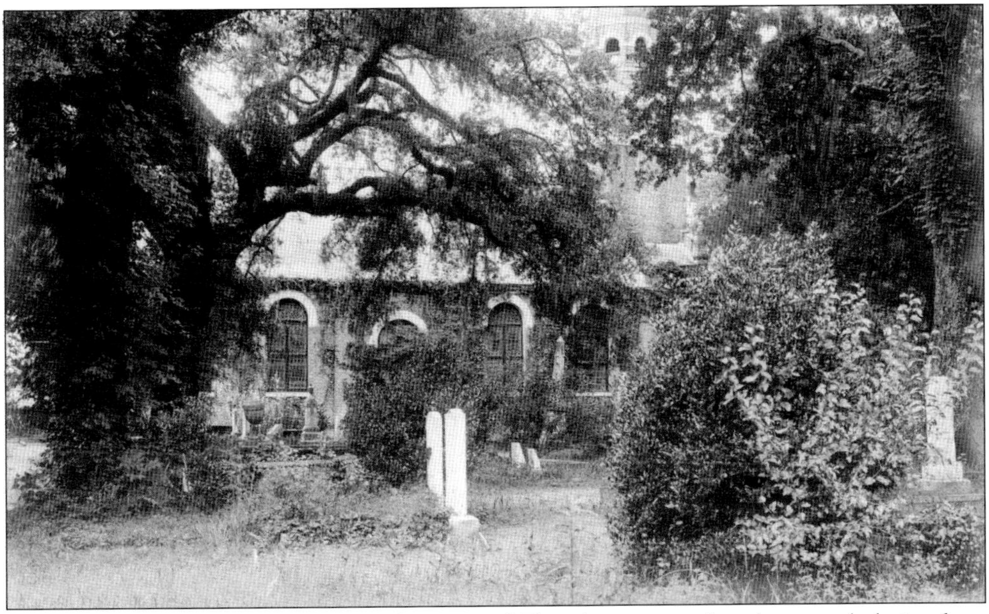

The cemetery of Prince George Winyah Episcopal Church is seen in this photograph dating from around 1900. This is quite a different scene from the manicured grounds of today. The church is seen in the background.

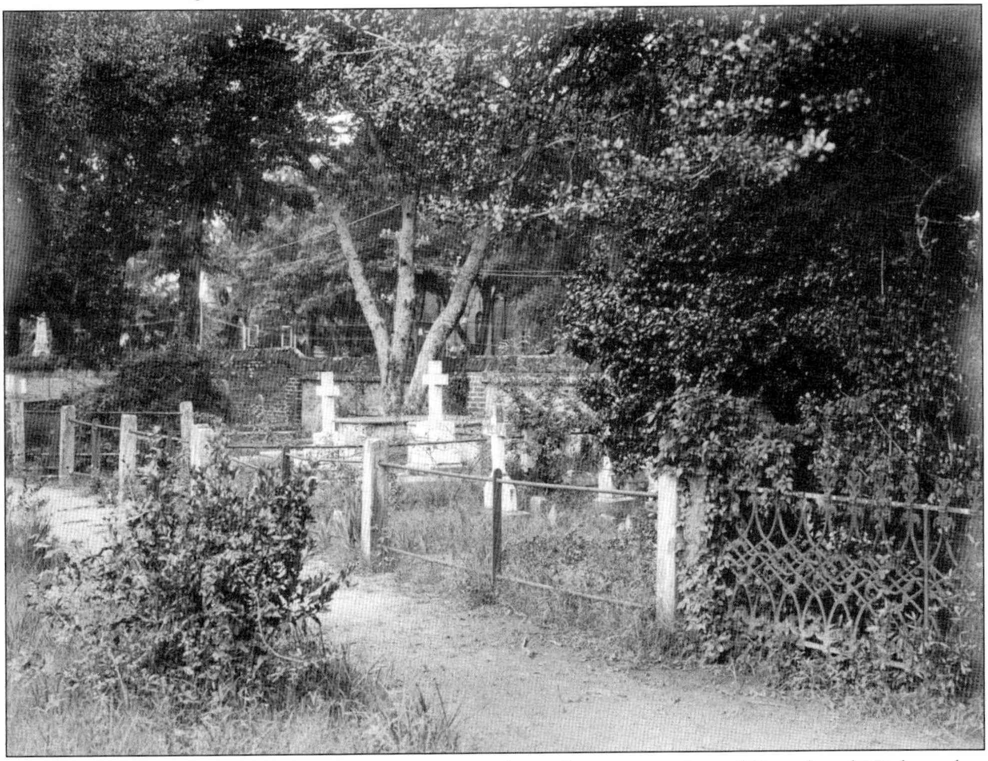

This photograph of the Prince George cemetery faces the intersection of Broad and Highmarket Streets. The wrought iron fence on the lower right corner surrounded the Morrison plot and was later moved to border the old Parish Hall and the present preschool building on Highmarket Street.

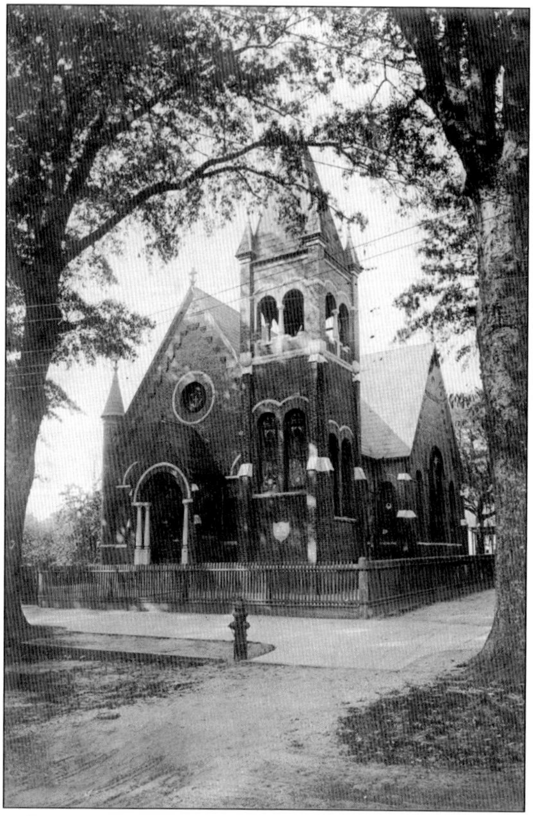

St. Mary's Roman Catholic Church is located on the corner of Highmarket and Broad Streets. The cornerstone was blessed on Thanksgiving Day, 1899. Before the sanctuary was built, Mass was offered in the homes of parishioners.

The Catholic congregation realized a dream on January 5, 1902, when St. Mary, Our Lady of Ransom was dedicated. This photograph shows the vestrymen and priests. Vestrymen shown from left to right are George A. Doyle, George A. Lohr, Daniel J. Crowley, James F. Doran, Patrick J. Doyle, Edward J. Whelan, and W. D. Morgan. Clergy pictured from left to right are Francis C. Clark (sub-deacon and editor of the *Saint Anthony Guild* in Florence, South Carolina), Rev. Joseph D. Budd (chancellor of the diocese, assistant priest), the Right Rev. Henry P. Northrup, D. D. (bishop of Charleston, celebrant), and the Rev. Charles D. Wood (missionary in charge, deacon).

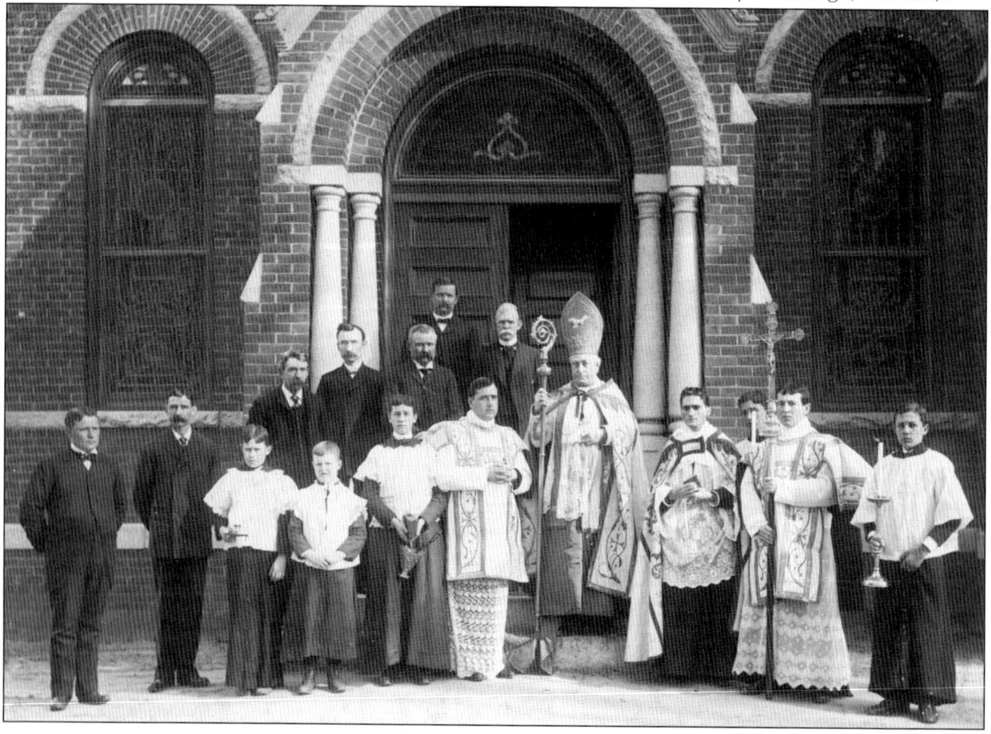

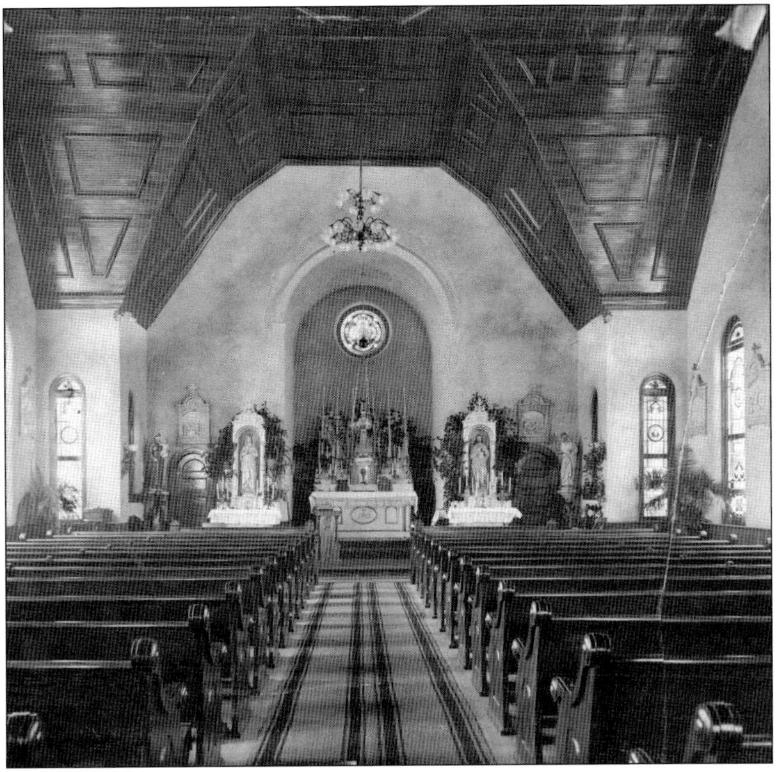

This interior view of St. Mary's shows the church as it existed until massive 1967 renovations. Capacity was increased from 150 to 350, and the original structure was practically rebuilt while retaining the original design. Care was taken with stained-glass windows to be incorporated into the new plans. And the entrance was changed from Highmarket Street to the present Broad Street location.

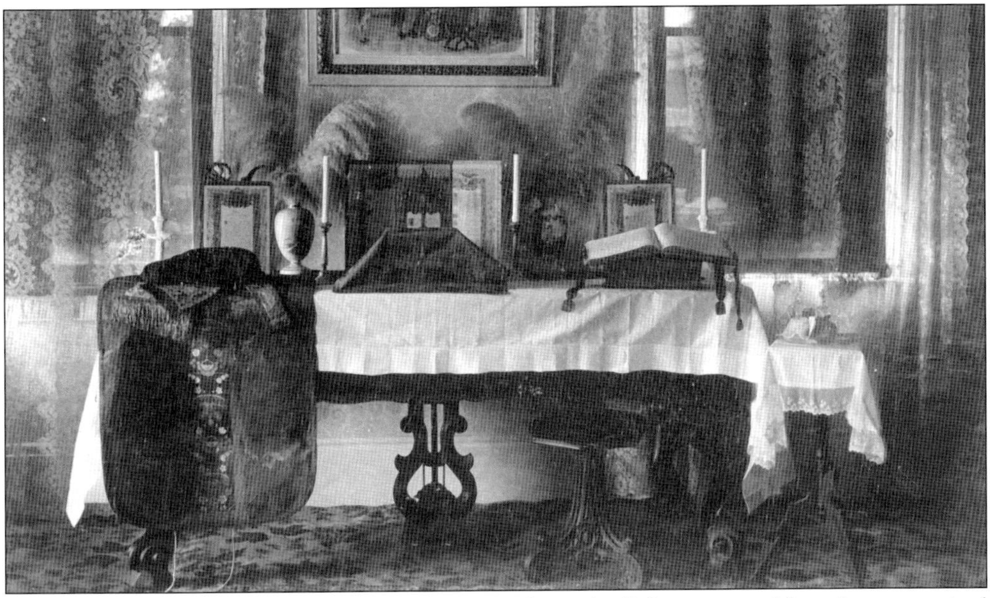

There have been Catholics in Georgetown since the early 19th century, although unorganized and without a sanctuary. After the Civil War, Mass was said in the home of Arthur Morgan (now the Kaminski House Museum on Front Street) until his death in 1878. Mass was then said in the home of his nephew W. D. Morgan. This photograph shows such an occasion in the house at Broad and Prince Streets before 1902, when St. Mary's Catholic Church at Broad and Highmarket Streets was dedicated.

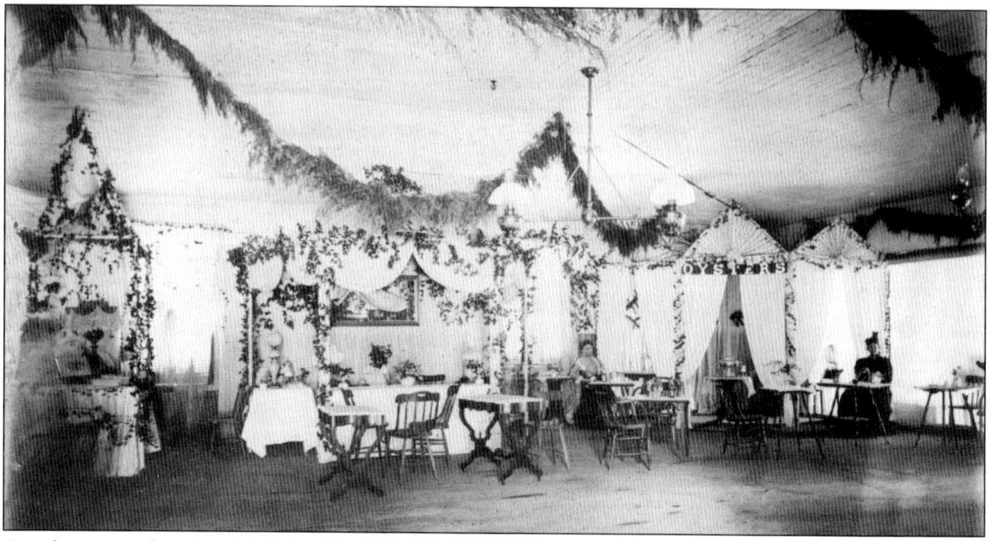

A gala atmosphere prevailed as Georgetown's Catholics, assisted by friends of all denominations, presented "A Grand Fall Carnival" December 4–7, 1900, at Walker's Rink. The purpose was to raise money to furnish the new mission church under construction. Extensive planning and preparations were made for the affair, which made a net profit of $971.85. Elaborately decorated booths dominated the hall, and one of the fanciest was the ice cream bower. Pre-carnival publicity boasted "2,900 articles of value" to be offered for sale. The special prize was a grand upright piano, valued at $500. Walker's Rink was located approximately where the patio area of the present church is now and housed the temporary mission chapel of St. Anne from 1899 until the permanent structure was completed in 1901.

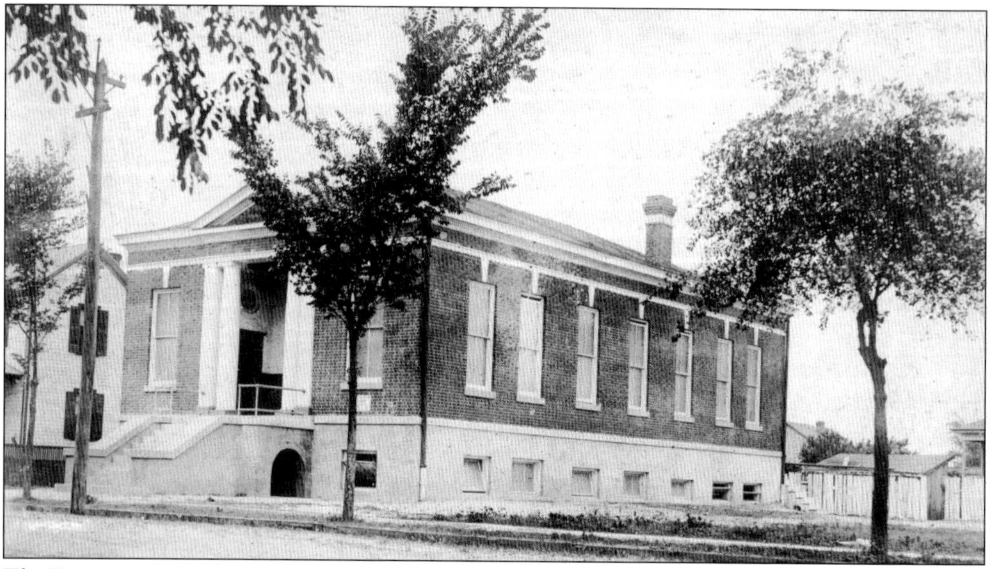

The Baptist congregation in Georgetown dates from 1729. A lot was set aside in the town plan for the Anabaptists to build their church along with the Presbyterians and the Church of England. In January 1845, a new Baptist church was dedicated on Highmarket Street near the corner at Queen Street. The church pictured here was erected in 1912 and faces Cleland Street near the corner of Highmarket Street. A larger sanctuary was completed in 1948, and this structure was converted into an educational building.

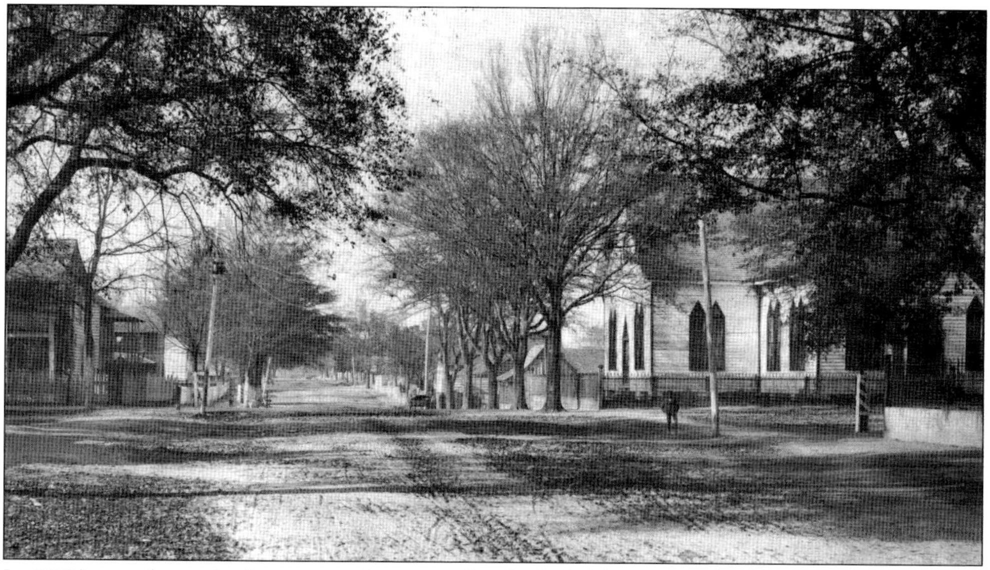

In 1865, members of what was to become the Bethel African Methodist Episcopal Church petitioned the denomination to start their own congregation. They purchased a lot at the corner of Broad and Prince Streets and built a small sanctuary. In 1882, they built a new church directly on the corner, as seen on the right in this photograph. In 1908, improvements were made to the interior, and a new brick facade was erected. This is one of the earliest A.M.E churches to be organized following the Civil War.

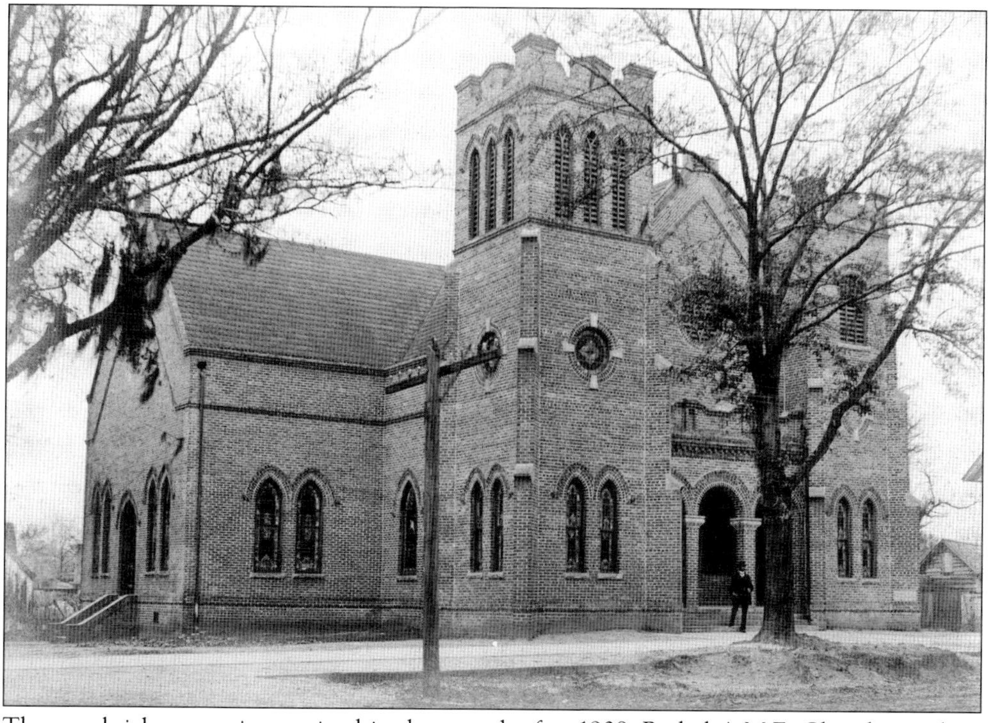

The new brick veneer is seen in this photograph after 1908. Bethel A.M.E. Church members enlarged and enhanced their sanctuary by adding beautiful hand-painted glass windows, a ceiling made of pressed tin tiles, and a magnificent pipe organ.

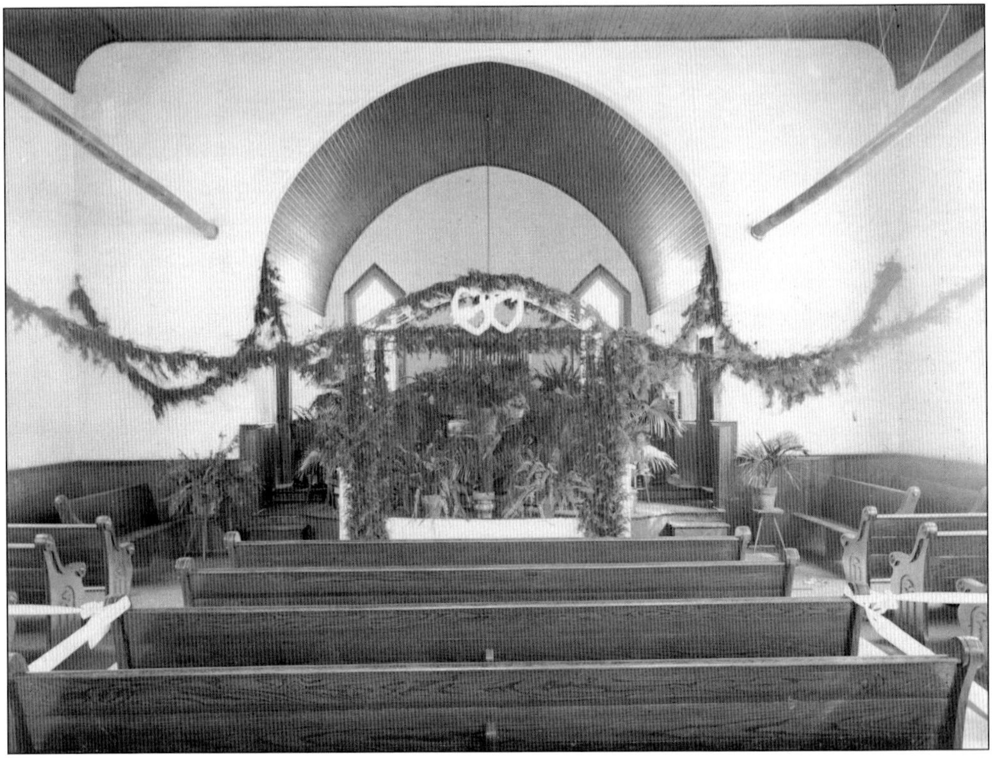

This is the interior of the Bethel A.M.E. Church before the renovation of 1908. This photograph shows the altar decorated with greenery, and the two interlocking hearts made of flowers indicate the occasion may have been a wedding.

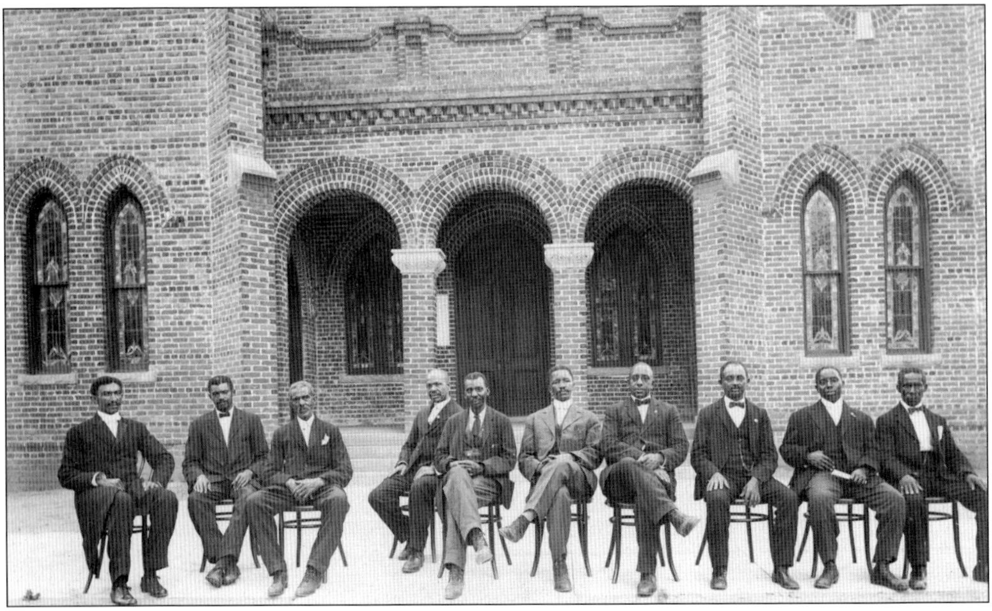

The pastor and trustees of the Bethel A.M.E. Church pose in front of the newly renovated building in 1908. Seated from left to right are J. E. Beard, pastor J. J. Burton, Adam Dunmore, J. B. Beck, R. B. Anderson, Dr. Brewington, J. Prioleau, J. B. Brockington, and Tony Allston.

In 1729, a lot was set aside on Church Street at the head of King Street for the Presbyterians to build their sanctuary. Little is known of these early members. In 1901, a handful of Georgetown Presbyterians were determined to build a church. They were not wealthy and were few in number, but they worked diligently to build this simple wooden structure in the west end of the city on Winyah Road. In 1906, this first Presbyterian church was destroyed by a hurricane.

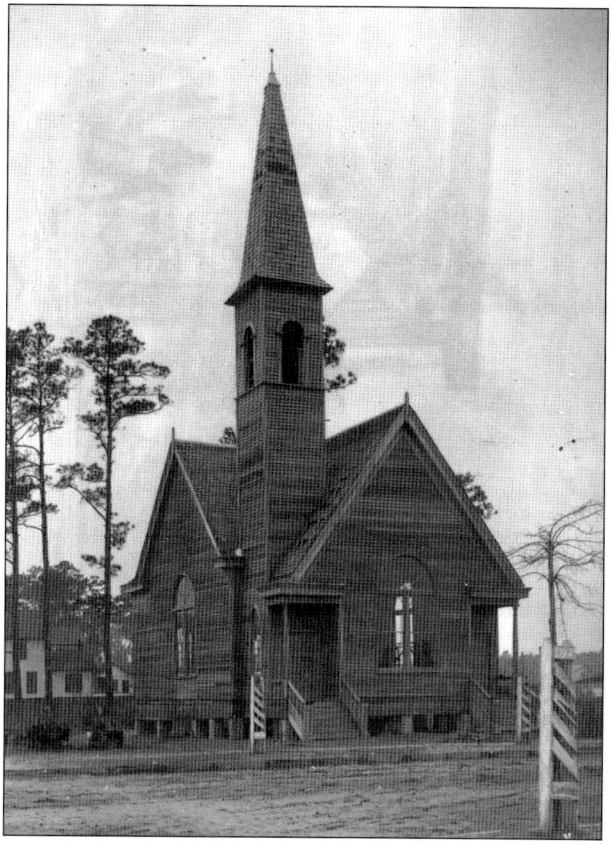

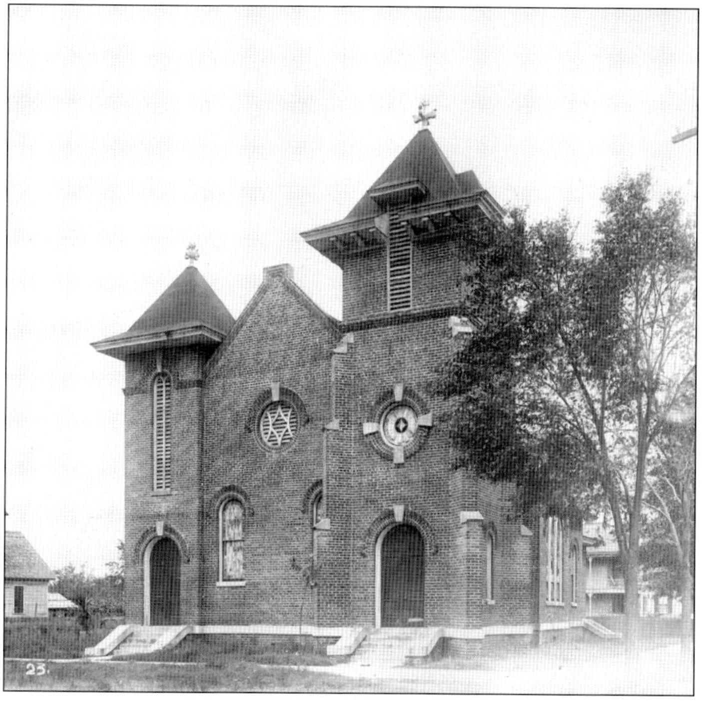

The present Presbyterian congregation in Georgetown dates from 1897, although Presbyterians have been here since the founding of the city. In 1907, this brick church was built on the site of the previous one, which was destroyed by a hurricane, at Winyah Road and Hazard Street. This was the sanctuary for Presbyterians until 1957, when the present church on Black River Road was completed. The house on the left remains. The one behind the church was torn down and a Sunday school building erected in the 1940s.

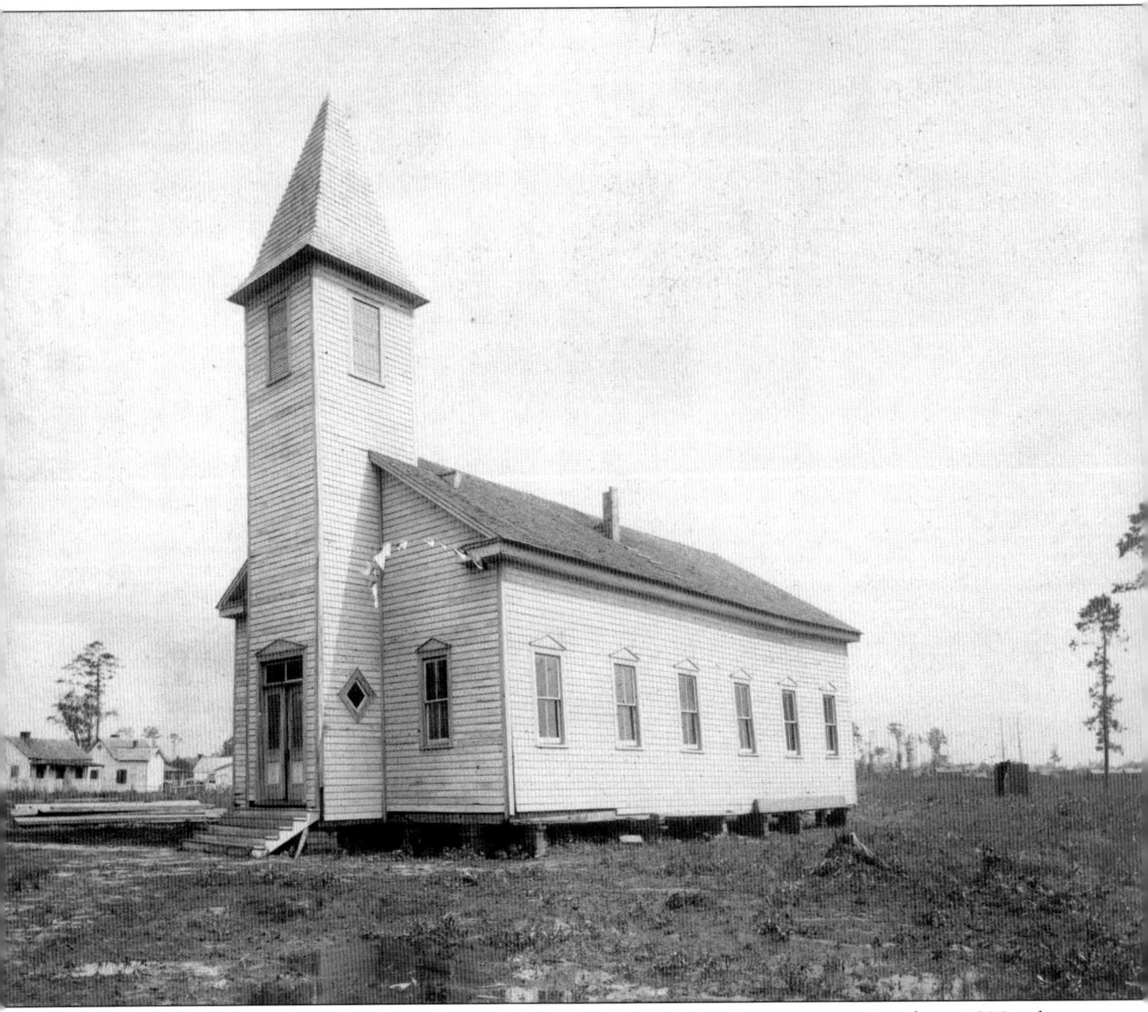

This building is believed to have housed the West End Methodist congregation from 1899, when it was started as a mission from Duncan Methodist on Orange Street, until 1910, when a new brick structure was completed. The houses built by the Atlantic Coast Lumber Company for its workers are seen in the background.

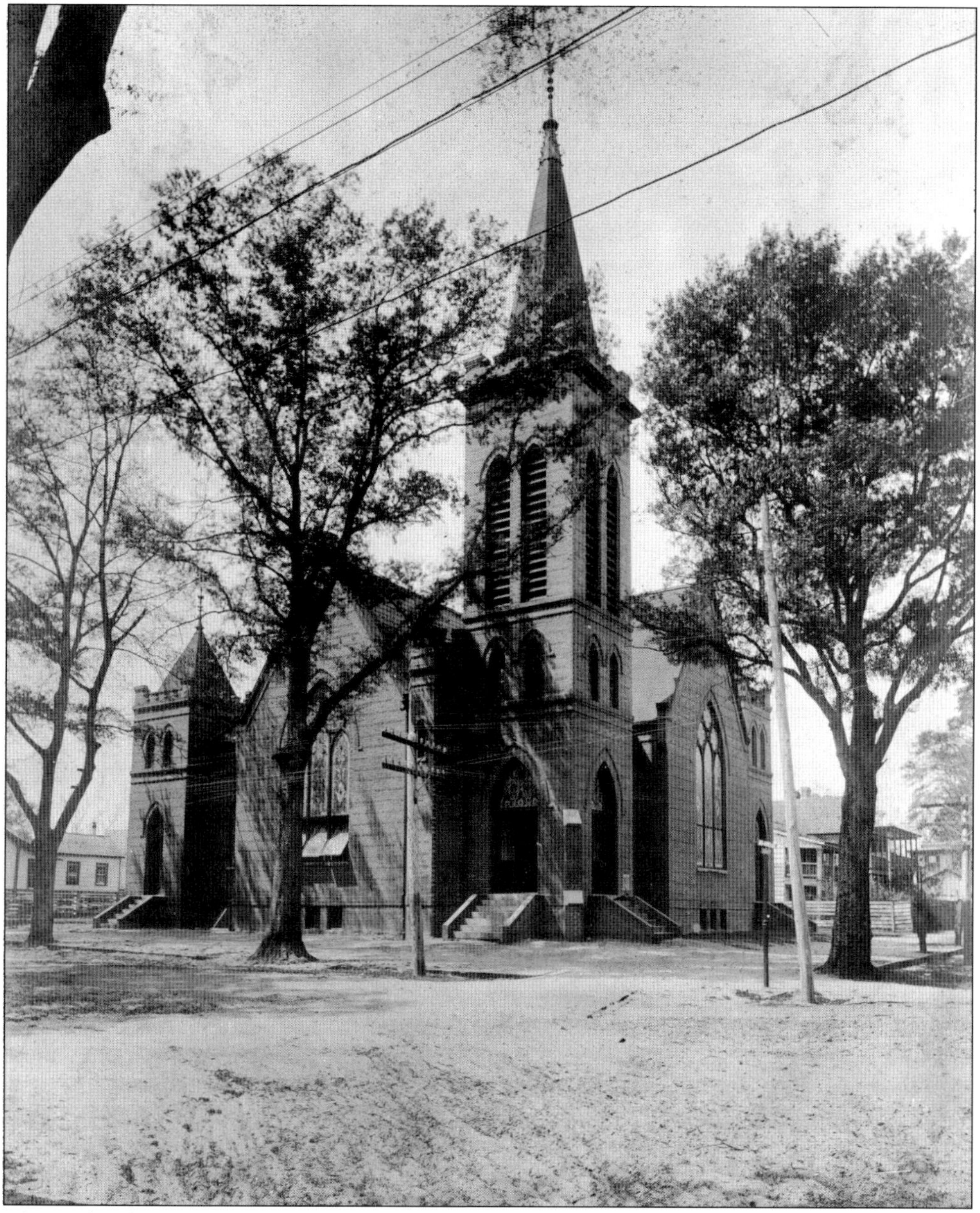

This is the third church building the Methodists have owned since the founding of the church in Georgetown in 1785 by Bishop Francis Asbury. William Wayne of Georgetown was the first Methodist convert in South Carolina and donated land on Orange and Highmarket Streets. The edifice pictured here was completed in 1901 and named Duncan after the pastor, Rev. W. M. Duncan. This occupies the southwest corner of Orange and Highmarket Streets across from the site of the original building. About 1922, a Sunday school building was added to the rear of the sanctuary.

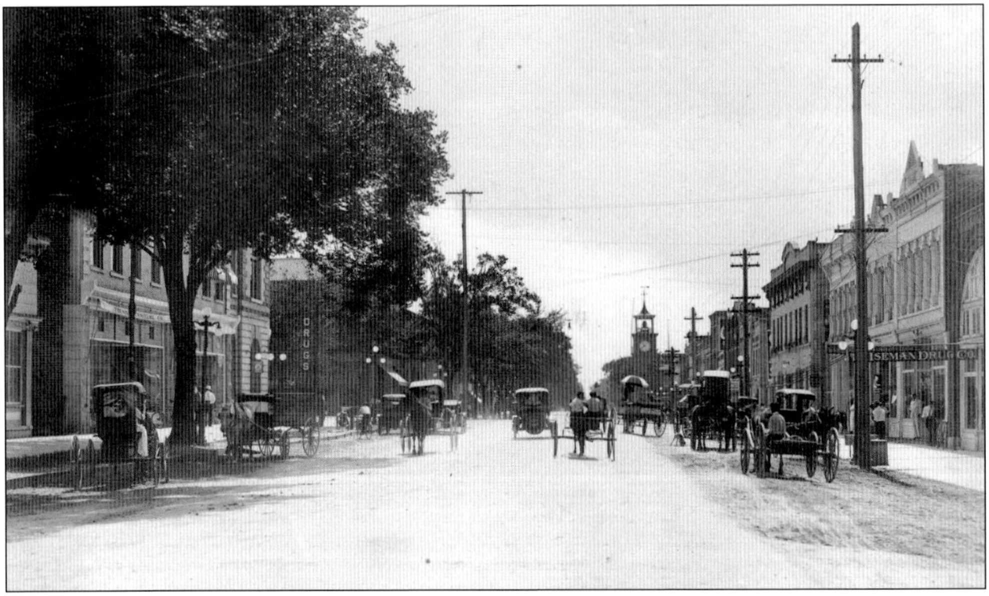

It was a busy day when a photographer captured this scene from the 800 block of Front Street. The city hall, built in 1911, is seen at the foot of Broad Street on the left. Georgetown's two banks in stately brick buildings, the Bank of Georgetown and the People's Bank, can be seen on either side of Broad Street near the "Drugs" sign. A diversity of transportation—buggies, Model Ts, wagons, and bicycles—is evident. Streetlights mounted on cast iron posts in the sidewalk added a charm to the street at night and date the photograph to 1914.

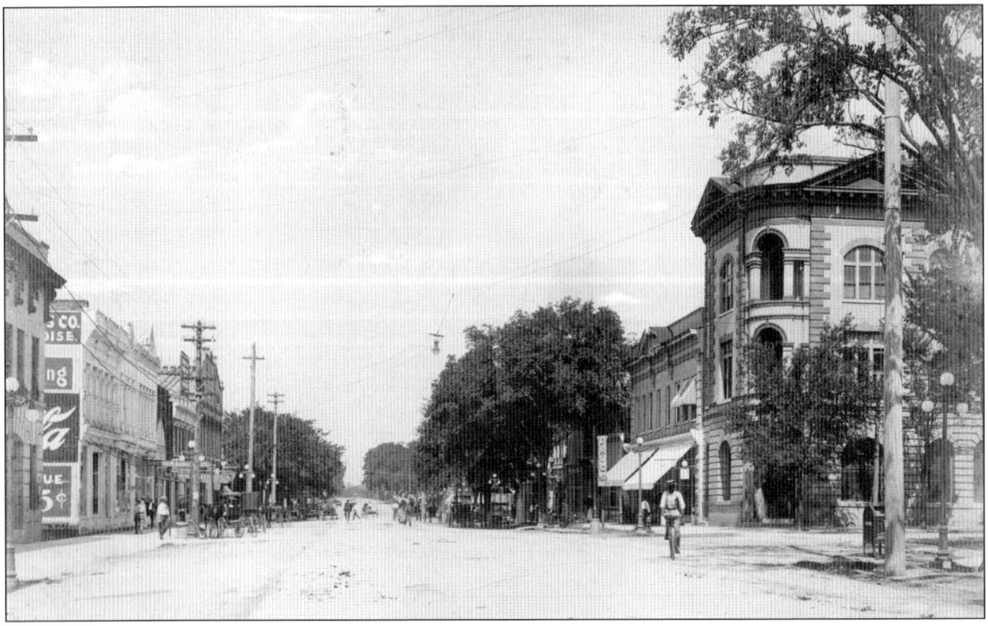

A bicycle or a horse and buggy offered the most reliable transportation when this photograph was taken. The three-story brick building on the right is the Bank of Georgetown, of which Mayor W. D. Morgan was president. Across Front Street at the extreme left of the photograph is the fire hall. Impressive trees lined the street as though in tribute to Mayor Morgan and some of his associates. The three-globe street lights along the sidewalk date the photograph to 1914 or later.

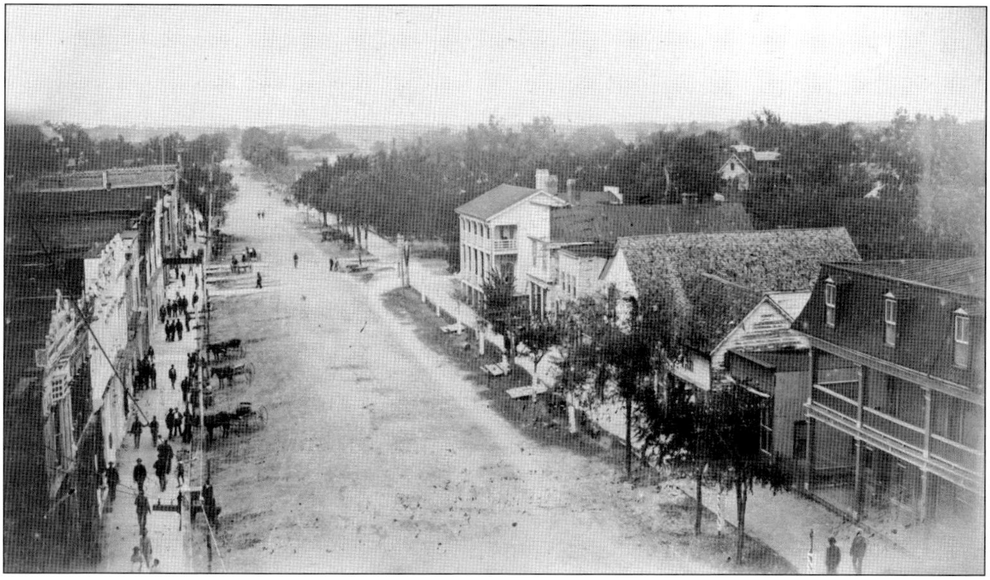

This early view of Front Street is particularly intriguing, as it must have been taken from the town clock, and yet the first third of the 700 block is not visible. The first building on the left is 709 Front Street. Interesting also is that all the business is taking place on the left where most of the stores were newer, having been built since 1885. On the right in the photograph's center is the Gladstone Hotel and at the far right, the Commercial Hotel. The house appearing from the trees on Broad Street is that built by M. Manheim in 1896. The concrete sidewalks and electric lights indicate progress in the city on the Sampit River.

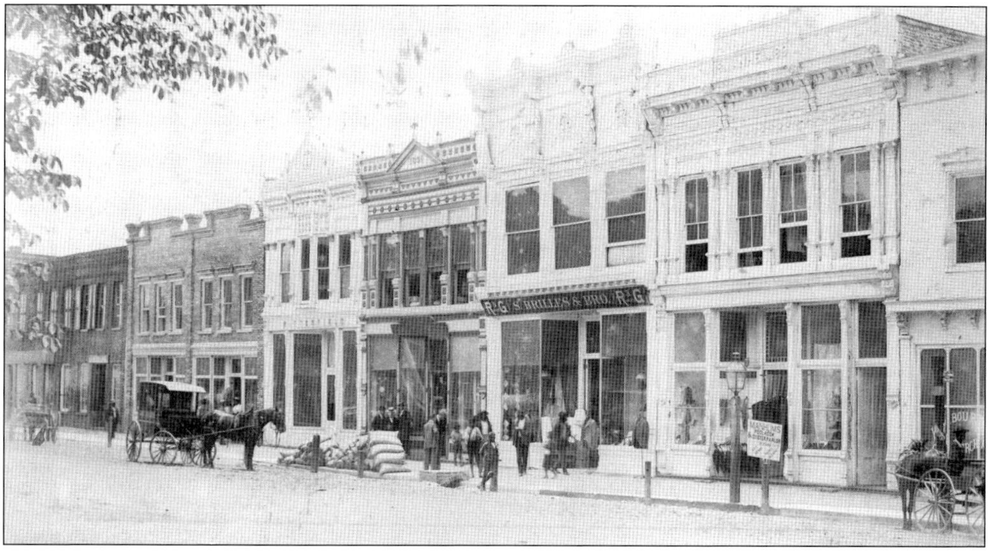

Downtown Georgetown presented an easygoing scene when this photograph of Front Street was taken, probably in the 1890s before the advent of electricity. The sign by the oil street lantern on the right proclaims Manheim's Pool Room and Oyster Parlor. Merchandise for sale in stores often was displayed on sidewalks, and storekeepers would scurry when a sudden rain blew up. The architecture of the buildings seen here is particularly interesting. The photograph shows the 700 block of Front Street. It shows seven Front Street stores, including S. Brilles and Brothers, Manheim's Pool Room and Oyster Parlor, and C. L. Ford Family Grocery.

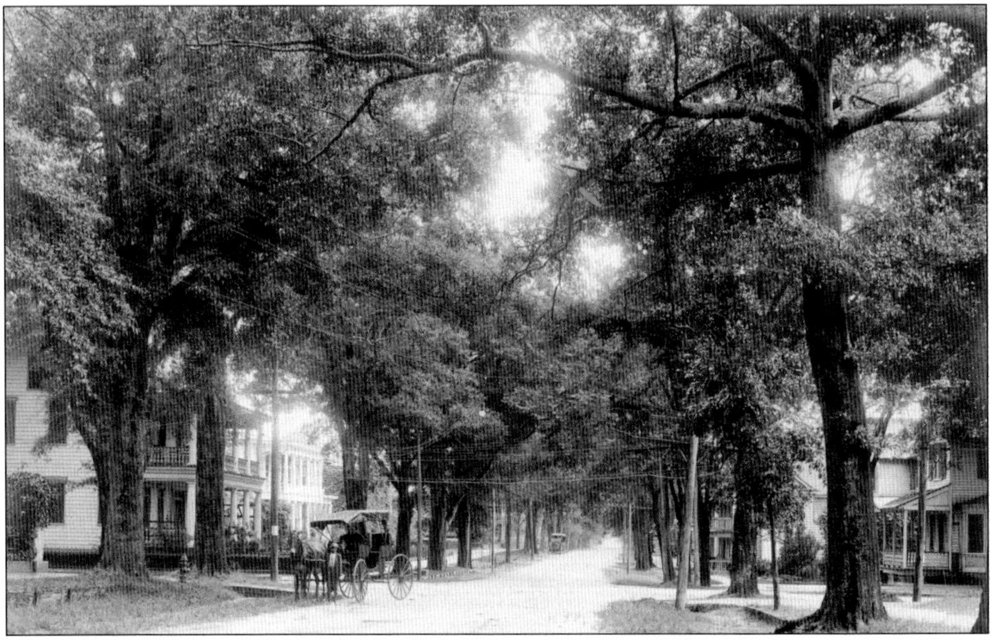

The shutters are all closed in this Prince Street scene, presumably to keep out the sunlight and hot air. This was a common practice in the South before air conditioning. There is little activity except for the young man attending the horse and buggy. William Doyle Morgan's home is on the left; all others visible are still standing.

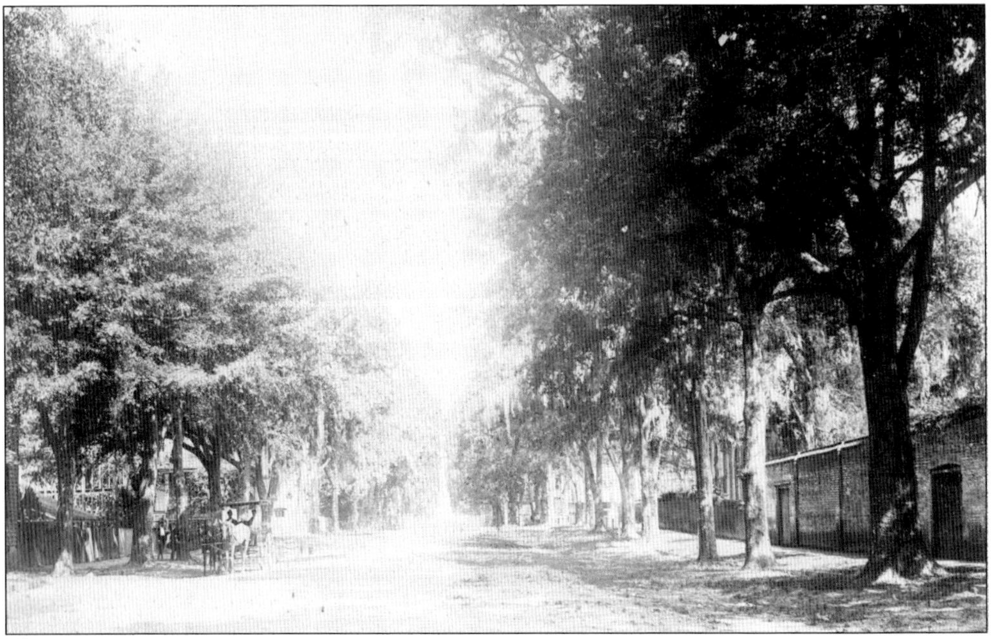

This view of the 700 block of Highmarket Street shows the high brick wall of the old jail on the right, then the wall and side of Prince George Winyah Episcopal Church. The first house on the left has been torn down, but the other, which would be on that corner, is still intact. The absence of light poles would date this before 1896. The Confederate monument can barely be seen in the distance.

This photograph shows the west side of the 200 block of Broad Street. The Rose Kaminski house, left, was probably built by the Carr family prior to the Civil War. Originally the house was located closer to the street, but Rose Kaminski moved it farther back on the lot and added the semicircular drive and the porte-cochere at the front. The children shown have books in hand and are ready for a full school day.

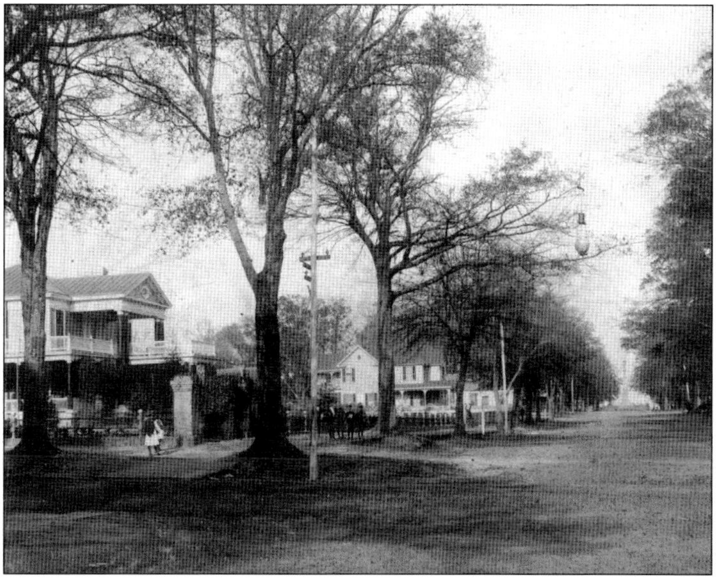

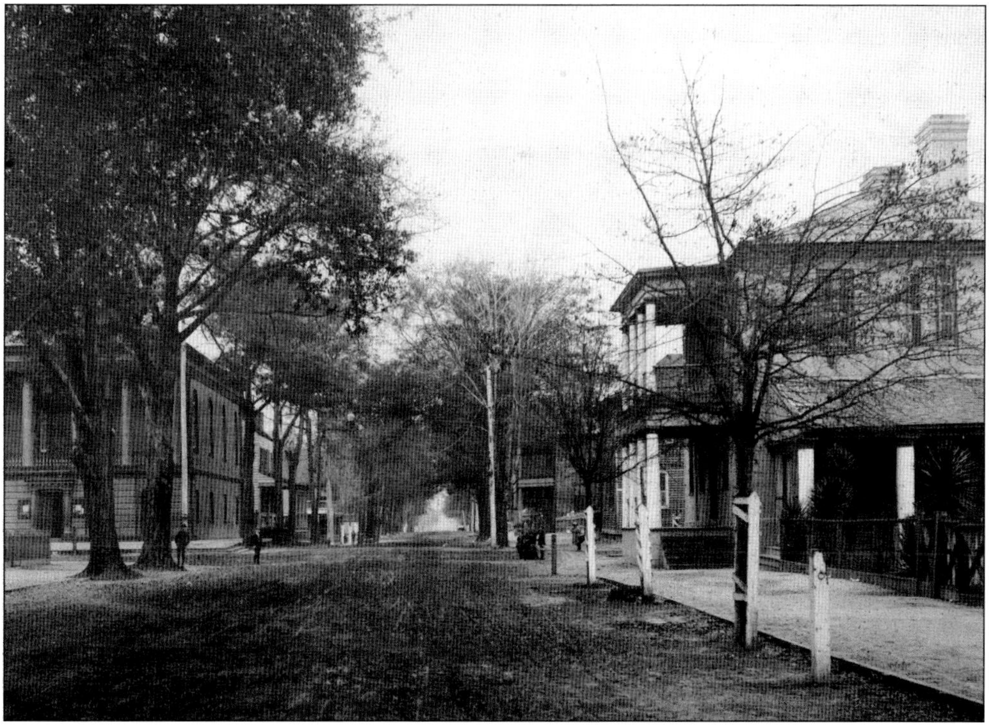

This view of Prince Street looking west across Screven Street shows that considerable change has taken place. The most obvious alteration is in the stucco building to the right. Though still recognizable, the top porch has been removed and the roofline completely redone. This was possibly done between 1910 and 1914, when it was used as an armory by the rifle guard. It was later the Masonic Lodge and at present houses the Georgetown County Museum. The house behind the Georgetown County Courthouse (left) has been torn down and the one opposite it moved back off the sidewalk. The other house on the left still remains in the same location (719 Prince Street).

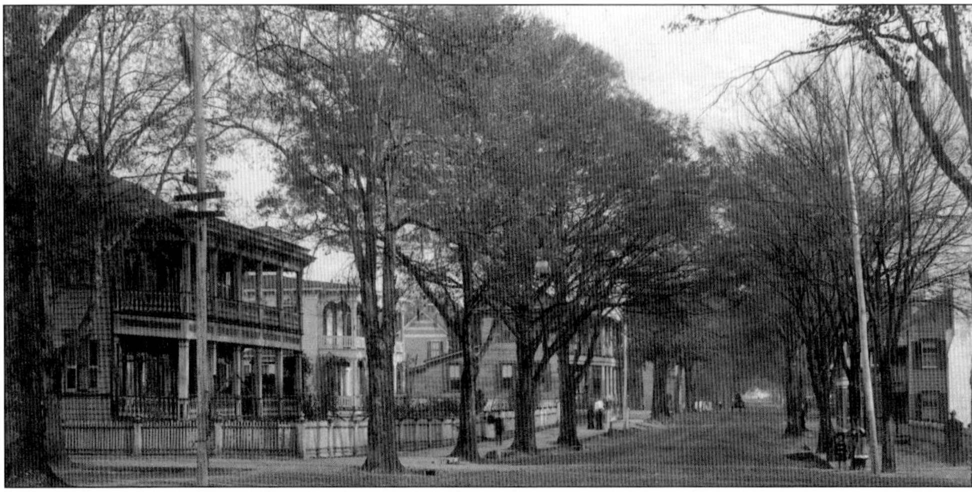

This view of Prince Street from just beyond the intersection of Broad Street looking east shows the W. D. Morgan house on the left corner. That and the next house, built by Mark Moses, remain very much the same as in this *c.* 1900 photograph. The Moses house, topped by a "Widow's Watch or Walk," was used at one time as a Jewish Church School. The third house was moved back in line and remodeled extensively about 1902 into its present character. Close inspection reveals what appears to be a woman carrying a large load balanced on her head on the sidewalk at left. The bare trees and dress of the children on the right corner suggest the season is winter.

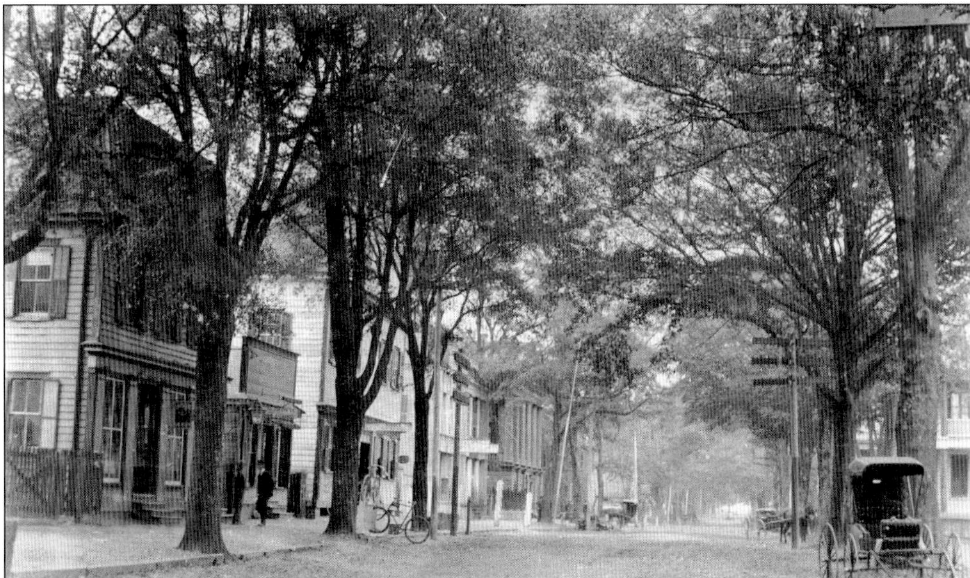

This view of the 200 block of Screven Street, looking north, was taken before one of Georgetown's worst fires in 1902. The first building on the left (west) side housed offices. The next was a barbershop in 1894 and a bicycle repair shop by the time of this picture. The third building was the post office and a printing shop. The next two were used for offices, and the Georgetown County Courthouse stands at the corner of Prince Street. On the right side, just over the top of the foremost buggy, is the porch of a house that may have been Georgetown's oldest. It stood on the site of William Screven's land. Screven is known to have lived on the site and is buried on the property. His son Elisha was the founder of Georgetown in 1729.

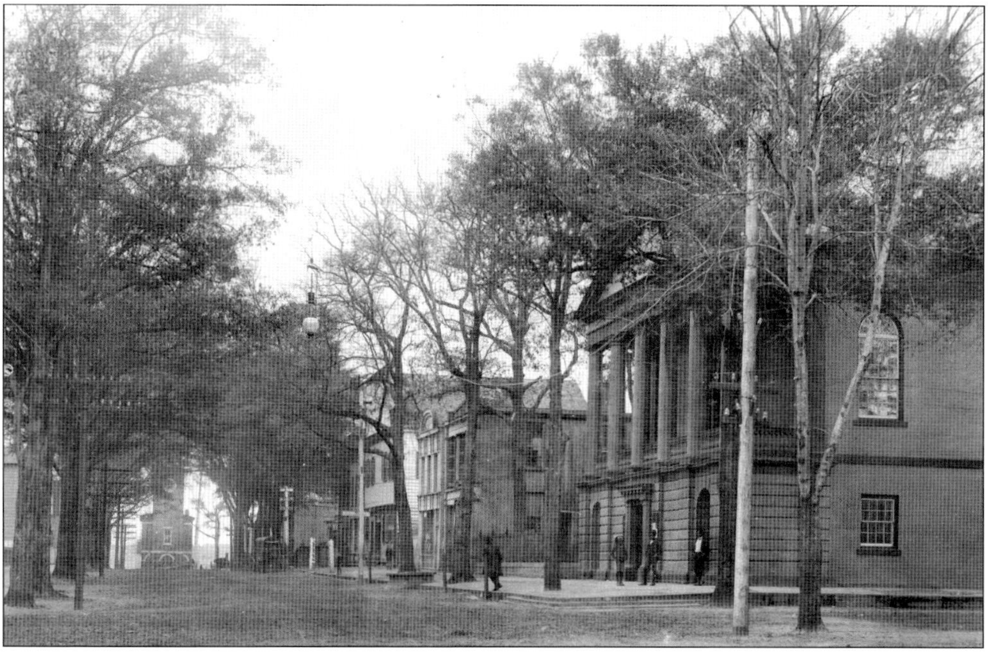

This photograph shows the same block involved in the fire of 1902 but from a view looking south. The fire began in the Southern Express Company building, near the center of the block, and spread to the *Georgetown Times* newspaper building next door. The inferno also engulfed three other buildings, which housed the post office and the law offices and libraries of L. G. Walker, M. W. Pyatt, and Walter Hazard. The J. R. Sparkman insurance firm, C. W. Rouse stationery store, Ingman and Bryan bicycle shop, P. M. Matthews's civil engineering office, and the Masonic Lodge were also lost. The loss of the five buildings was estimated at $16,500. The stucco building next to the courthouse was built prior to the revolution and became the sheriff's office after earlier use by rice brokers, a bank, and as a lawyer's office.

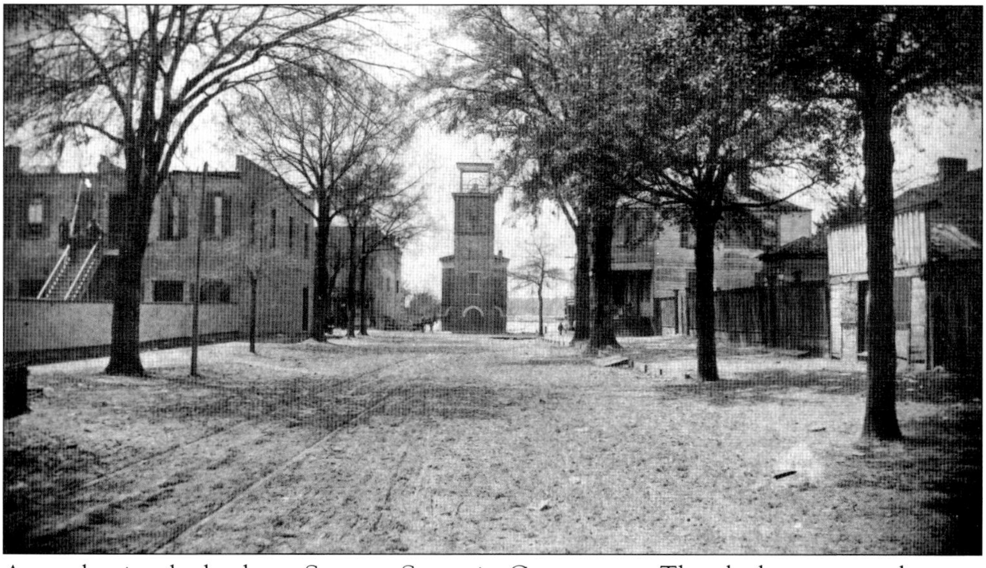

An early view looks down Screven Street in Georgetown. The clock tower can be seen at center.

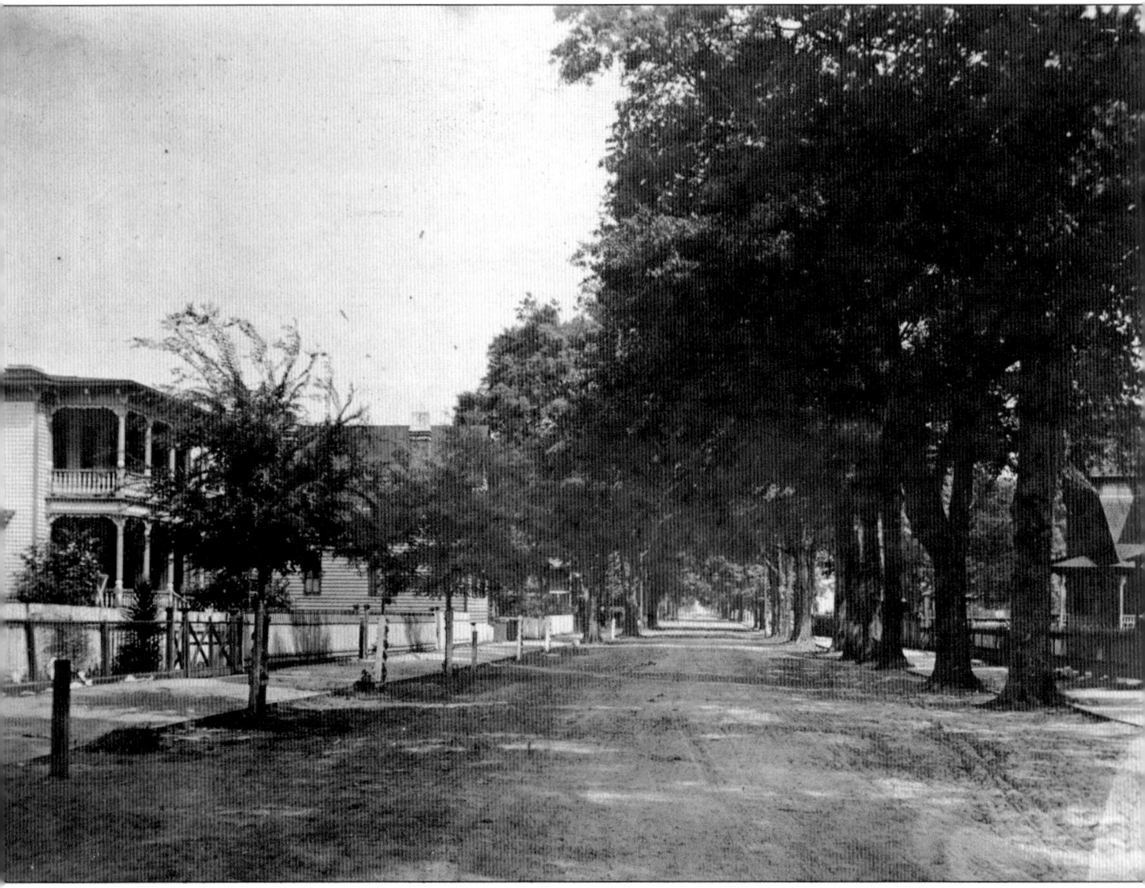

Looking eastward in the 600 block of Prince Street, the two houses on the left still stand, as well as the one on the far right, though altered. It is remarkable the number of houses seen in this 1890s collection that still remain and are in use.

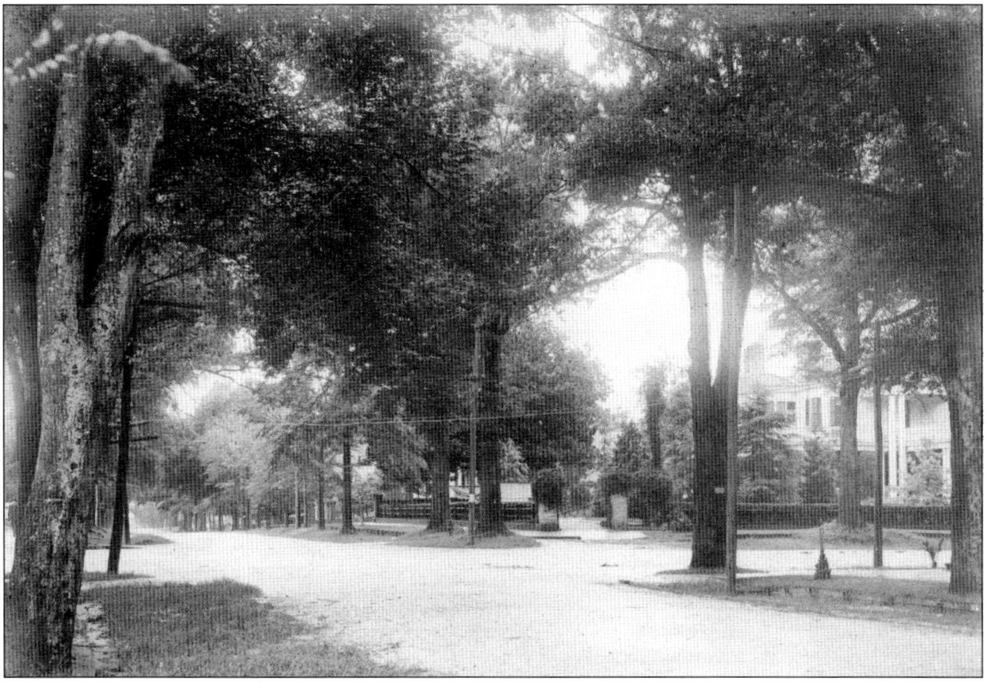

The Heiman and Rose Kaminski house is seen in this photograph of the corner of Prince and Broad Streets looking west. Power lines date the photograph after 1896, when Georgetown became electrified.

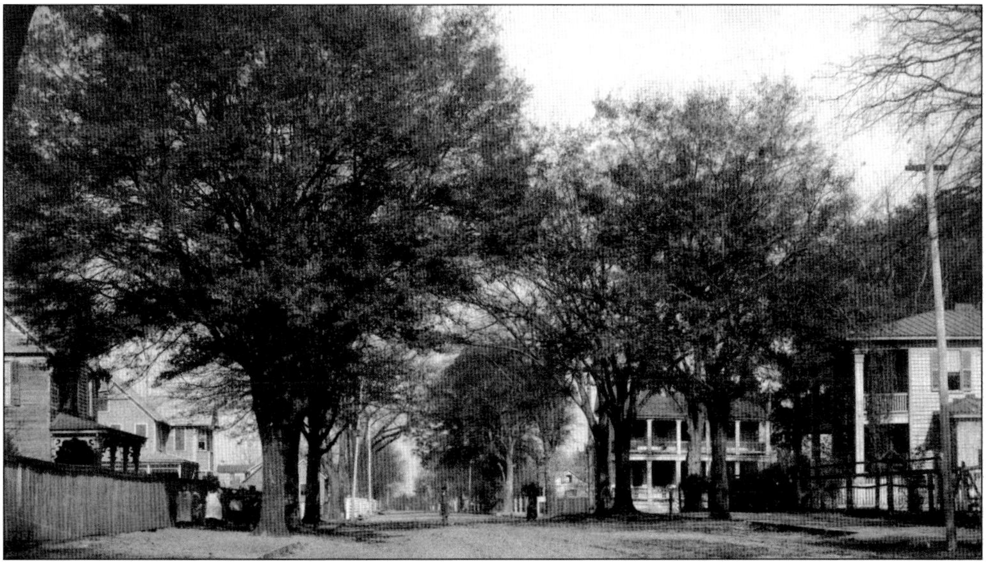

This view of King Street at the intersection of Highmarket Street facing north is hardly recognizable today, although three of the four houses still remain. The house on the left behind the high fence was built in the late 19th century and was once owned by James A. Bowley, a state representative from 1870 to 1872. Bowley, with R. O. Bush, also edited the *Georgetown Planet*. The second house was built in 1897 by prominent attorney and noted public speaker Walter Hazard, editor of the *Georgetown Enquirer* from 1880 to 1889. The third corner house has been torn down. The fourth was extensively remodeled in the 1950s, and the top porch was removed.

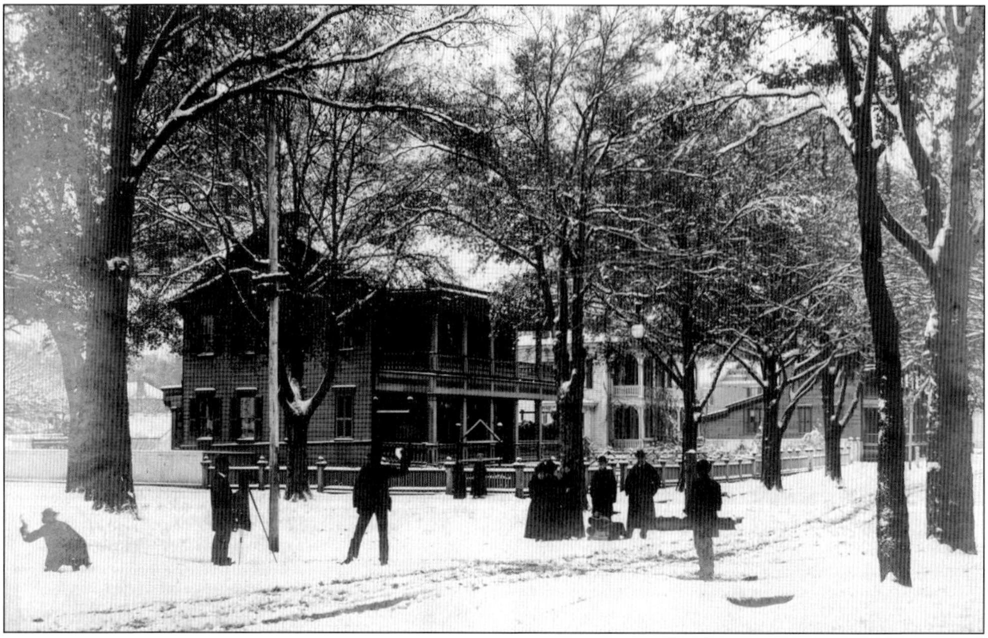

A special report to the *State* newspaper from Georgetown, February 15, 1899, says: "The weather in intensity of coldness, fall and duration of snow is said to be unprecedented in Georgetown. Snow fell to a depth of 6 to 12 inches, which offered no end of pleasure to all classes. The children were ubiquitous. Boats drawn by horses and improvised sleighs and sleds gave a picturesque effect to the scene." Most interesting in the photograph is a photographer getting ready to preserve this scene for posterity. The adults seem to have enjoyed snowball throwing as well as posing for pictures.

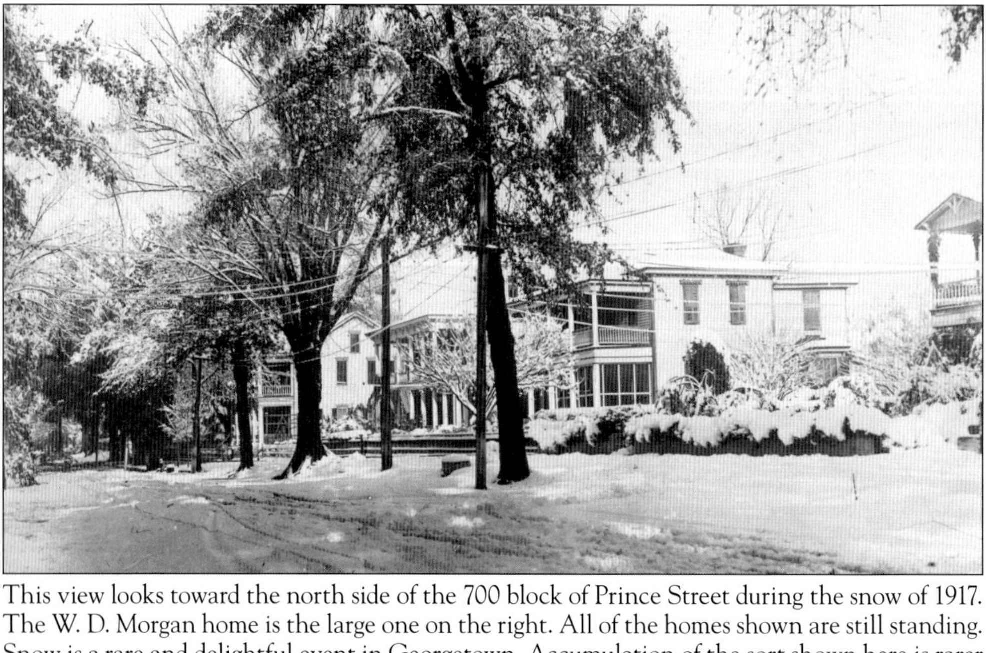

This view looks toward the north side of the 700 block of Prince Street during the snow of 1917. The W. D. Morgan home is the large one on the right. All of the homes shown are still standing. Snow is a rare and delightful event in Georgetown. Accumulation of the sort shown here is rarer still and provides recreational diversions usually unavailable to Georgetonians. This street scene is remarkably quiet, given the excitement generally created by snowfall in Georgetown.

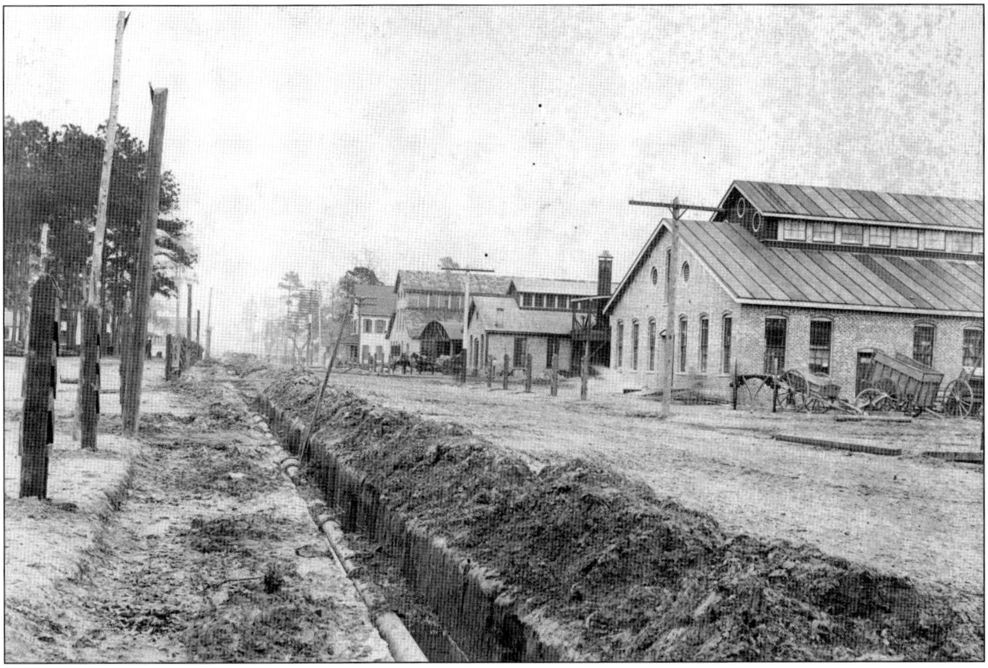

At the intersection of Fraser and Hawkins Streets around 1904, a sewer is being laid. On the left side, the large building in the distance is the Atlantic Coast Lumber Company Store that carried nearly everything. This saved the workers a trek downtown. The large buildings on the right belonged to the ACL and were used in its business. Judging from the wagons, the horse was still a major transporter.

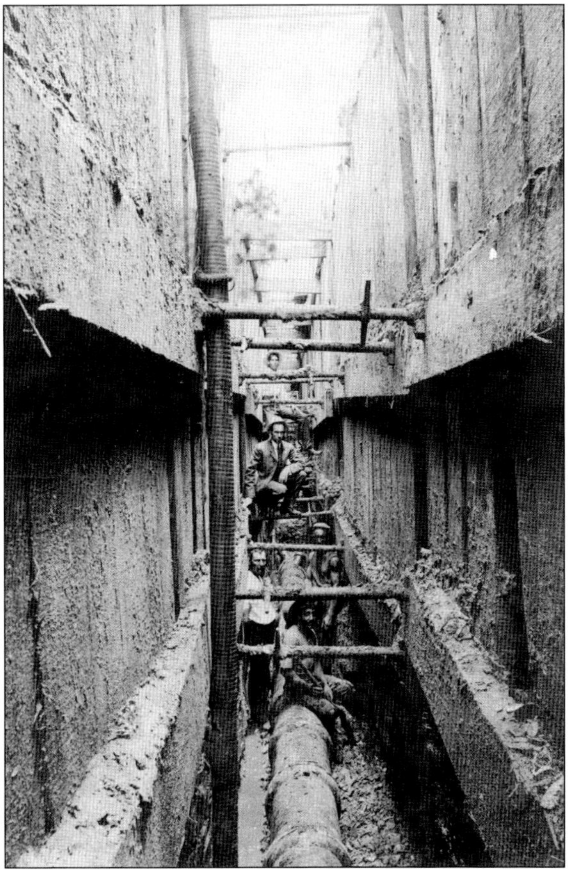

This photograph shows the installation of the sewer through Vinegar Hill, the highest spot in Georgetown, near the intersection of Front and Wood Streets. Recent estimates place this pipe about 22 feet below street level. Primitive methods of construction made this a dangerous undertaking. The sheeting on the sides, reinforced with rangers and braced with screw jacks, was under tremendous pressure. The vertical pipe on the left was connected with a suction pump. The gentleman in the suit may be J. L. Ludlow, civil engineer for the project.

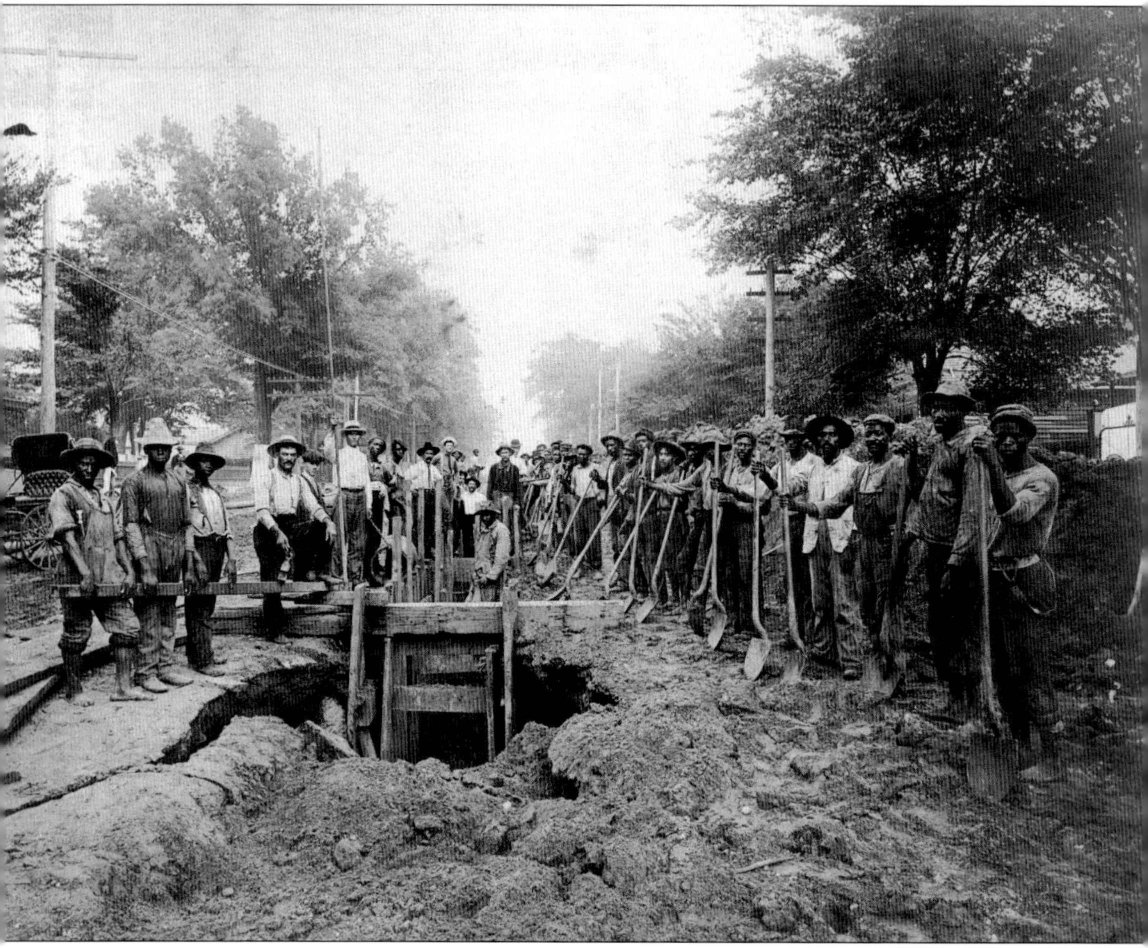

The crew that installed the sewer in this section of Front Street at Wood Street deserves to be immortalized on film. This is the highest ground in town and in order for the sewer to function, the pipe is laid some 22 feet deep. It was hard and dangerous work but has served Georgetown since the installation in 1904. The city had floated a bond issue for $75,000 for this purpose in 1903. No one in the photograph has been identified.

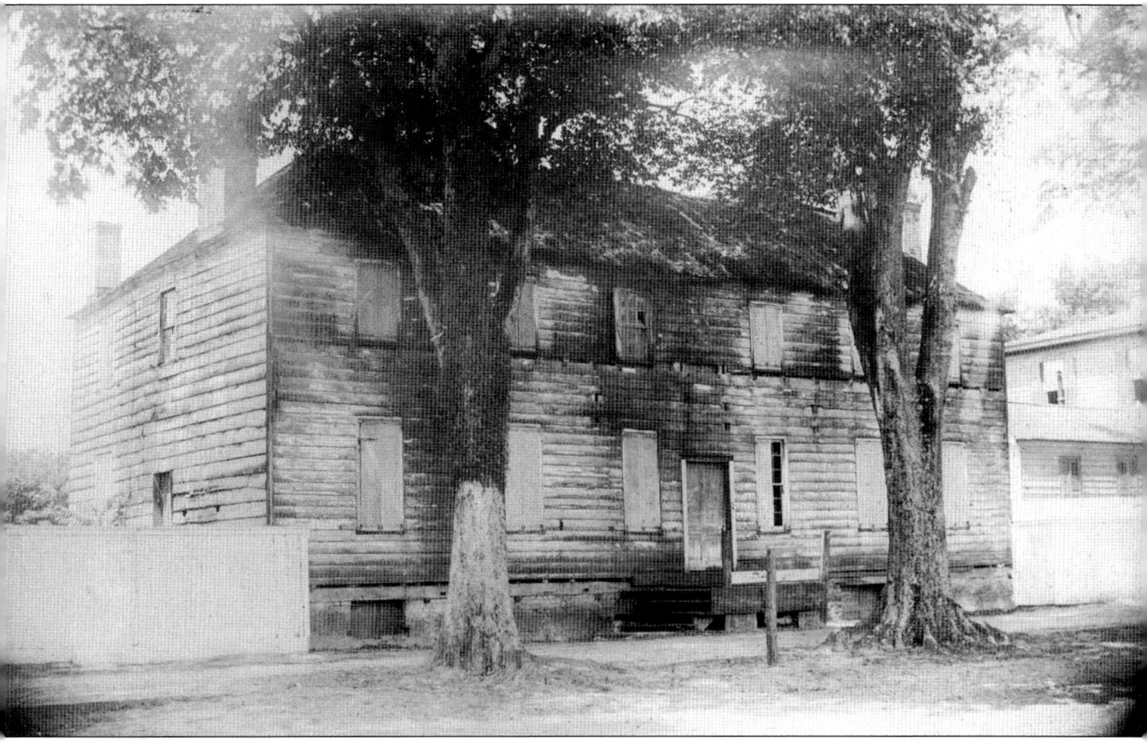

This building is no longer in existence. It was a hotel at one time and was connected to the house on the right, which stands on the corner of King and Highmarket Streets. Rebecca Susan Byrd (1787–1890) inherited the house and lot from her parents. She and her husband owned and operated the property as a hotel on Highmarket Street directly behind their house. Their daughter Alifair D. Hawkins married William Henry Dorrill, who moved into the hotel. A long room connected the hotel to the home, and the front room was used as a bar room for the hotel. In December 1856, the local newspaper printed, "the Dorrill House is very nearly completed, so much so that the house is open to the traveling public. The house is made up of two distinct houses—facing upon different streets—but connected by a long and spacious dining room. The main entrance is upon Highmarket Street, while the entrance in King Street is set apart for ladies, where a neat and comfortable parlor awaits them."

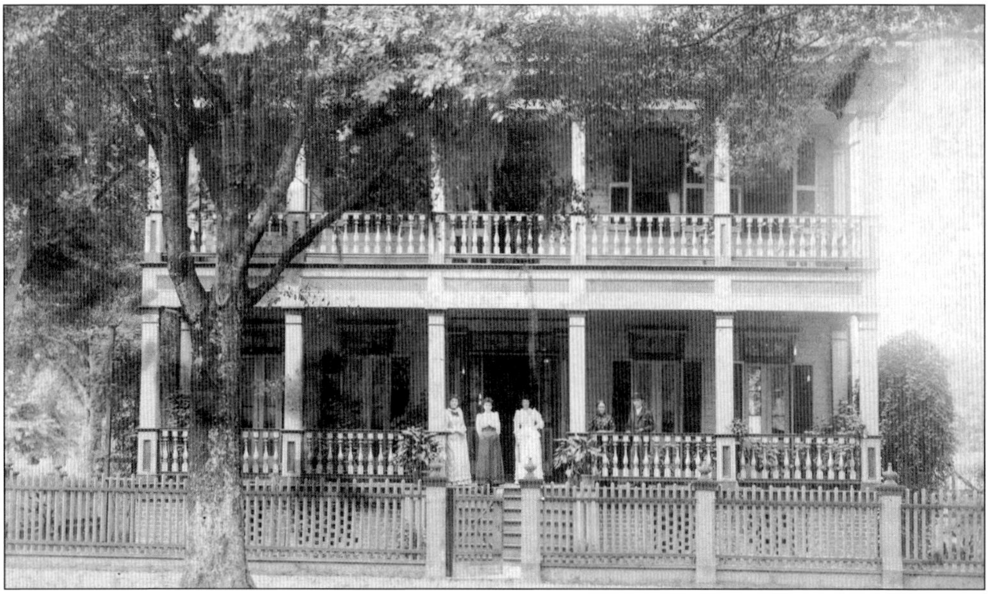

William Doyle Morgan served Georgetown as mayor from 1891 until 1906. His home, located on the corner of Prince and Broad Streets has always been one of the most attractive in town. As Irish Catholics, the Morgan family was privileged to celebrate Catholic Mass here before a sanctuary was constructed. In this picture of a leisurely summer's day get-together, Morgan is the gentleman and two of the ladies may be his sisters Kate and Agnes. Kate conducted a school for young children, held for some time in the Winyah Steam Fire Engine Company's upstairs meeting room on the corner of Front and Queen Streets. Agnes married Dr. Eugene Wasdin of Georgetown, who was on the faculty of the Medical College of South Carolina and later helped conquer yellow fever in the Panama Canal Zone.

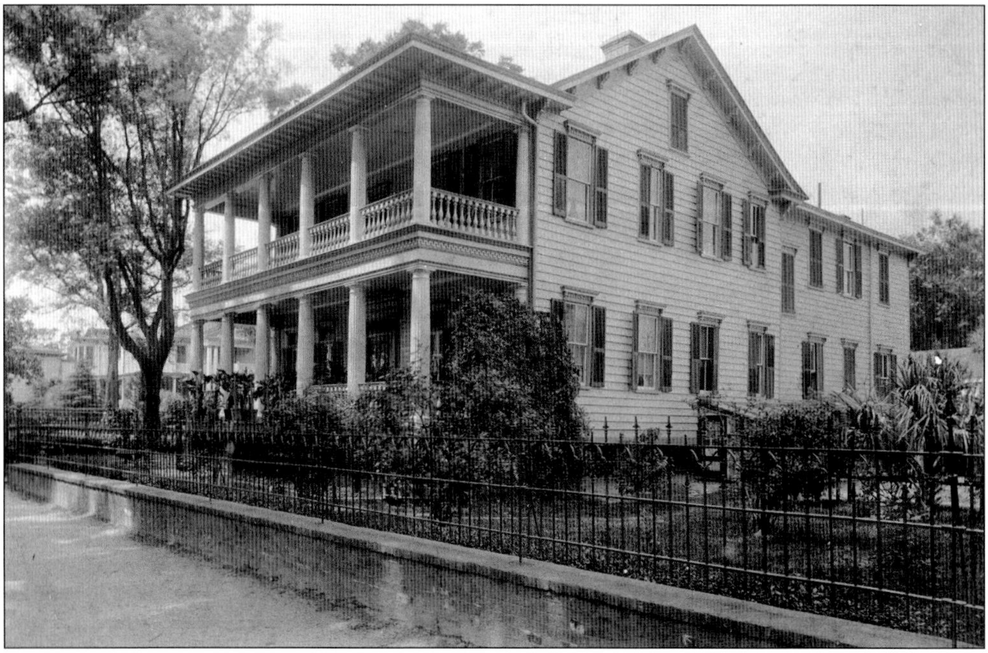

This photograph shows the side view of the W. D. Morgan house.

This two-story colonial dwelling stood on the northeast corner of Front and Broad Street until the beginning of the 20th century, when it was razed for a bank building. Tradition cites this as the British headquarters in Georgetown during the American Revolution. The British occupied Georgetown from June 1780 until May 1781. In 1780, Mayor John James of Williamsburg confronted British commandant John Ardesoif about British raids in the backcountry. During the stormy interview, James assaulted Ardesoif with a chair and escaped from this house to join Francis Marion when the British officer threatened to arrest him. The absence of electrical lines dates the photograph to before 1900.

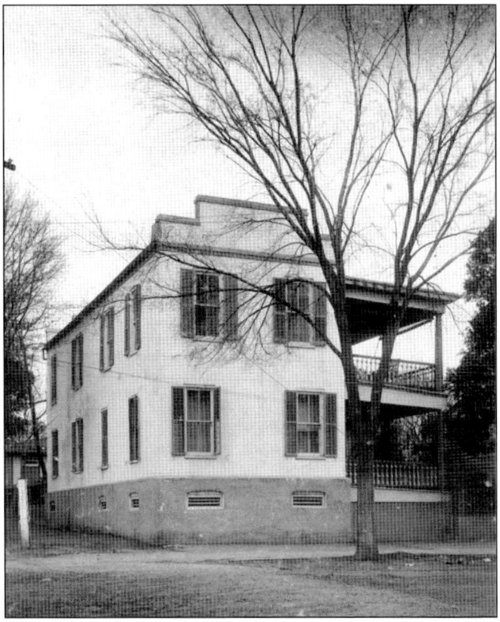

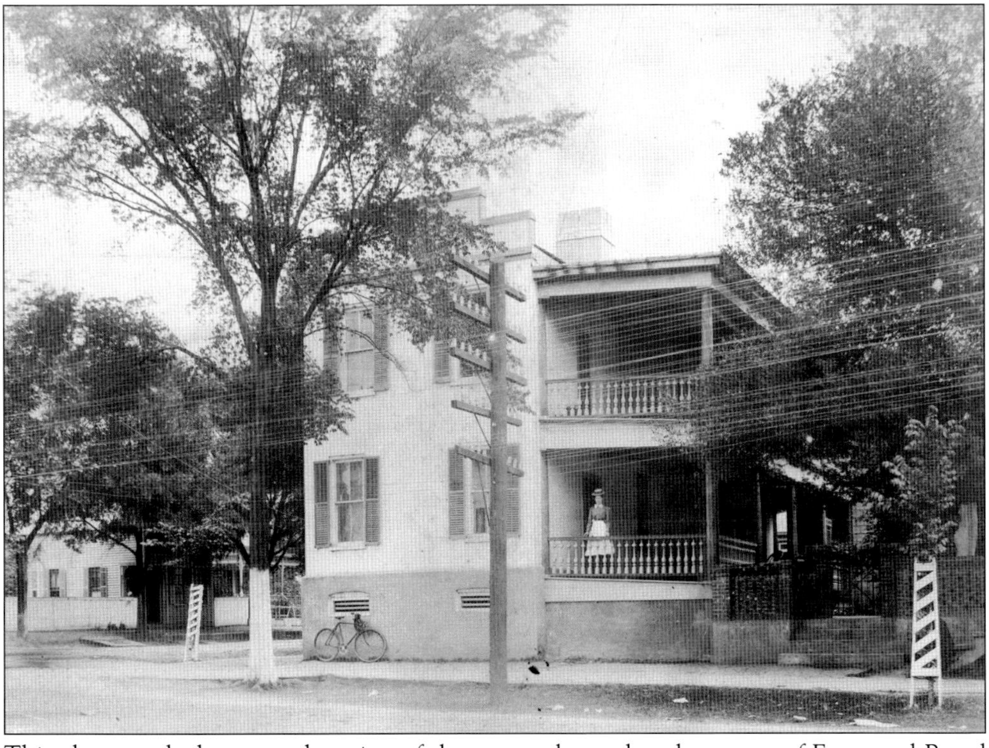

This photograph shows another view of the tavern, located at the corner of Front and Broad Streets where the People's Bank was later erected. It is deeply steeped in the history of Georgetown County. The Winyah Indigo Society held its meetings in this masonry building from 1750 to 1857, when the present Winyah Indigo Society Hall was constructed. Young trees on Front Street are protected by white boards, and numerous electrical lines are strung overhead. These details date the photograph to shortly after 1900. The woman on the porch is unidentified.

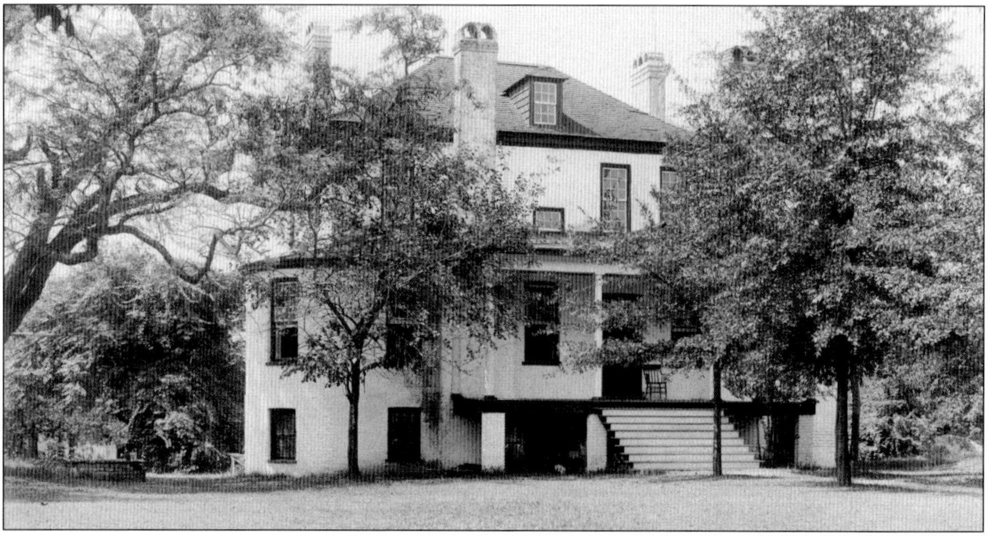

The Robert Stewart House is the two-and-a-half-story stuccoed brick structure seen in this photograph. It faces the Sampit River near the bend of the river behind Front Street. Scratched on a windowpane in the dining room bay is the inscription "J. W. Pawley, Sept. 2nd, 1851." Built in portions, the original section of the house was constructed between 1740 and 1770. Tradition has it that Pres. George Washington was briefly entertained here in 1791 as he passed through on his way to Charleston.

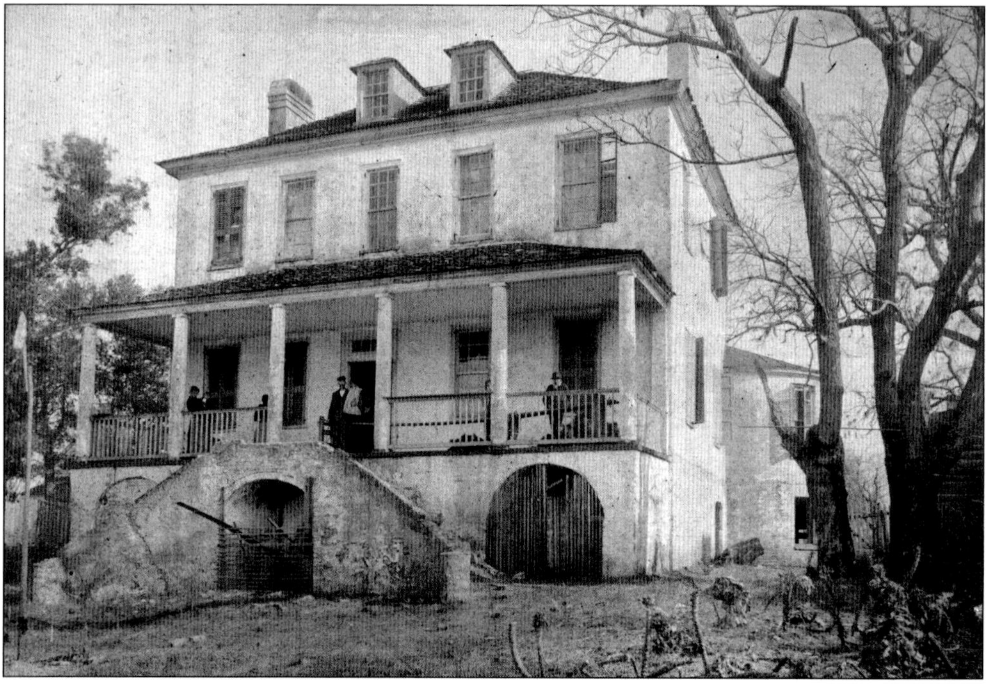

This front view of the Robert Stewart house, which faces the river, shows one of Georgetown's first brick homes. This handsome dwelling at 1019 Front Street still stands. The unusual round room is seen to the right. The rectangular bay toward the back was added later and is matched by another on the other side. The joggling board on the porch probably offered many hours of fun for the unidentified folks seen here.

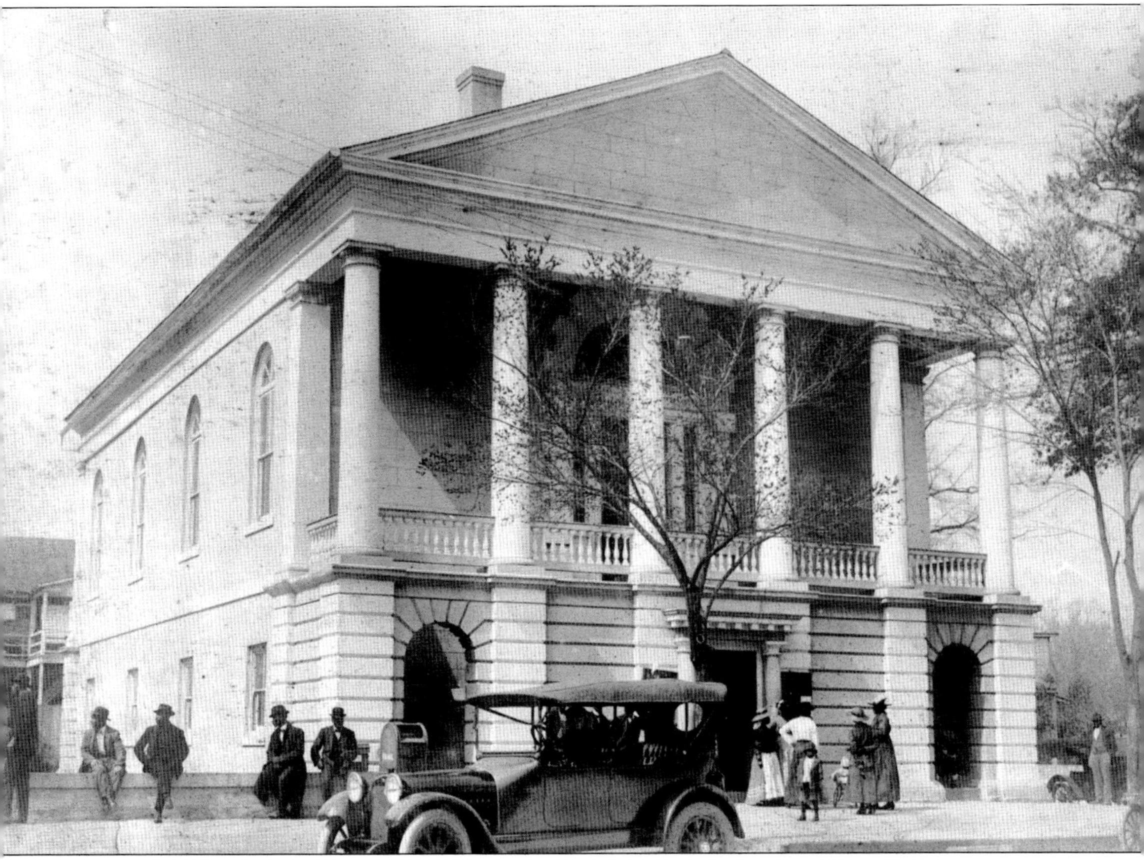

After a devastating hurricane in 1822, the Georgetown County Courthouse located on Duke and Broad Streets was severely damaged. A new one was constructed in 1824 on the corner of Prince and Screven Streets. It was designed by architect Robert Mills, designer of the Washington Monument. It is an example of the Greek Revival style that was prevalent in the United States between 1825 and 1860.

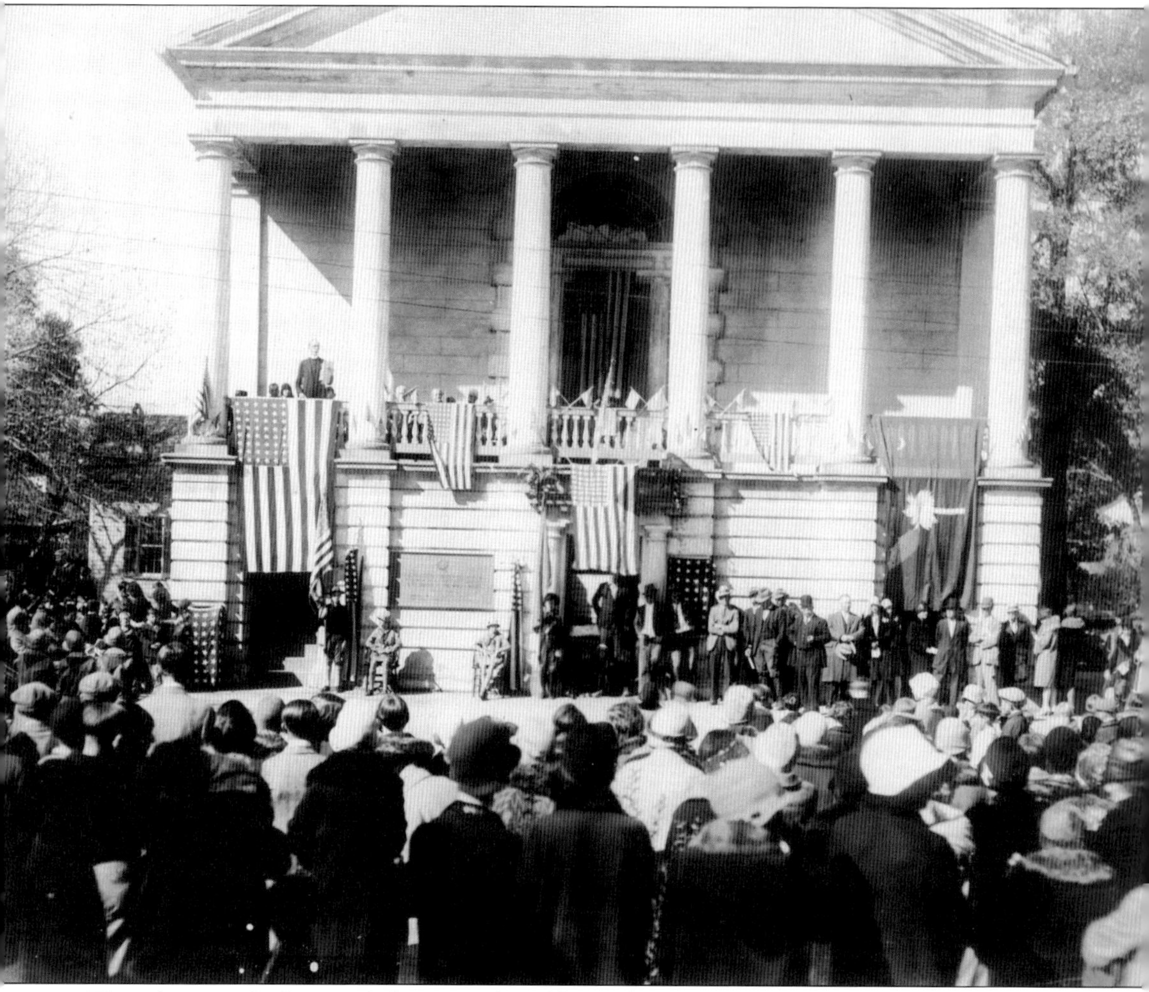

This photograph shows a dedication of a tablet at the courthouse honoring Georgetown men who fought in World War I.

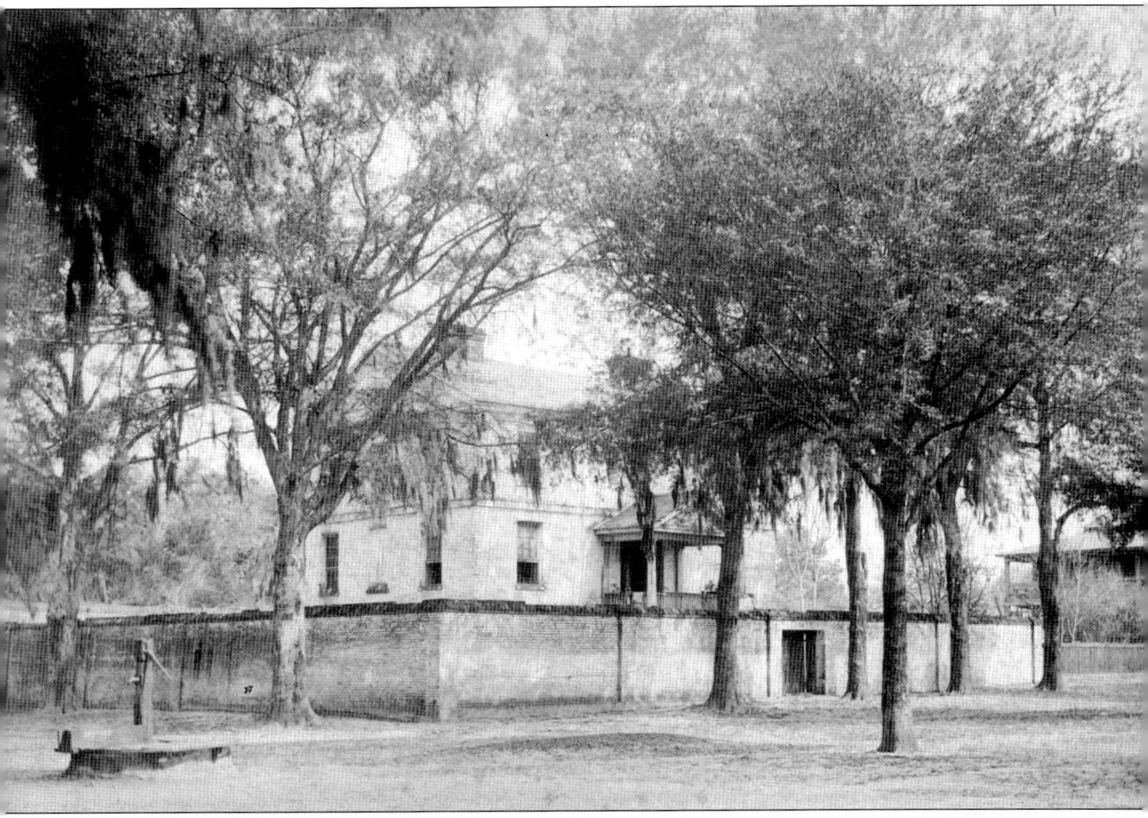

By 1840, Georgetown was in dire need of a new jail. Requests for appropriations were finally granted, and in 1845 the new state-of-the-art building was opened on the northwest corner of Screven and Highmarket Streets. The third floor housed four cells, the second floor was the sheriff's office, and the ground floor was the residence for the sheriff's family. The nine-foot wall surrounded the entire property, and the gallows were somewhere inside the enclosure. In the 1950s, the building became the Georgetown County Library, and in the 1980s it was purchased by Prince George Winyah Episcopal Church to be the parish hall and church offices. The home at the far right is dated 1770 and was purchased by the church to be the rectory in 2007.

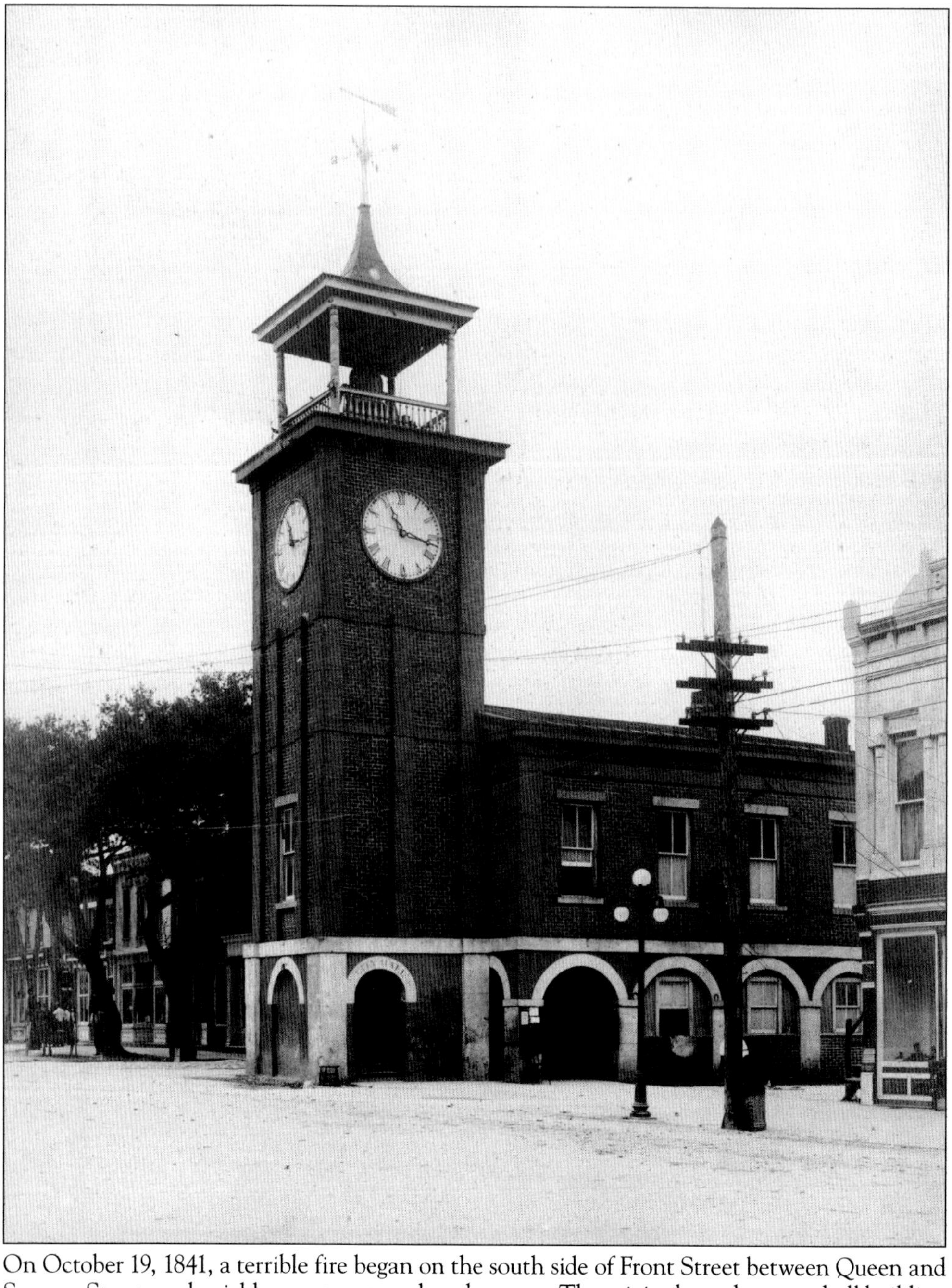

On October 19, 1841, a terrible fire began on the south side of Front Street between Queen and Screven Streets and quickly swept westward up the street. The original wooden town hall building was pulled down by ropes, and the fire stopped there. This building was constructed in 1842, a replica of the former one. Again it was the town hall on the second floor, and the city market occupied the open-air ground floor. The clock and bell were added in July 1857. Today the Rice Museum operates on the second floor, and the first floor contains offices.

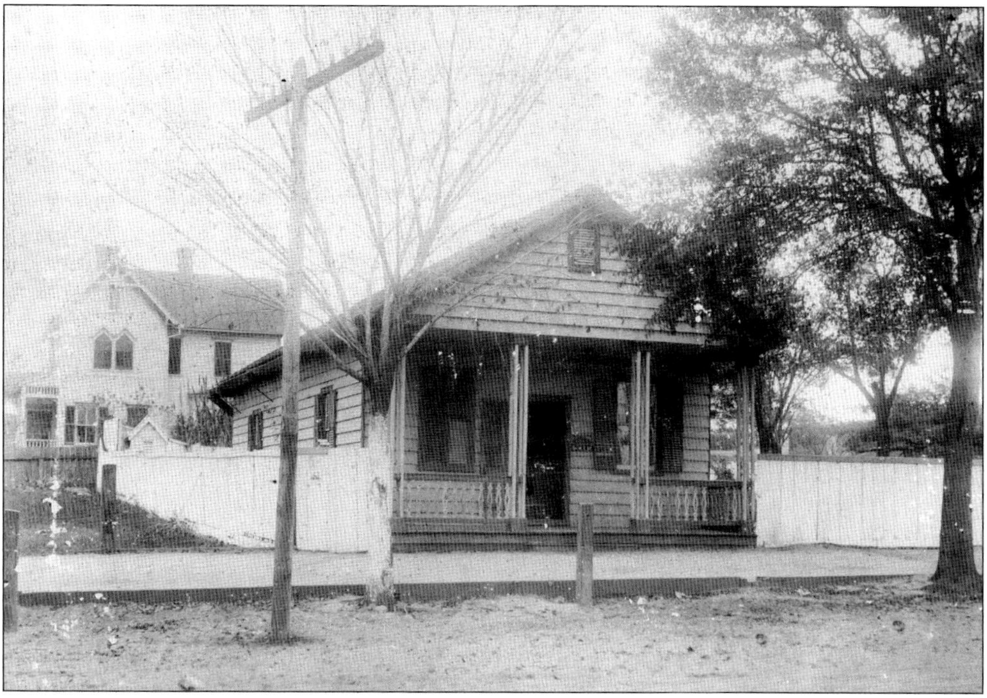

Dr. Thomas P. Bailey, who died in 1904, practiced in this frame building in the 800 block of Front Street, near where Tomlinson's department store stands today. Bailey was quite active in the post-Reconstruction life of Georgetown. Trees were still being planted and maintained in the main business section when this photograph was taken, which dates it around 1900.

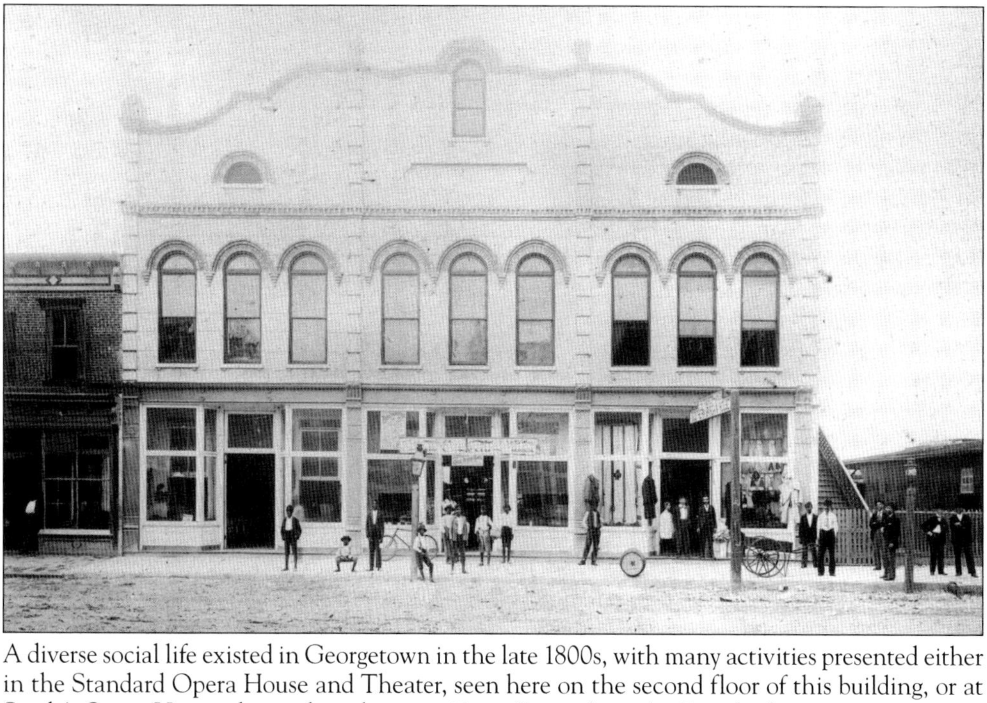

A diverse social life existed in Georgetown in the late 1800s, with many activities presented either in the Standard Opera House and Theater, seen here on the second floor of this building, or at Steele's Opera House almost directly across Front Street from the Standard.

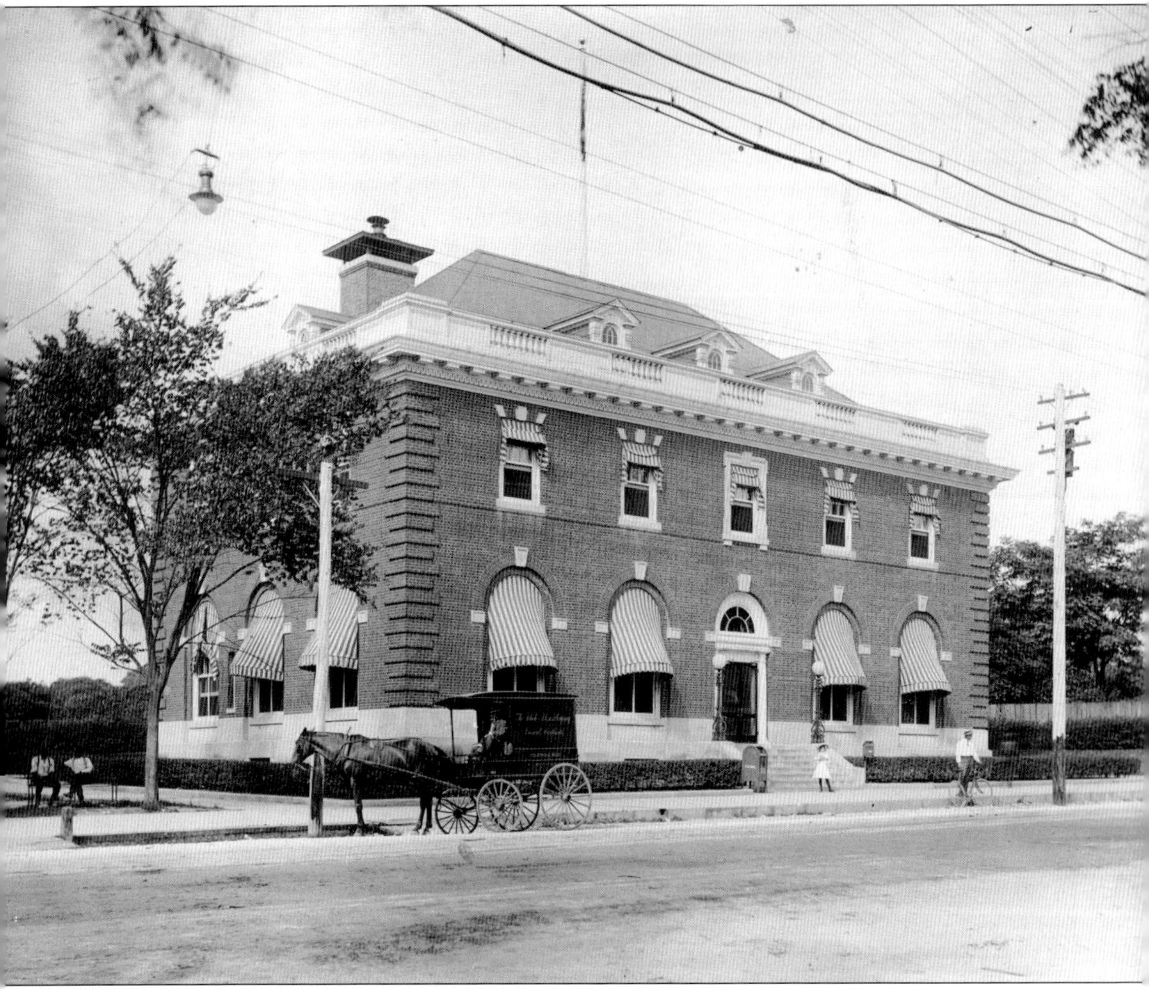

This large, handsome structure, erected in 1906, is considered one of the most substantially built in Georgetown County. The post office occupied the main floor with a customs office upstairs. There is great use of marble and brass throughout. A new post office was constructed in 1967, and this building was adapted to commercial use. It is a Georgetown landmark, adding character to the main business district.

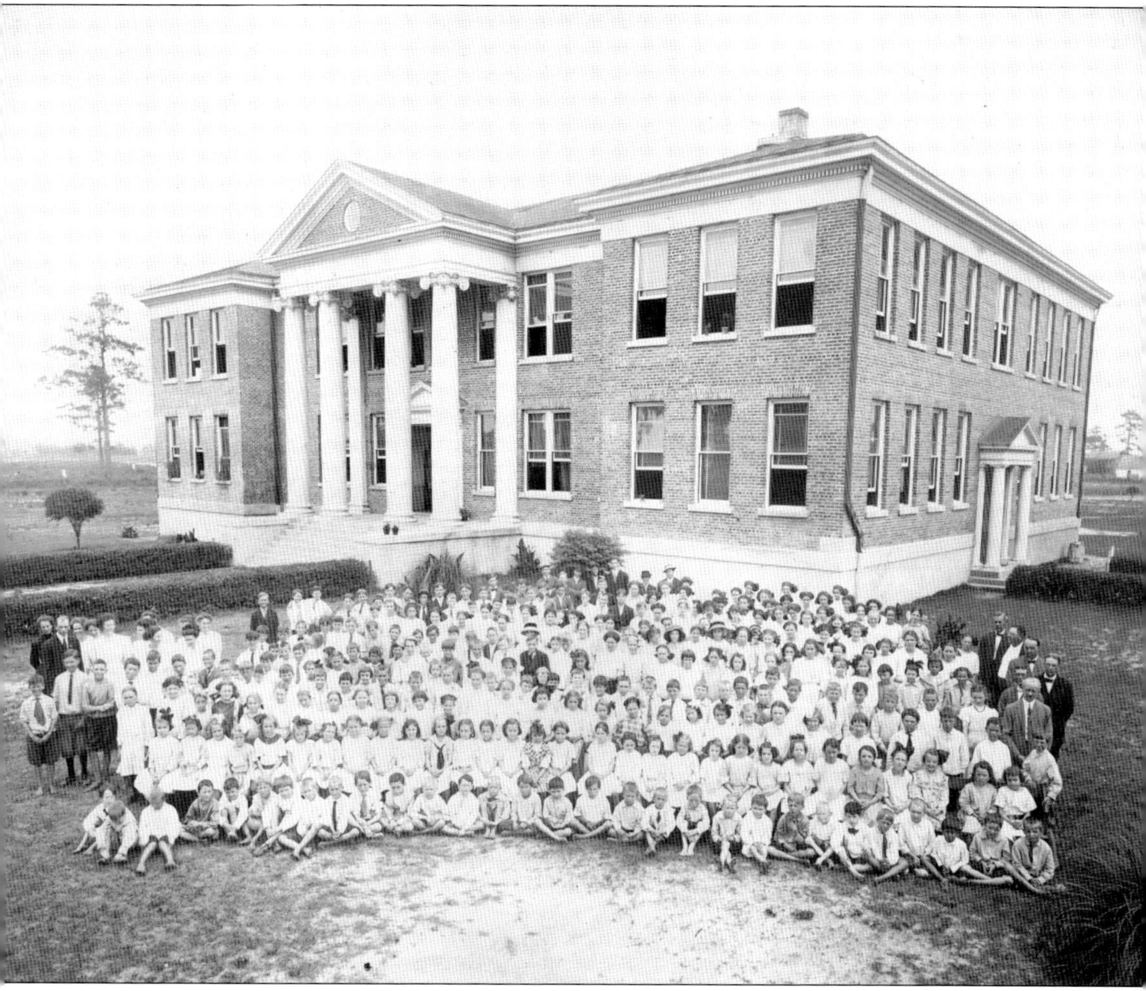

This grade school at the corner of Highmarket and Cleland Streets was completed and opened in 1908. Before that, classes were held at the Winyah Indigo Society Hall. In this building there were 12 classrooms and eight cloakrooms. The carefully manicured privet hedges on either side of the two walkways were maintained just as it looks here until the death of the longtime superintendent William C. Bynum in 1946. It served as the auditorium for Winyah High School, which was located next door until that building burned in the early 1980s. Although plans for renovation are still in the initial stages, some space has been opened to medical offices. It is hoped that the auditorium will be opened for the use of the community after restoration.

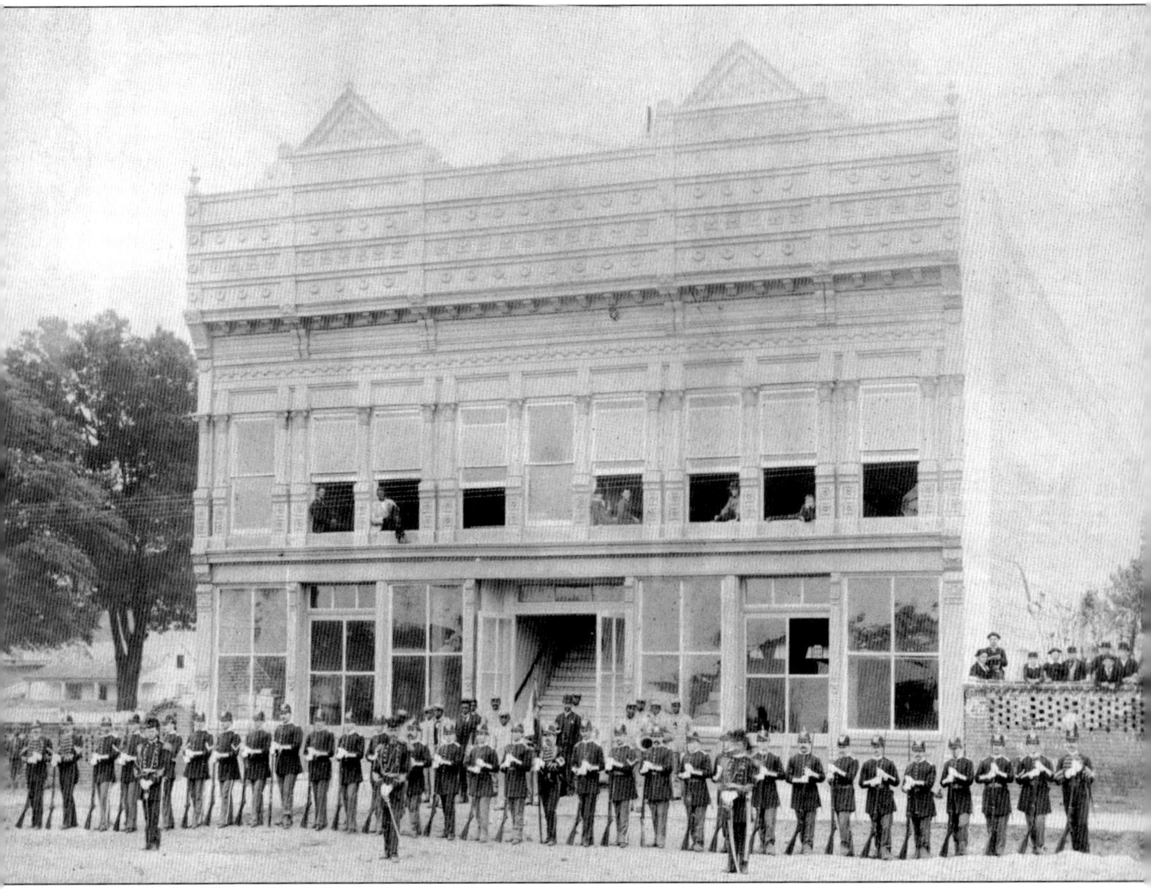

The rifle guards appear, with drawn bayonets, in the 800 block of Front Street in front of Steele's Opera House. The opera house was located on the second floor of this building, which stood on the north side of Front Street. A dispensary operated on the first floor to the right and a dry goods store to the left. Note the central staircase leading to the second floor.

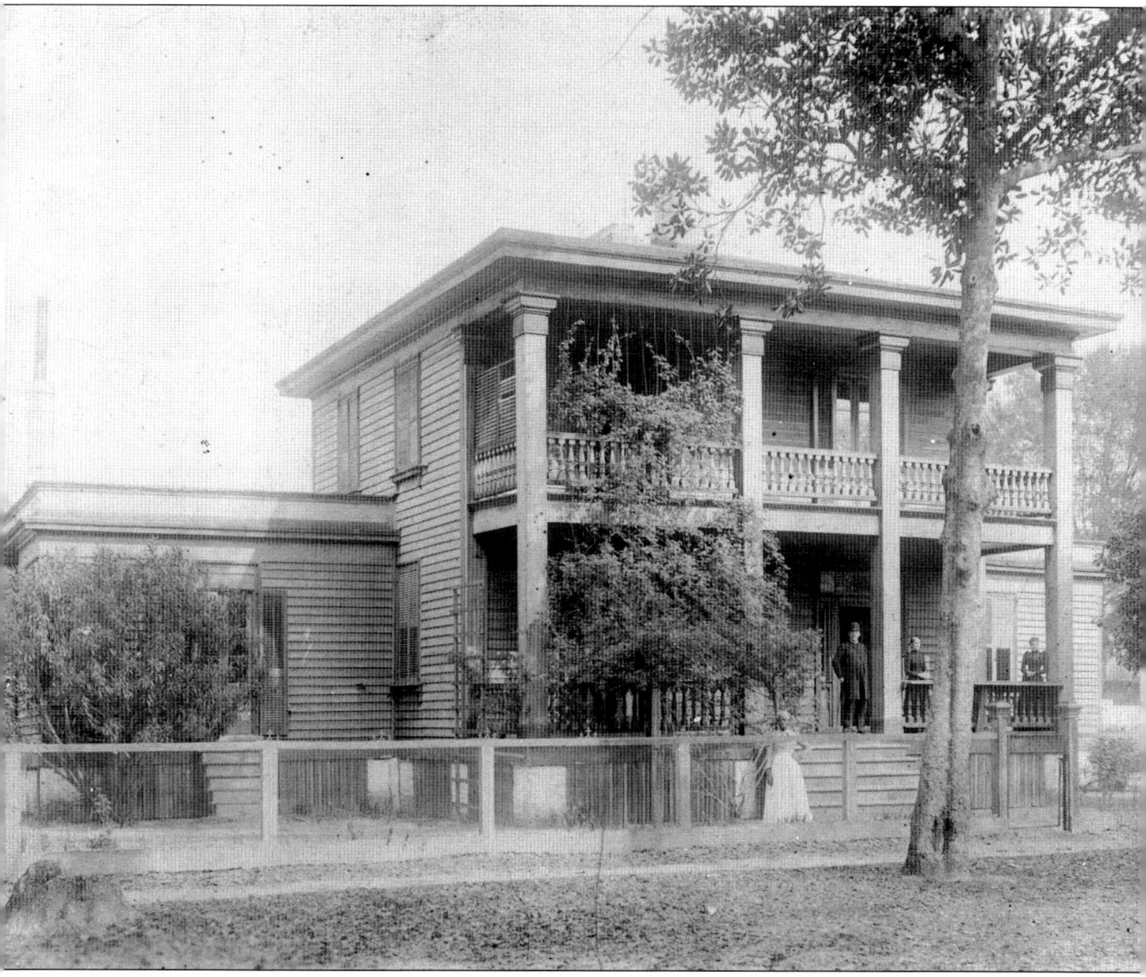

This handsome dwelling at 223 Queen Street served as the home for the ministers of historic Prince George Winyah parish until 2007. It was built around 1825 and has the unusual feature of a single huge chimney in the center of the house that serves all the main rooms, upstairs and down, with fireplaces for heating.

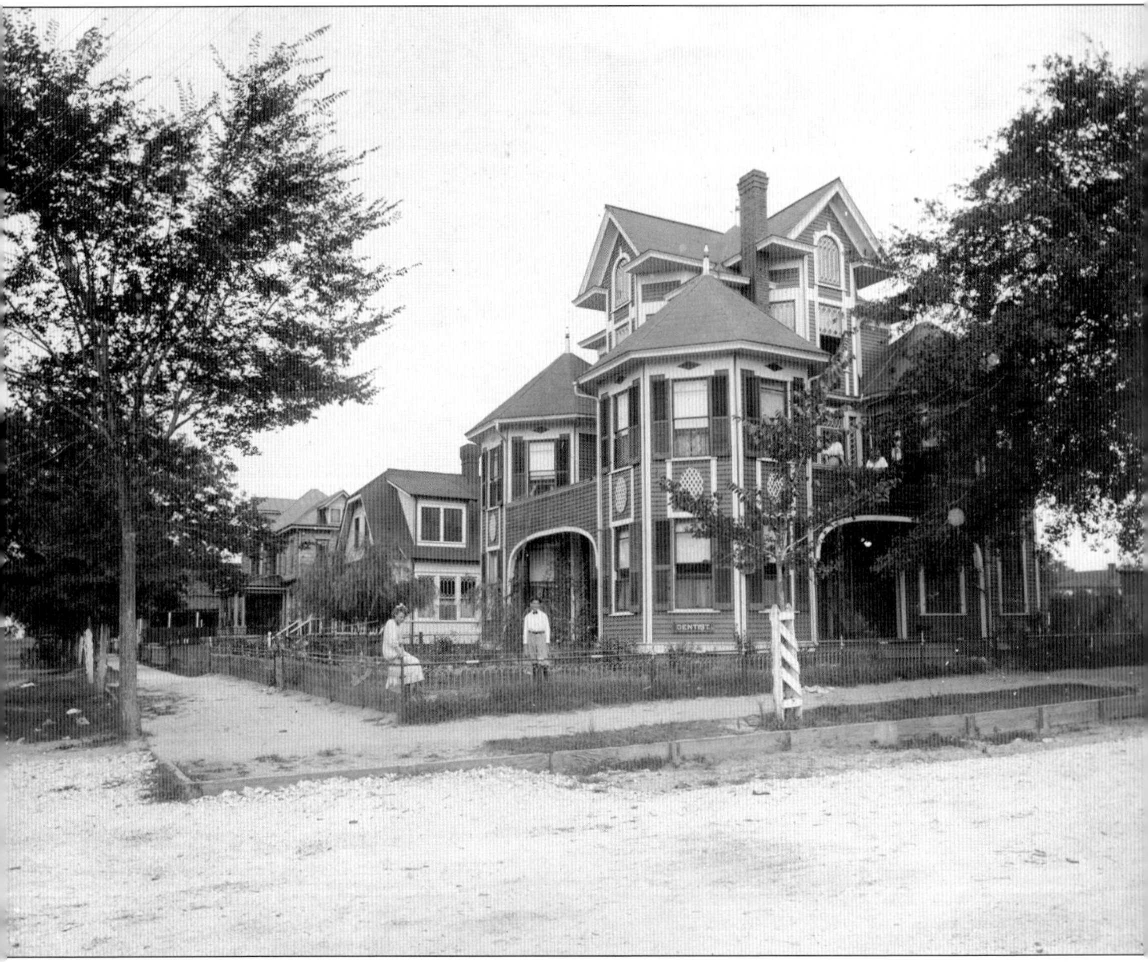

This unusual house, located on the northeast corner of Front and St. James Streets, was built by Dr. H. A. Farris, a dentist. It served as home and office. There was one large room in the center of the house on both floors, with four doors leading to the four octagonal rooms and four more doors leading to the porches. Each octagonal room had five windows and one door. The third floor had 12 windows, three over each porch, and the attic had four decorative ones. The oval pieces, painted to resemble latticework, are unique. This was razed in 1953, and the Presbyterian manse built on the site.

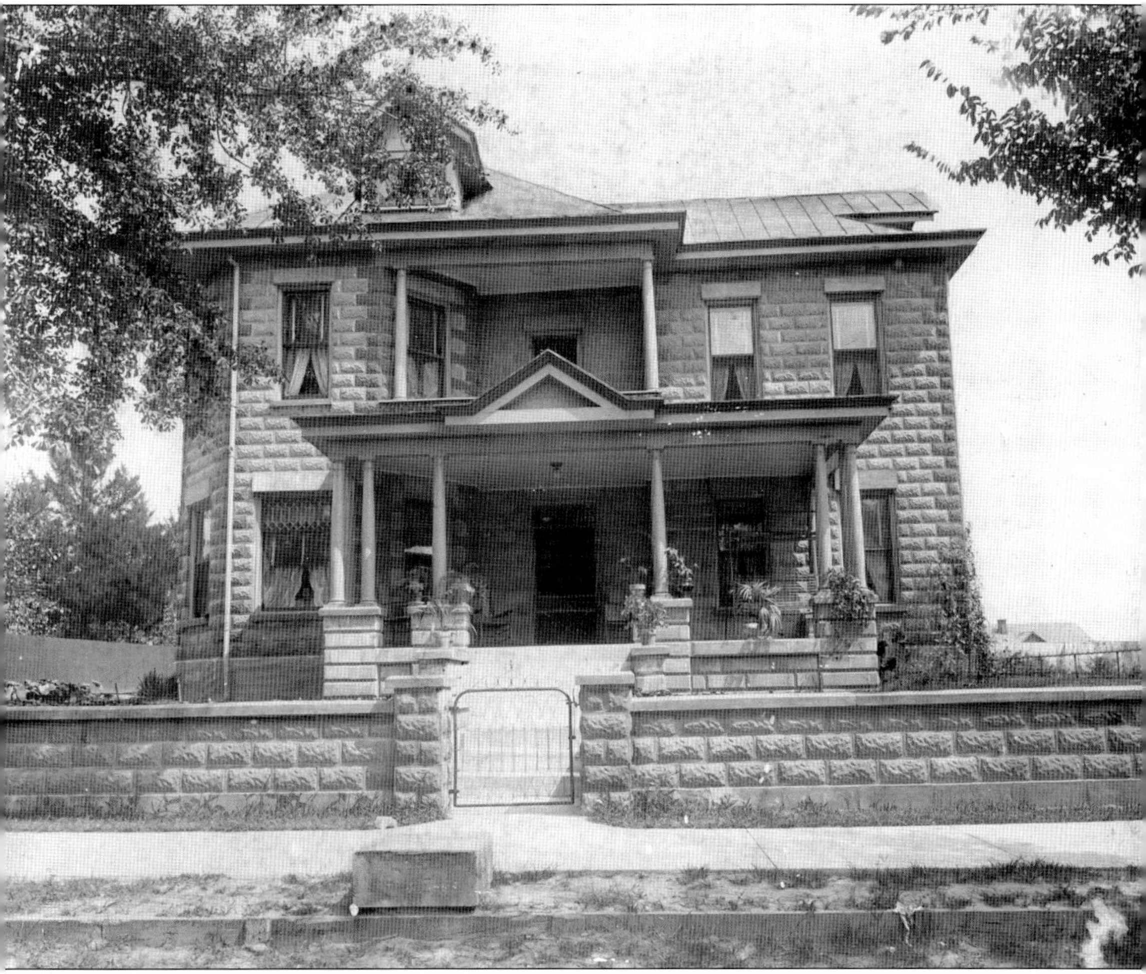

Another unusual house located in the 200 block of St. James Street on the east side still stands. The siding, which gives the appearance of large stone blocks, is really concrete blocks. Fred Brickman, a local furniture dealer, built the house around 1900. It is the only home in Georgetown of its kind.

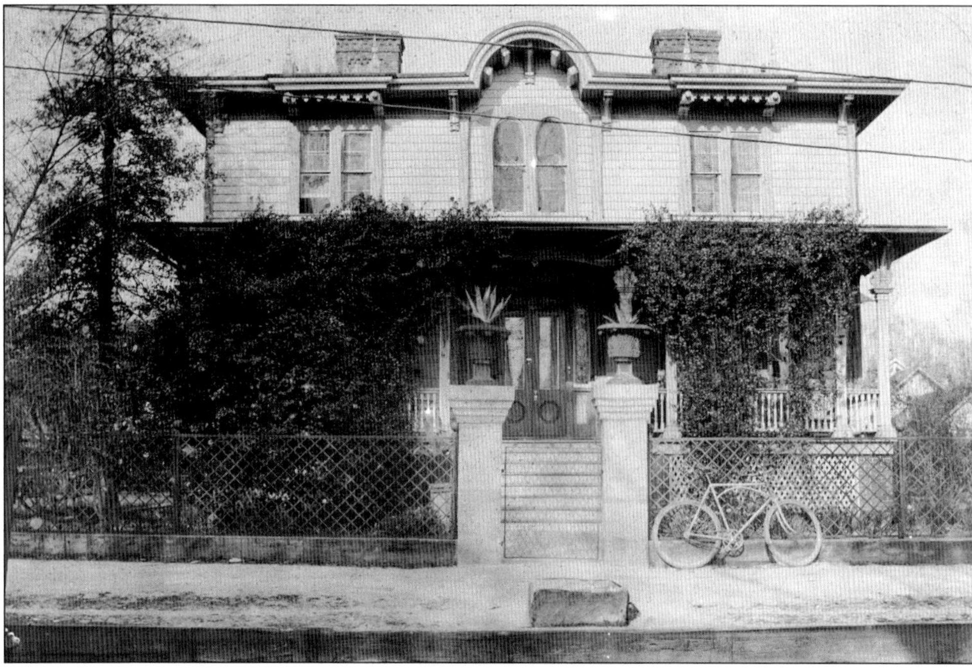

The Joseph Schenk house is located in the 800 block of Prince Street. This photograph reflects some remodeling with the most notable change being the replacement of an original picket fence with the metal one shown and the addition of imposing gateposts. The roofline and finishing details reflect high Victorian taste. The house was modernized at a later date, and none of these embellishments remain. This house was used in the film *Pied Piper Malone*, a silent movie made in the 1920s in Georgetown.

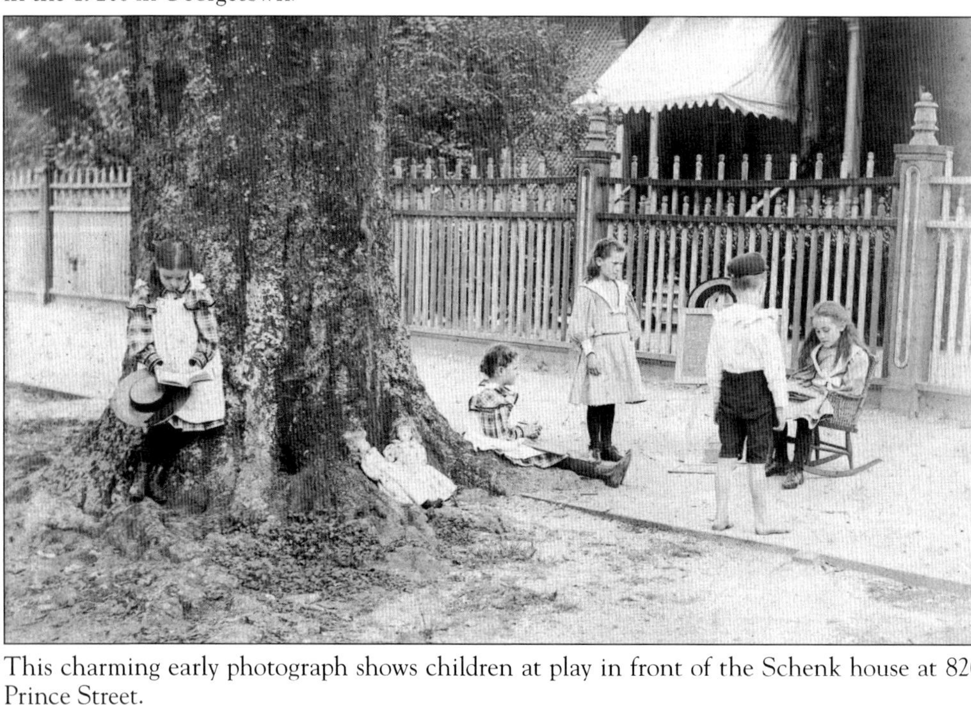

This charming early photograph shows children at play in front of the Schenk house at 820 Prince Street.

The Davis house is at 722 Prince Street. Trees near the street are surrounded by protective fencing. A widow's watch, or belvedere, sits above the roof.

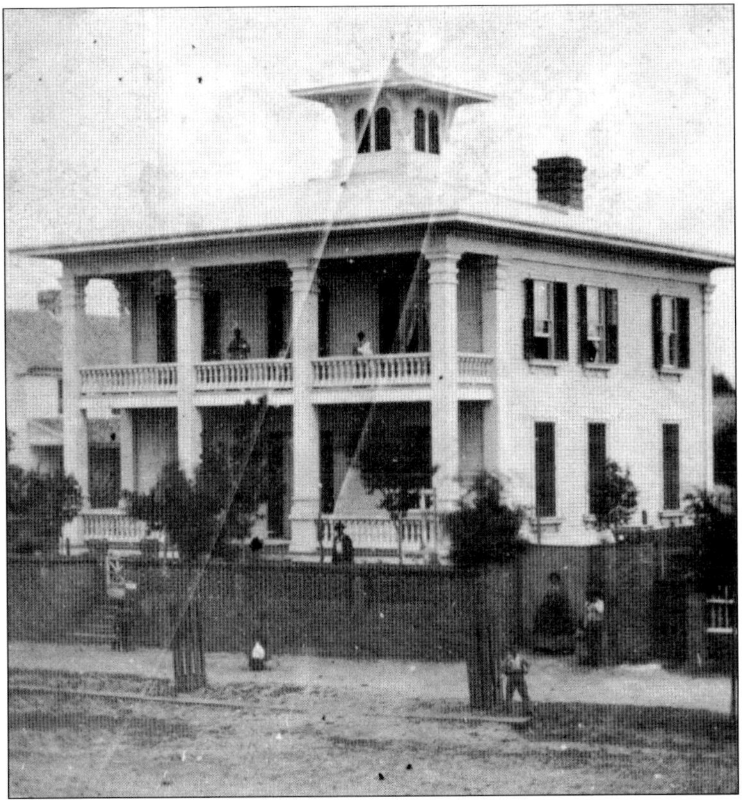

Sarah Trenholm stands in front of her home at 811 Prince Street. She was the daughter of Alfred G. Trenholm; his photographs are throughout this book. George A. Trenholm, Alfred's grandfather, was secretary of the Confederate treasury and is believed to be the basis for Rhett Butler in *Gone With the Wind*.

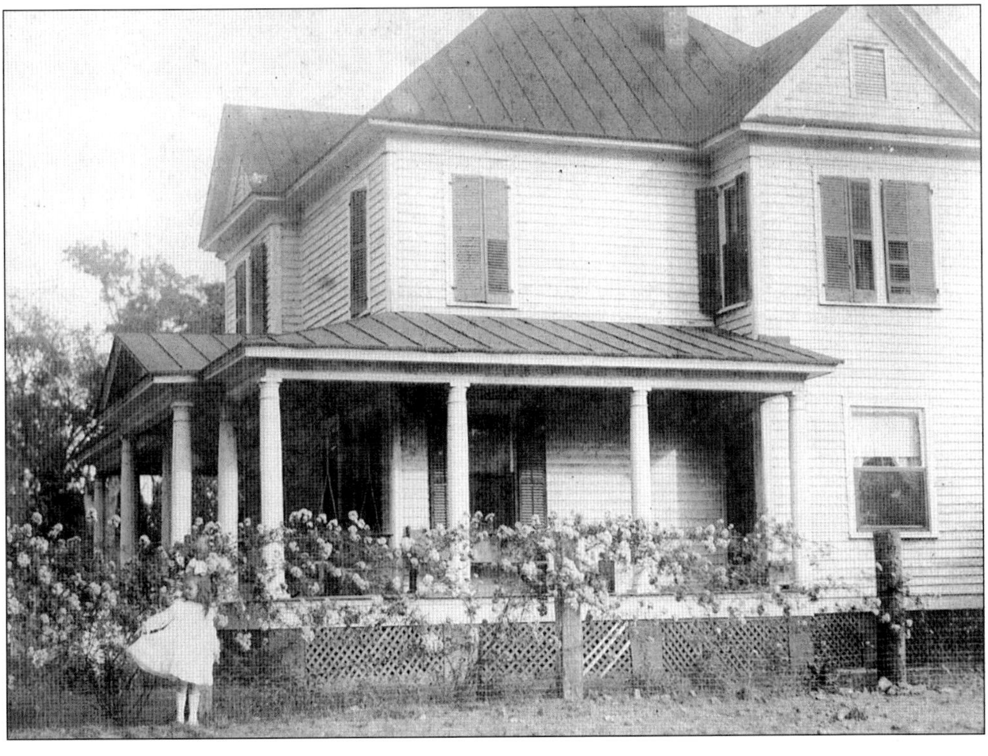

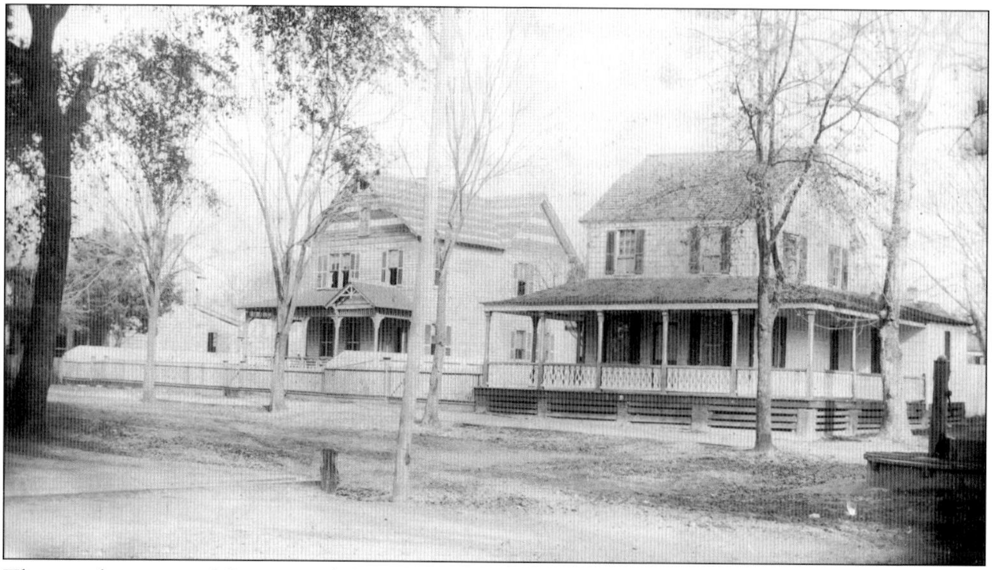

The north corner of Prince and Orange Streets is pictured about 1900. The house on the left remains and has been remodeled, as has the house in the middle. The painting of the eaves and the roof in stripes is certainly an interesting feature. The house on the right, which belonged to the Levy family, was replaced by a brick residence in the 1940s. The community pump occupies the center of the unpaved street. The sidewalks are paved.

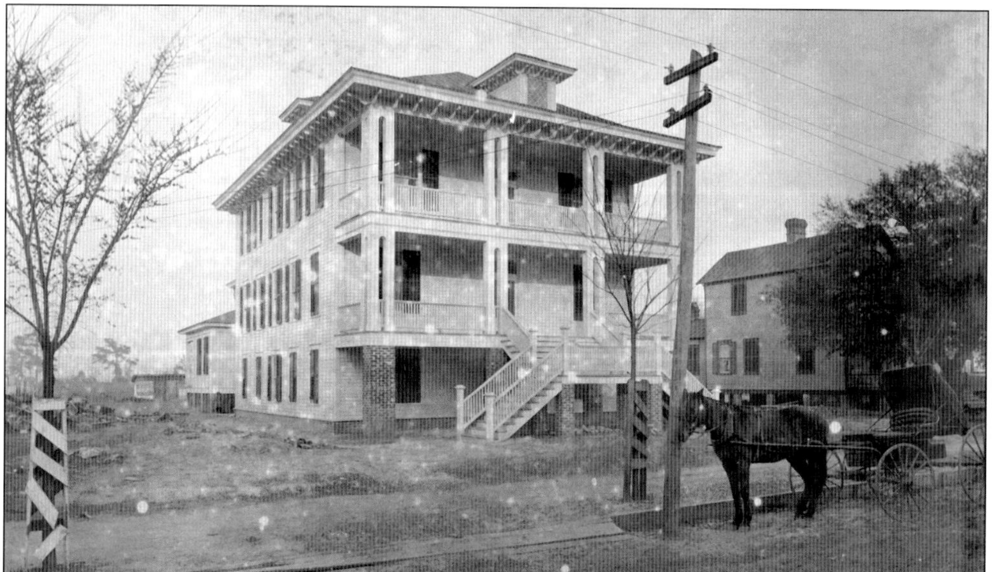

In the early 1900s, several Georgetown doctors, including Dr. W. M. Gaillard and Dr. M. P. Moorer, built the structure pictured here in the 1100 block of Highmarket Street for a hospital. It was operated until 1911, but faulty finances forced it to close. A boardinghouse operated here for several years but also lacked financial success. The property became part of the Georgetown school system in 1919 and was used as the high school until the addition was made behind the auditorium to Winyah Grade School. The school outgrew its quarters again, and this building housed overflow classes until Winyah High School was completed in 1938. The Georgetown County Health Department later occupied the building for some time.

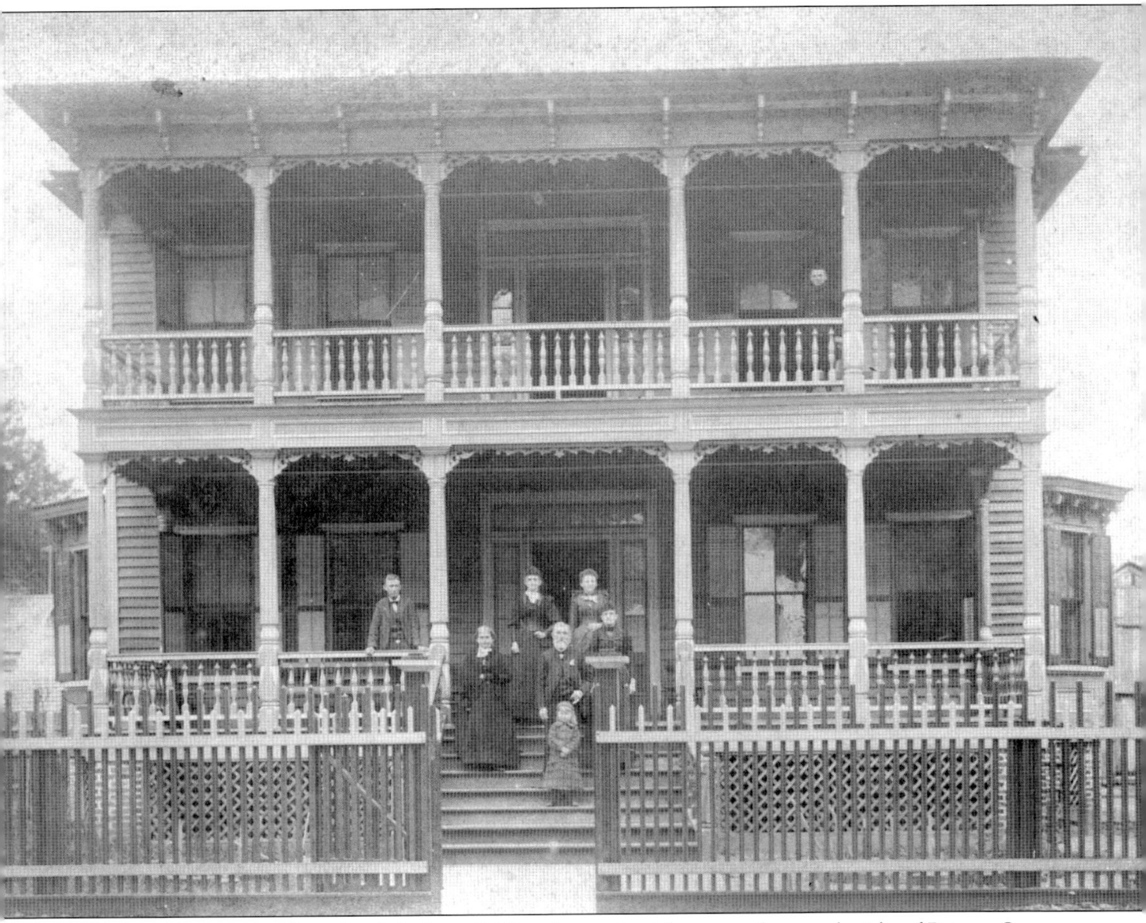

This handsome dwelling, built before 1900, is located midway on the north side of Prince Street in the 600 block. The builder is unknown, but it is known that it served as an annex to the Winyah Inn (now the Georgetown County Museum) when there was an overflow of guests. One Georgetonian recalls that the Dorrill family lived there, and as a child walking by, she was always fascinated by how far James Dorrill could spit his tobacco juice from his habitual seat on the downstairs porch. The upper porch has been removed and columns added. The family pictured is unidentified, but the clothes date this photograph around 1900.

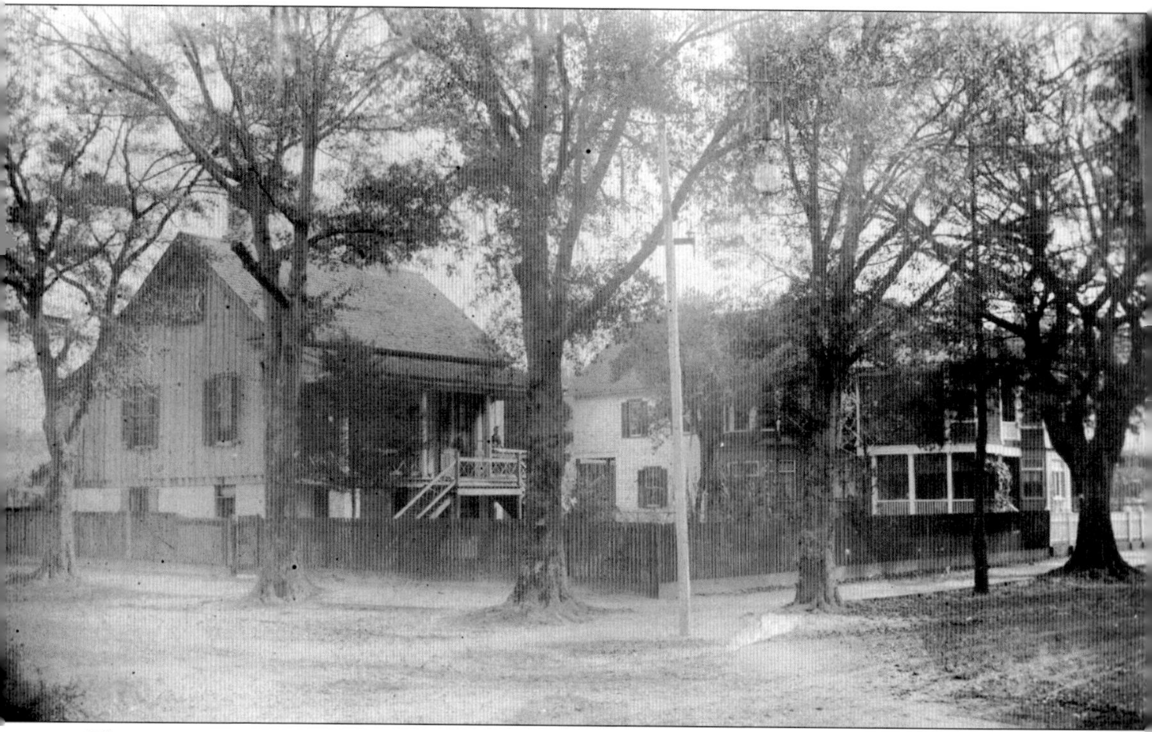

This scene is no more but was etched on the memory of several Georgetonians as children because it was the location of a big fire. The house on the corner of Prince and Queen Streets was occupied by Minnie Daggett; the next one by Mayor W. H. Andrews; the third house belonged to A. P. Webber, a druggist; and a fourth house, not seen, was occupied by Dr. M. P. Moorer and his family. Between 4:00 a.m. and 5:00 a.m. on December 17, 1914, the furnace—the first in Georgetown—in the Andrews home caught fire and spread rapidly. Although the fire companies answered the call for help immediately and were out in full force, they were unable to do much because the weather was so cold the water froze, rendering the pump useless. According to the *Progressive Democrat*, Chief McDonald pressed into service the old Winyah Steam fire engine, which forced a magnificent stream of water through the hose for a block and a half from the Sampit River. This helped save other homes in the neighborhood, but these four were completely destroyed. Damage was estimated at $50,000.

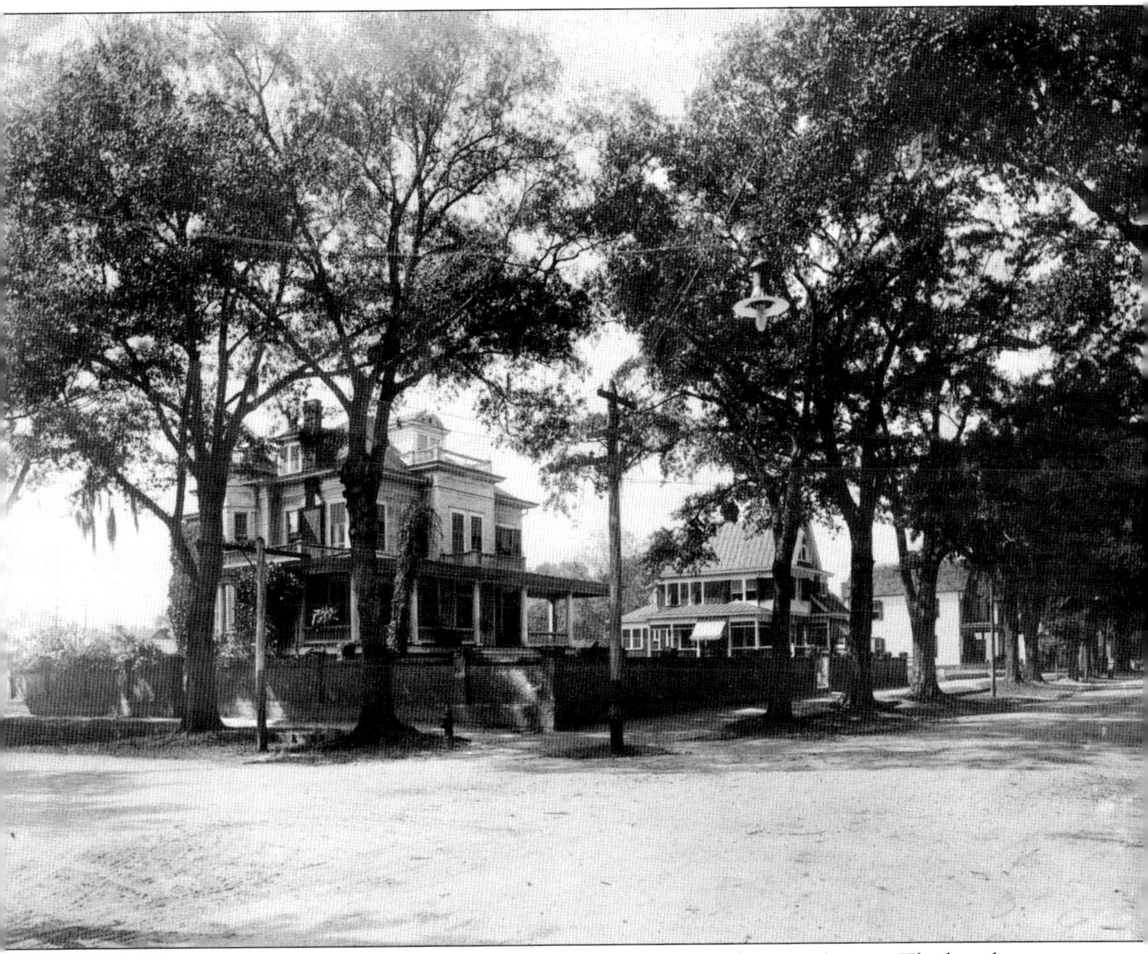

This photograph shows the south side of the 600 block of Prince and Queen Streets. The handsome dwelling on the corner was built by George R. Congdon in 1903 and still stands behind its high brick wall surveying the comings and goings of many. The next house was greatly altered, stuccoed, and painted pink and was always referred to locally as "The Pink Elephant." It was razed in 1970, and the area is presently used for parking. The third house remains in use as an office, but it was built to house overflow guests from the Winyah Inn just across the street.

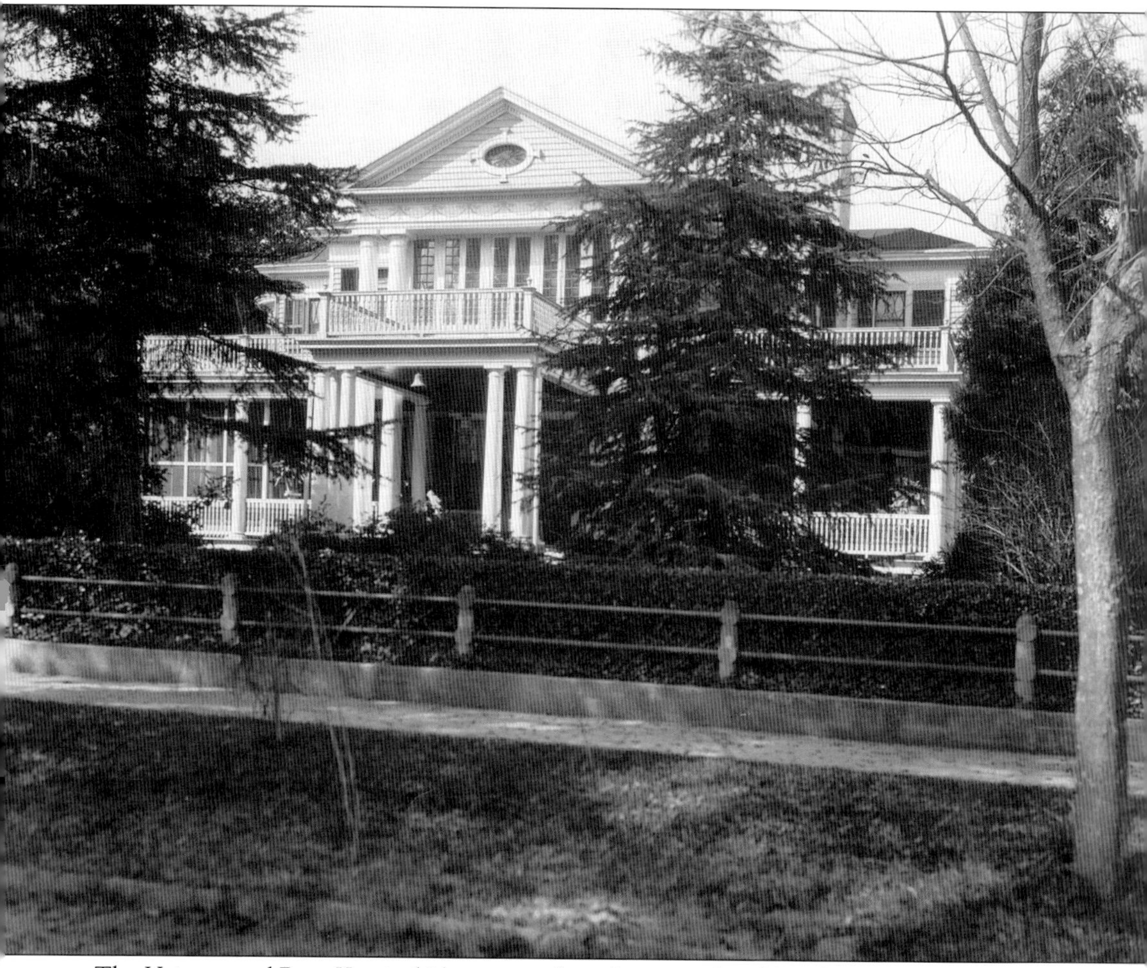

The Heiman and Rose Kaminski house stood on the west side of Broad Street in the 200 block. It was originally on the street, but Rose Kaminski moved it back, adding a semicircular drive and porte-cochere at the front. When the last owners died with no heirs, the house was sometimes rented to organizations, but finally fell into such disrepair that the city was forced to demolish it in the mid-1970s.

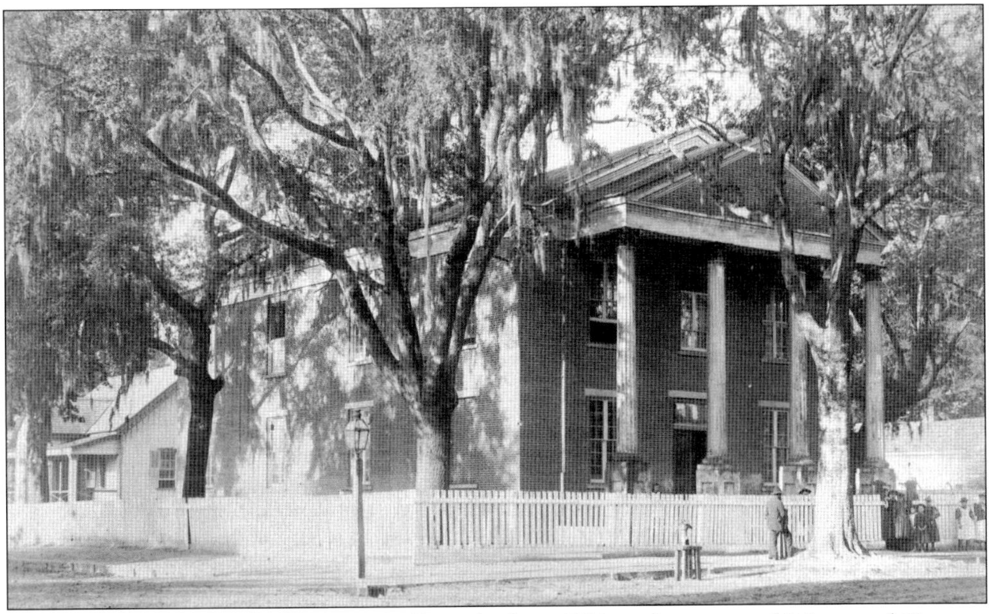

The historic Winyah Indigo Society Hall was built in 1857 on the corner of Prince and Cannon Streets. A school sponsored by the society of Georgetown indigo planters began in 1755 and was housed in several buildings prior to 1857, when this structure was erected. The first president of Winyah Indigo Society was Thomas Lynch, a delegate to the Second Continental Congress, where he helped draft the Declaration of Independence. For many of its early years, the Winyah Indigo Society School was the only educational institution between Charleston and Wilmington, North Carolina. The school continued until 1886, when it was incorporated into the public school system, but a private school operated in this building until 1908.

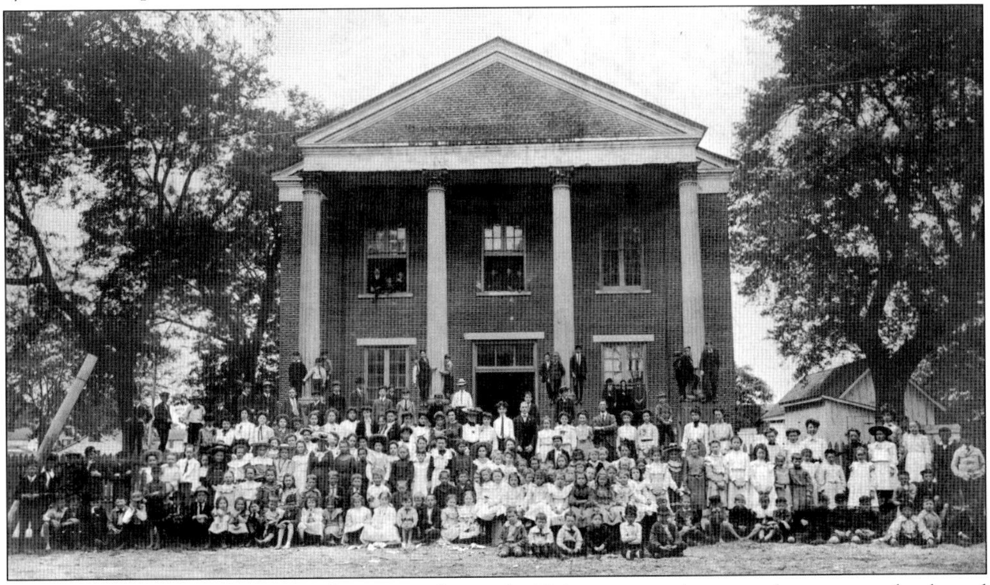

The Winyah Indigo Society Hall, seen in this early-20th-century photograph, was greatly abused by federal troops during Reconstruction during the occupation of Union troops from 1865 to 1868. The photograph shows the large student body and faculty. Notice the boys in the second floor windows and standing precariously on the columns.

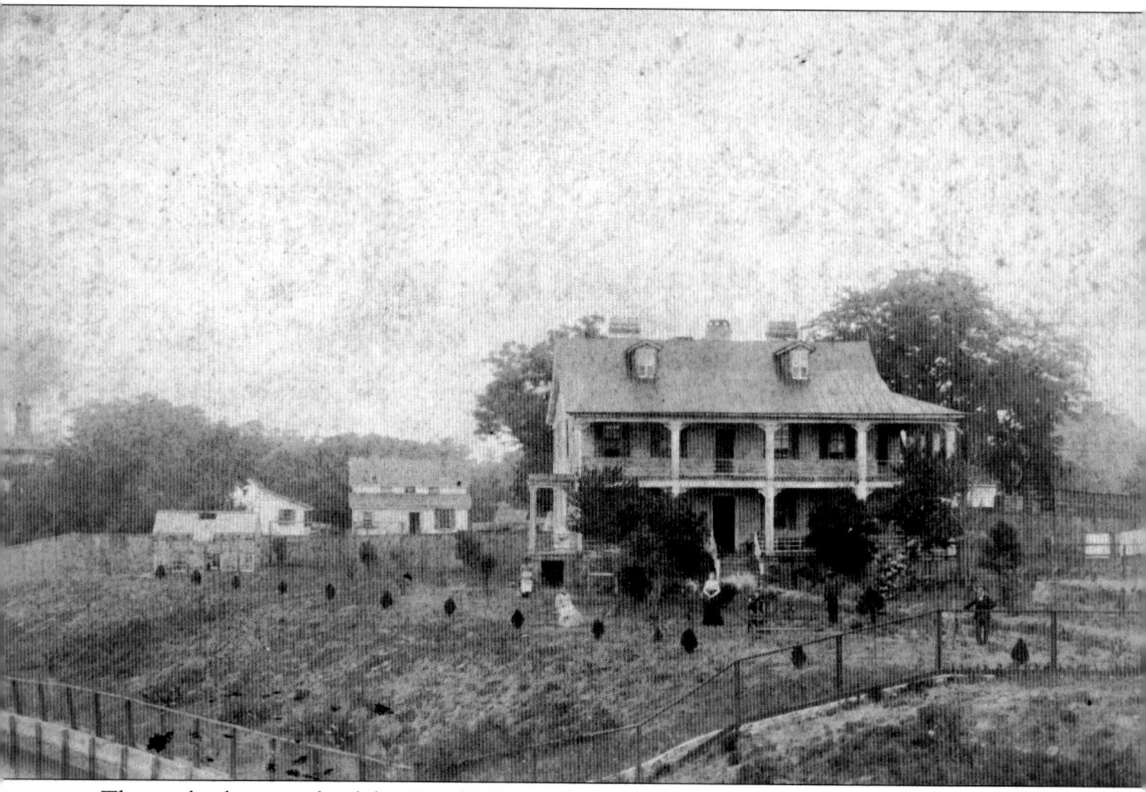

This early photograph of the Harold Kaminski house must have been taken from the deck of a ship docked in the Sampit River. The lovely home, added on to later, still stands and is now a museum. It occupies the highest ground on the Sampit River. To the left the Georgetown Rice Mill is visible. The one-story cottage is gone, but the neat house remains on Wood Street. The chimneys of the Robert Stewart house can be seen over the roof.

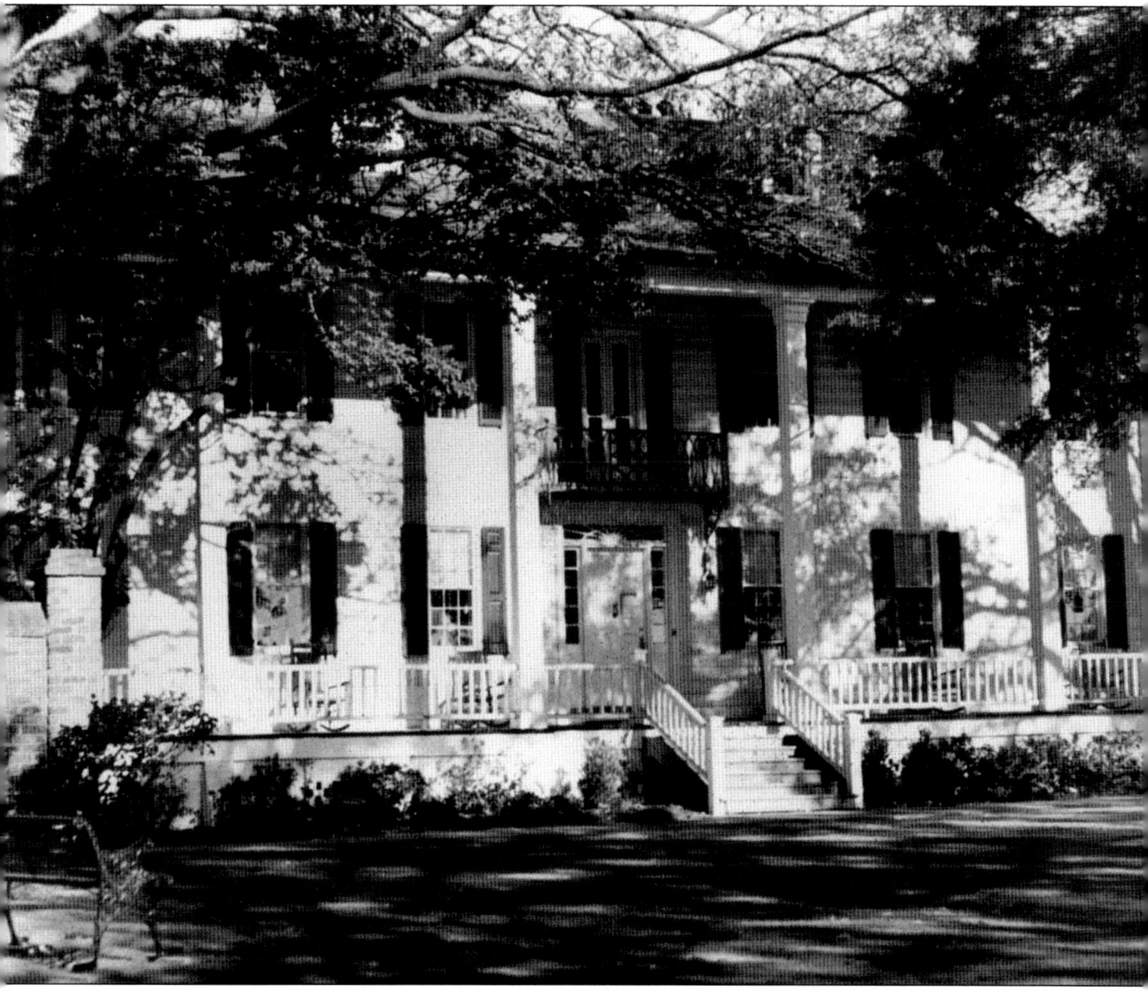
A more modern photograph of the Harold Kaminski house shows it as it is today. It was originally built by the Trapier family in the mid-1700s. The house, located at 1003 Front Street, passed through the Keith family and eventually was purchased by Harold and Julia Kaminski in 1931. At Julia's death in 1972, she left the house and contents to the City of Georgetown. Today it operates as a house museum containing priceless American and English antiques. (Courtesy of the Kaminski House Museum.)

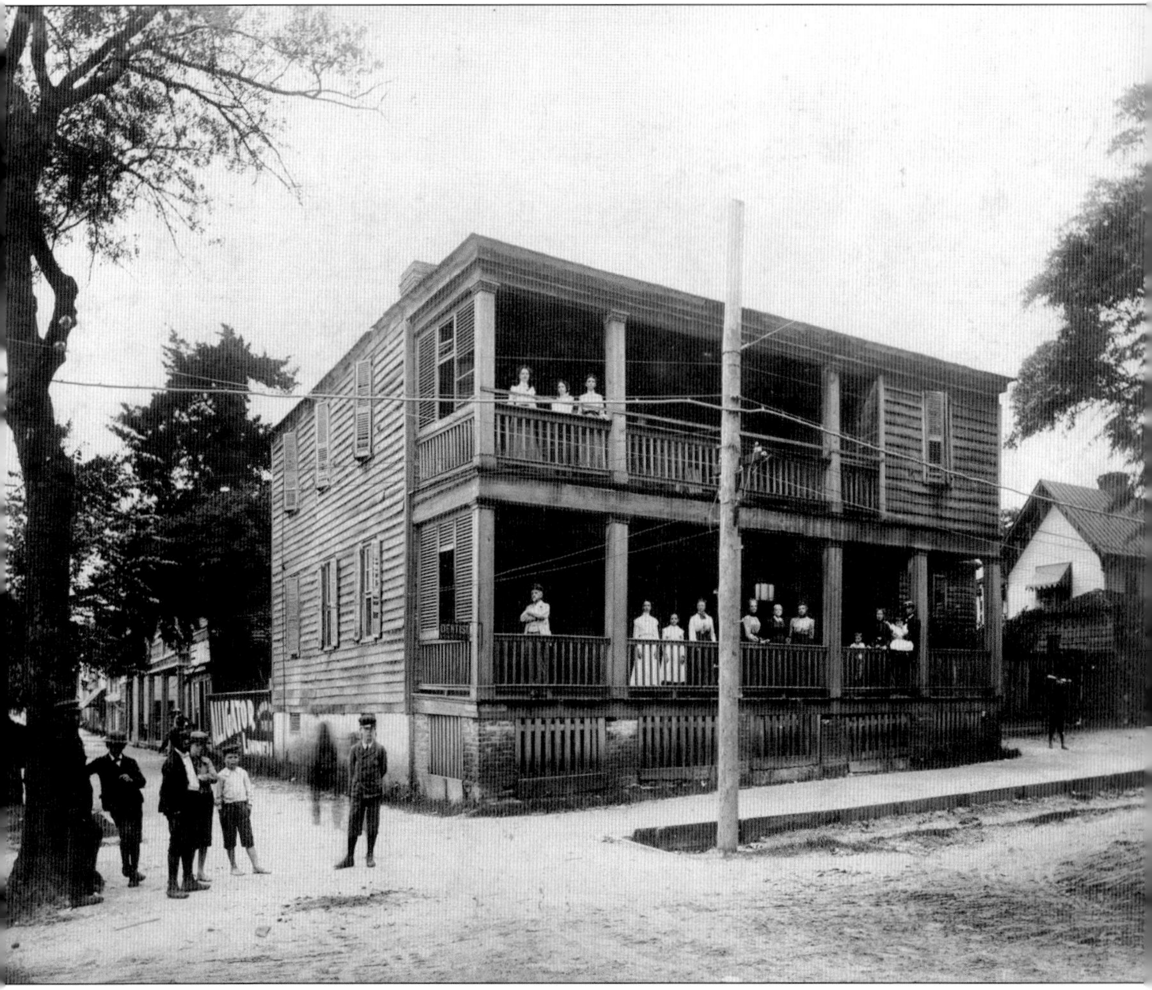

This two-story home, owned by the Blair family before it was torn down in 1902, stood on the northwest corner of Front and Screven Streets across from the town clock. The porch actually extended into the sidewalk area onto city property, which was not uncommon with older Georgetown houses. The house was also known as the Anderson-Generette house.

Two

Port of Georgetown

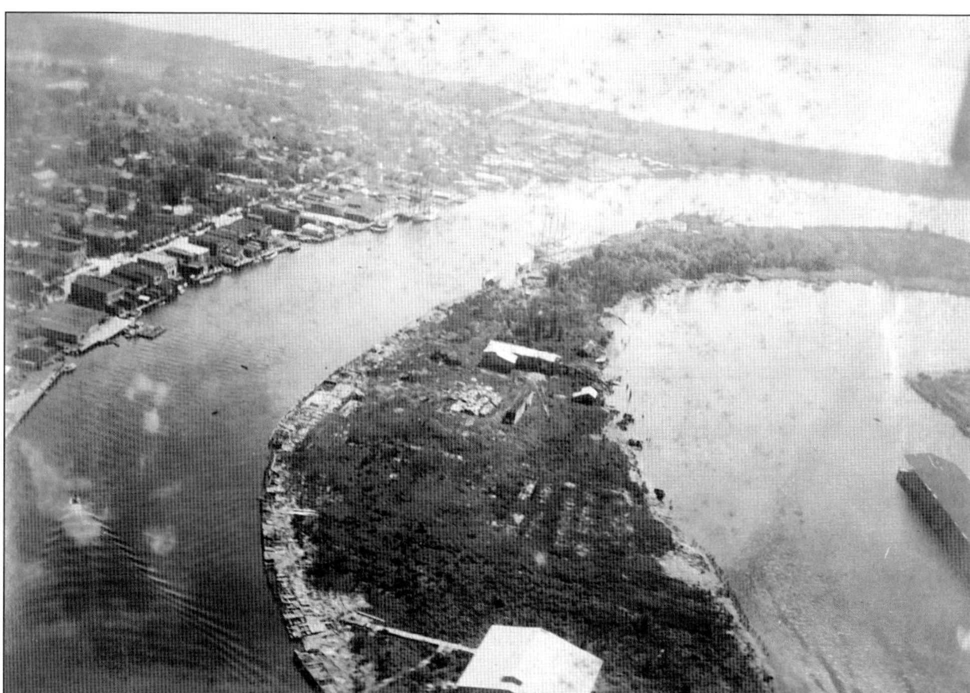

This is an aerial photograph showing the peninsula of land known today as Goat Island. This picture was taken by A. G. Trenholm in 1920, showing the Gardner and Lacy Lumber Company docks and mill site on the peninsula. The city of Georgetown is shown in the upper left corner of the picture, and in the lower left corner is part of the loading docks of the Atlantic Coast Lumber Company. Georgetown had many "commodity kings;" the most important in the 1920s were lumber products. Rice, indigo, cotton, tobacco, fish, and naval stores were important export products that were shipped worldwide from this thriving port.

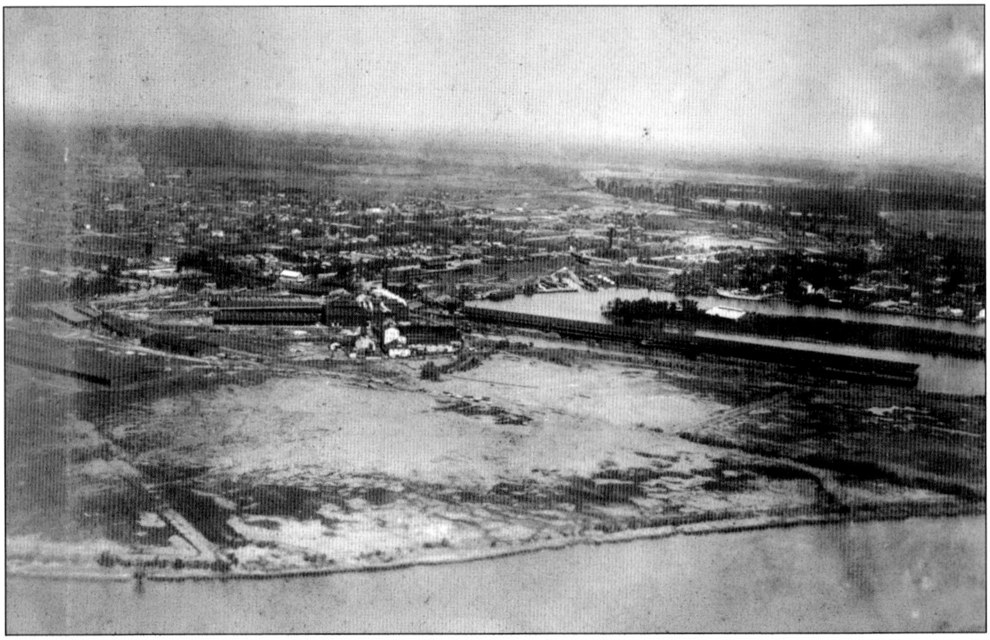

The land in the foreground of the aerial photograph is the present-day location of the South Carolina State Ports. The long straight building is the shipping and receiving docks of the Atlantic Coast Lumber Company. The loading dock building was almost a quarter of a mile long and could accommodate vessels on both sides of the building and dock.

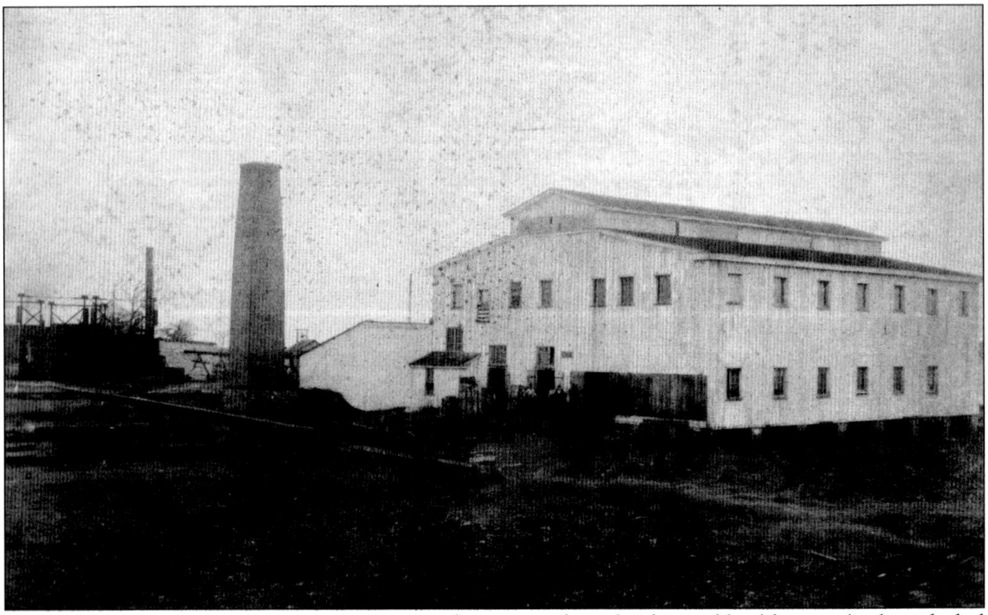

The Atlantic Coast Lumber Company was a large complex of industrial buildings, which included a steam generating plant for electricity and a dry kiln, which is shown here in this photograph. A planing mill, foundry, stackers, machine shop, pattern and woodworking shop, commissary, and offices covered more than 56 acres and accessed more than 8 miles of standard-gauge electric railroad track. This vast lumber-making complex could produce 200,000 board feet of finished lumber per day.

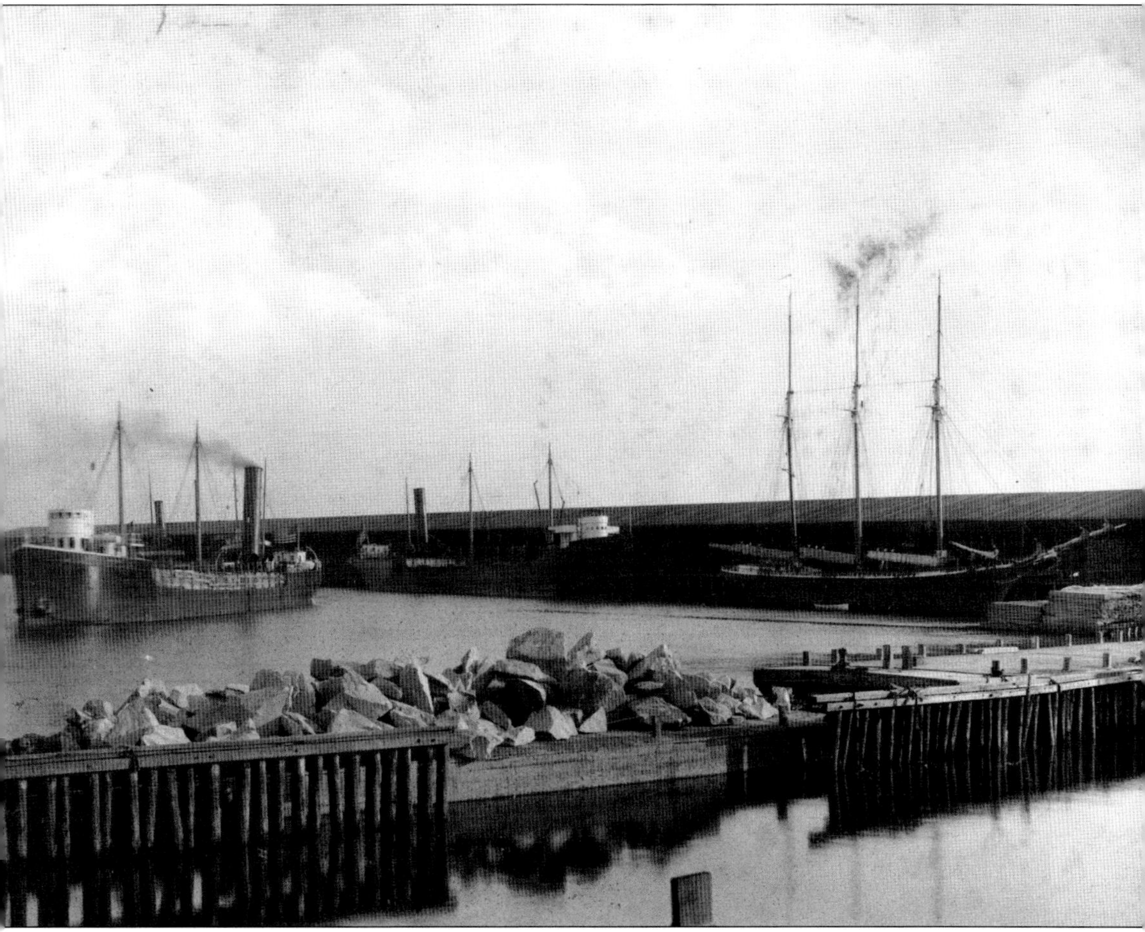

This is a scene from 1900 showing a merchant steamer and a three mast merchant schooner loading lumber at the Atlantic Coast Lumber Company docks on the Sampit River. In the foreground are barges loaded with rock for the jetty stabilization project at the ocean entrance to Winyah Bay.

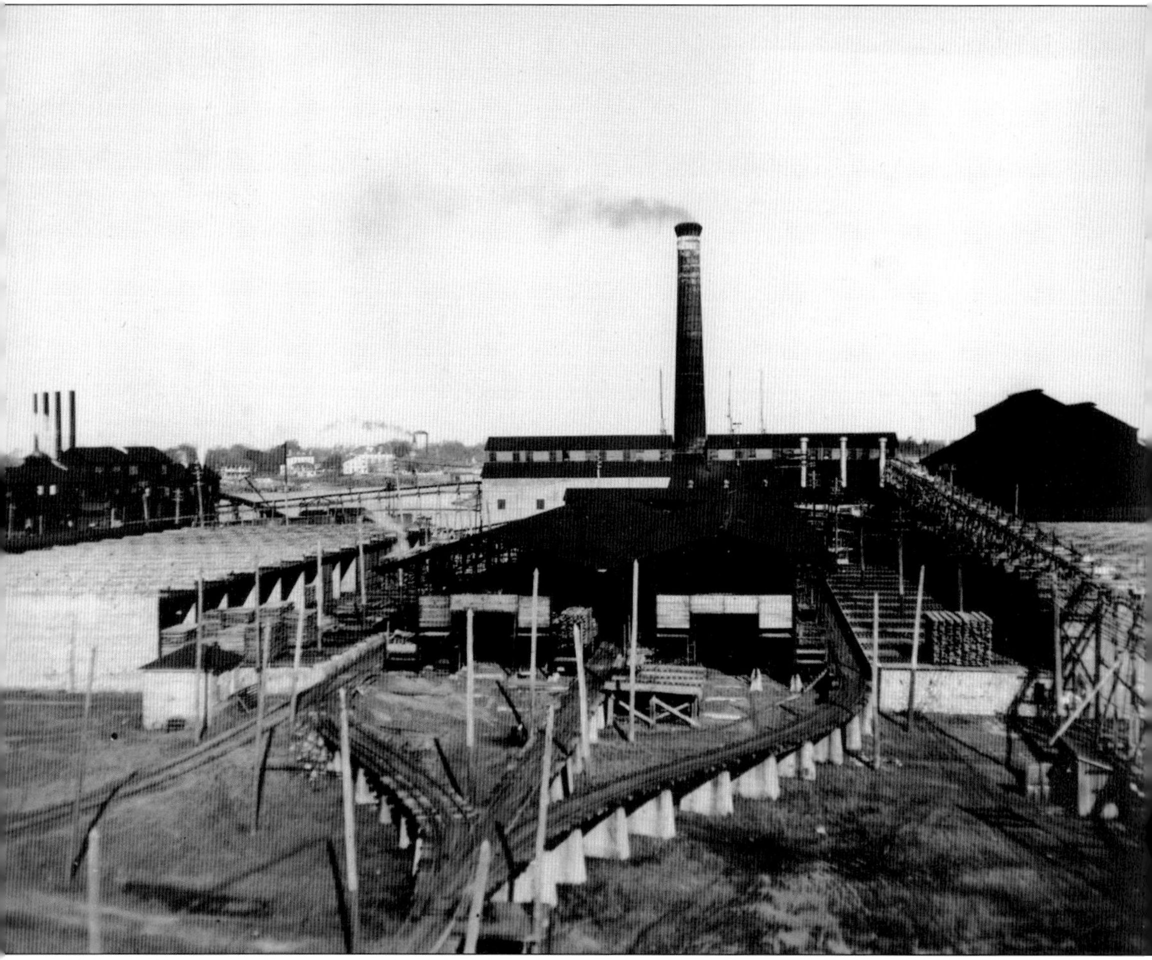

This photograph shows some of the 36 miles of narrow-gauge rail that ran through the Atlantic Coast Lumber Company complex. The rail line is shown running down both sides of the immense dry kiln operation. The dry kiln building is the light-colored structure on the left in the photograph. The dry kiln had 14 rooms on either side of the building, each 20 feet wide and 160 feet long. At the time (*c.* 1915) these were the largest dry kilns in the world.

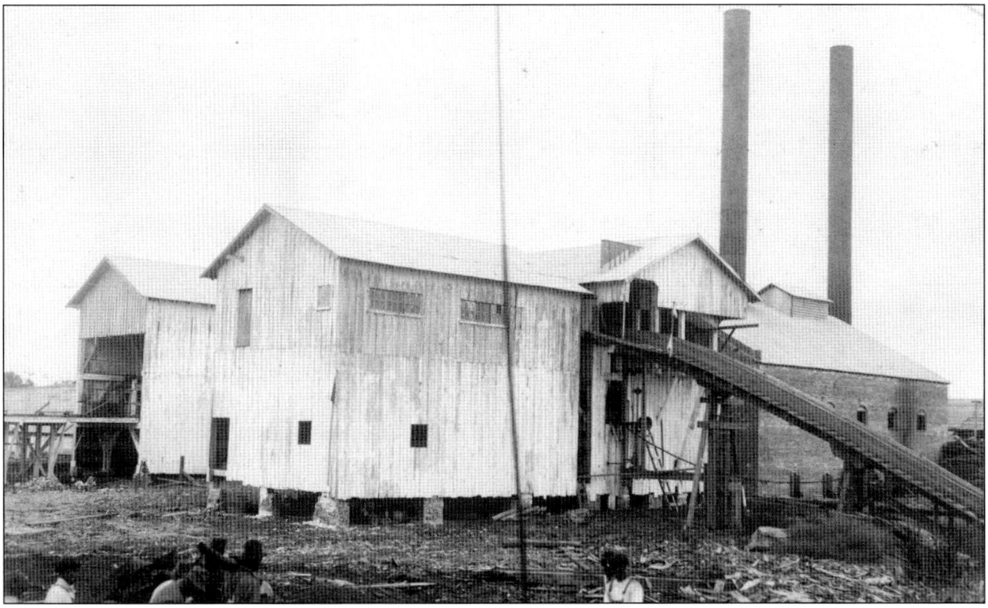

This is a photograph of one of the large storing and stacking buildings for finished lumber at the Atlantic Coast Lumber Company. Smokestacks seen behind the large white buildings mark the steam generating plant for the electric turbines. Sawdust was burned to generate electricity and to fire the foundry. The mill was completely vertical, capable of producing its own power source to operate machinery and burning the by-product of production to create energy to run the mill.

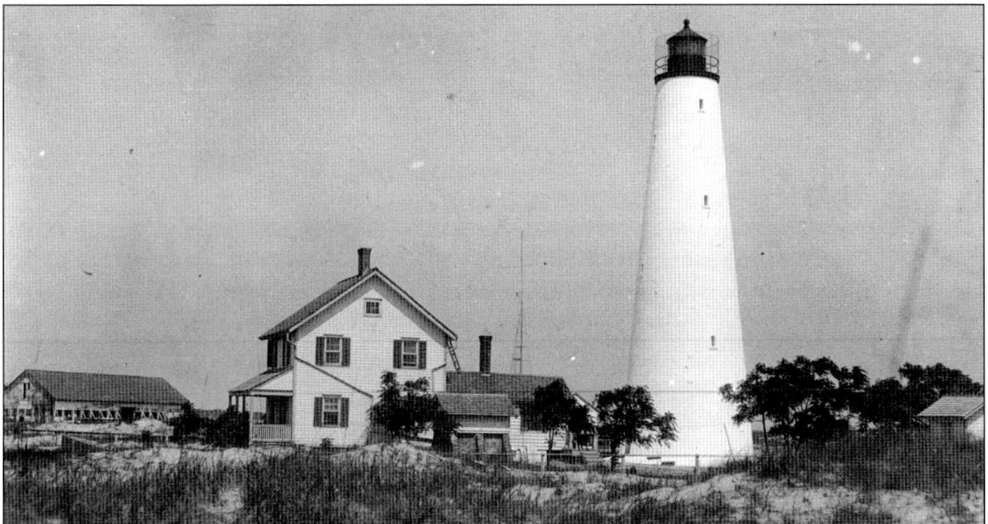

The Georgetown lighthouse is located on North Island, the north side of the entrance from the ocean to Winyah Bay. As early as 1746, the House of Commons Assembly was petitioned by the British Board of Trade to erect beacons or landmarks near the harbor entrance. The first lighthouse was built on the present site between 1795 and 1801, and the light was fueled by whale oil. That light was destroyed by a gale in 1803, and a second brick lighthouse was erected in 1812, suffering severe damage during the Civil War. The present lighthouse was erected in 1867. This *c.* 1900 photograph shows the lightkeeper's house, which no longer exists. It is the oldest active lighthouse in South Carolina.

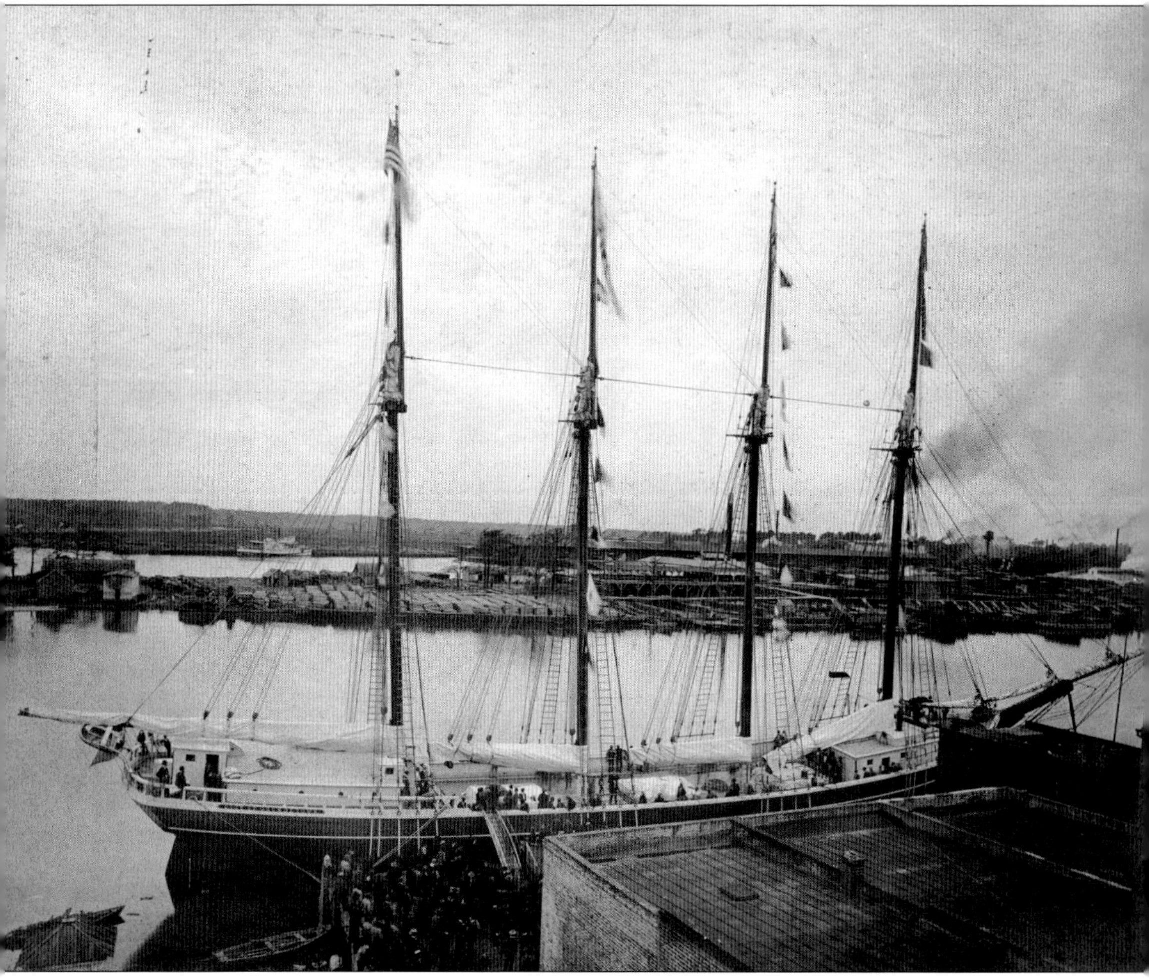

This idyllic waterfront scene pictures the schooner *City of Georgetown* docked behind a Front Street wharf. The *City of Georgetown* was built to carry lumber products to northern ports and on return trips bring coal, machinery, and support supplies for the lumber industry in Georgetown. This *c.* 1902 scene was probably during the open house, when the vessel first arrived in Georgetown. In the background can be seen the vast inventory of logs on the Gardner and Lacy Lumber Company receiving docks.

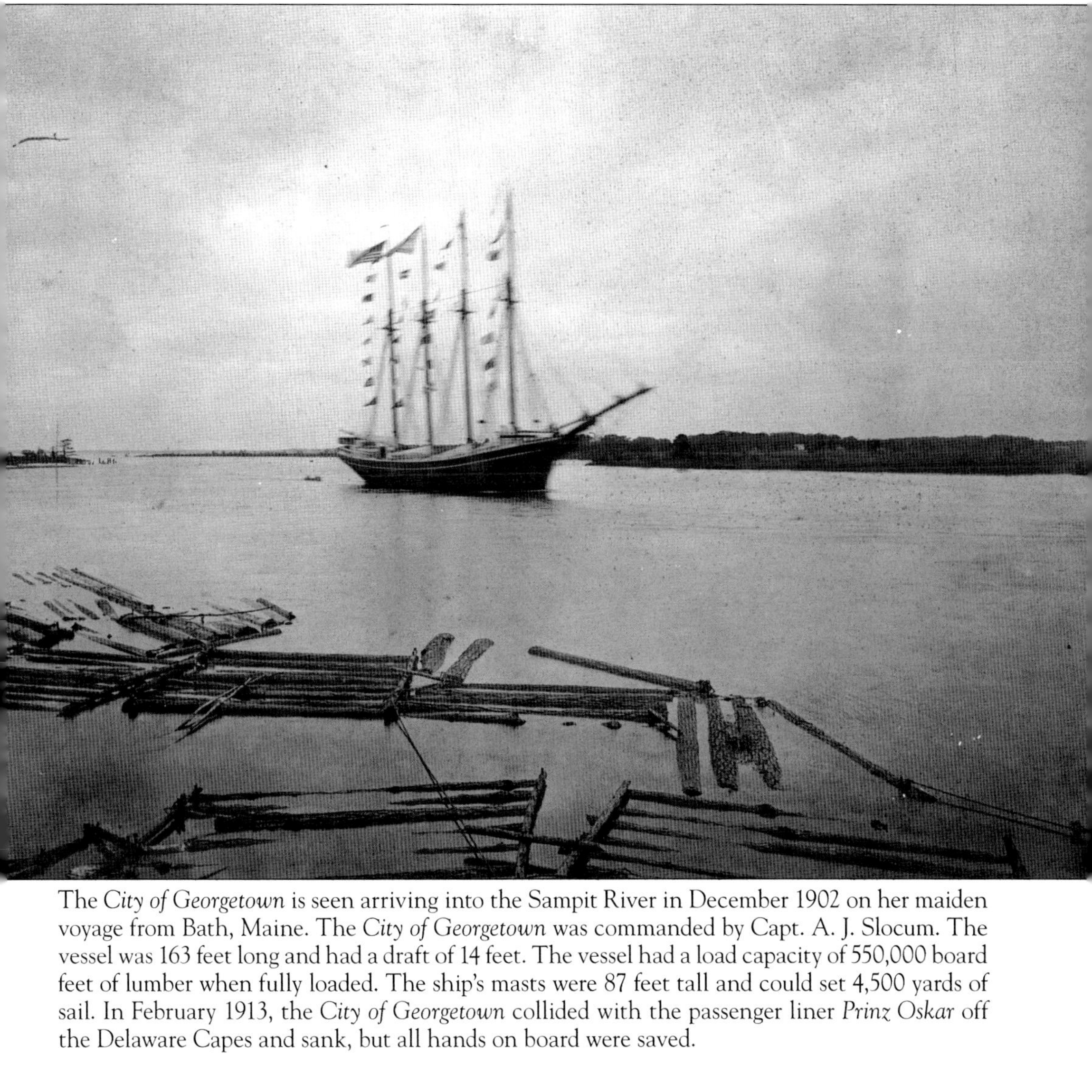

The *City of Georgetown* is seen arriving into the Sampit River in December 1902 on her maiden voyage from Bath, Maine. The *City of Georgetown* was commanded by Capt. A. J. Slocum. The vessel was 163 feet long and had a draft of 14 feet. The vessel had a load capacity of 550,000 board feet of lumber when fully loaded. The ship's masts were 87 feet tall and could set 4,500 yards of sail. In February 1913, the *City of Georgetown* collided with the passenger liner *Prinz Oskar* off the Delaware Capes and sank, but all hands on board were saved.

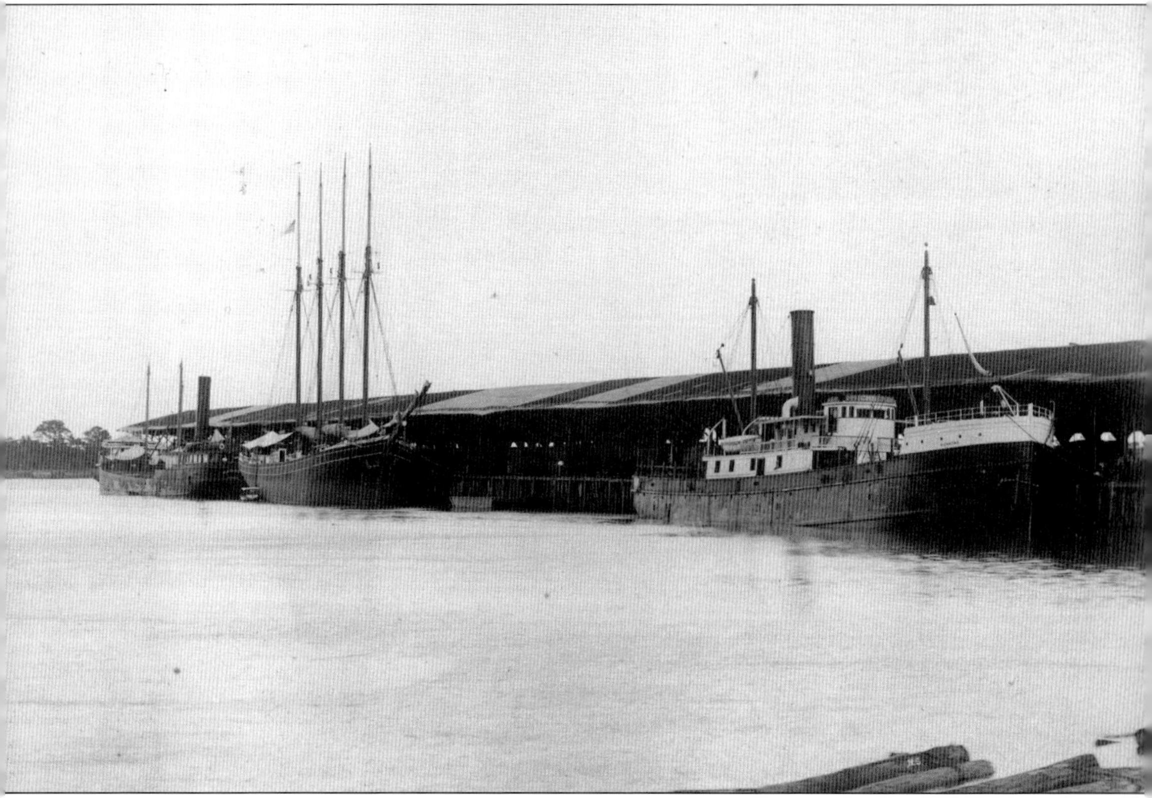

The *City of Georgetown* is moored between two steam-powered freighters at the Atlantic Coast Lumber Company docks on the Sampit River. It is interesting to note that the sailing merchant trade was soon becoming a thing of the past. Steam power was faster and more reliable, and with the expanding lumber trade, steam-powered freighters could be loaded with more cargo and be shipped for less expense.

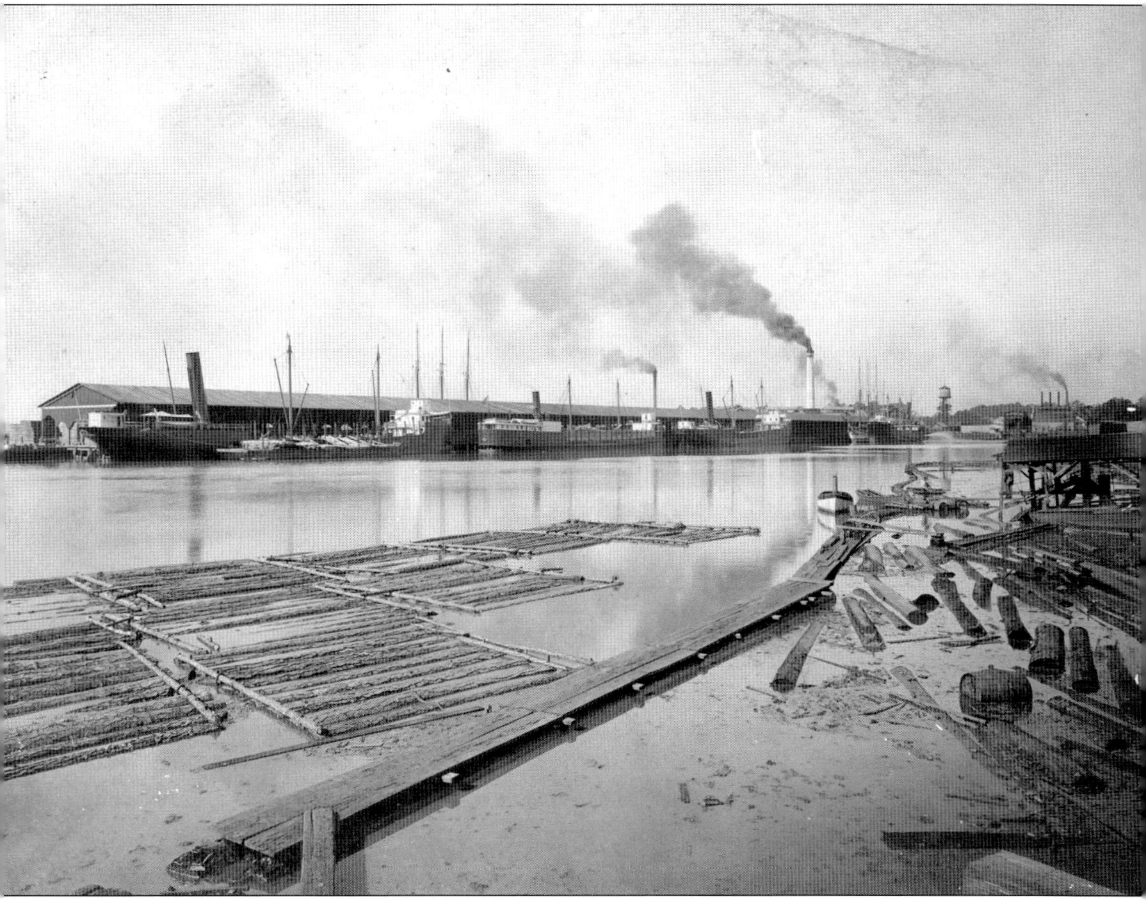

Pictured are two large schooners and three steam-powered freighters moored at the Atlantic Coast Lumber Company dock alongside the 1,200-foot-long loading shed. This scene also shows the south side of Goat Island. In the foreground are rafts of logs and a walkway of the Gardner and Lacy Lumber Company. These two large lumber mills transformed the vast timber acreage of the Georgetown County area into lumber products shipped worldwide.

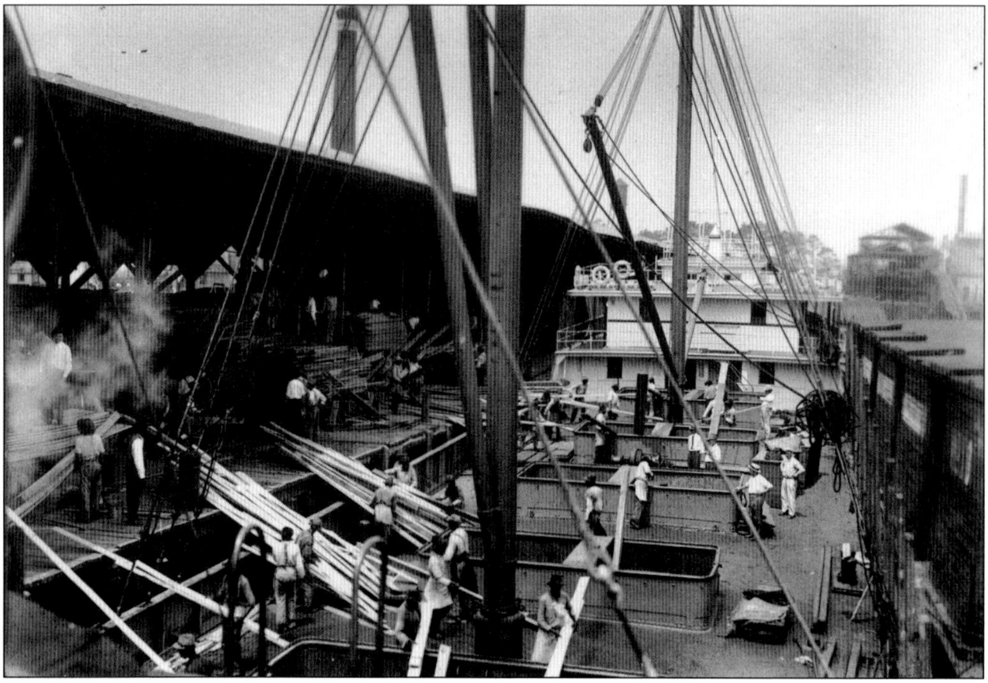

Lumber is loaded onto a cargo ship docked at the Atlantic Coast Lumber Company loading shed adjacent to the Sampit River. This scene is facing west up the river across from the south shore of Goat Island. During maximum production, mills had to ship almost daily to keep finished inventory from overcrowding the production facilities. Millions of board feet were produced weekly. This scene was probably from the mid-1920s.

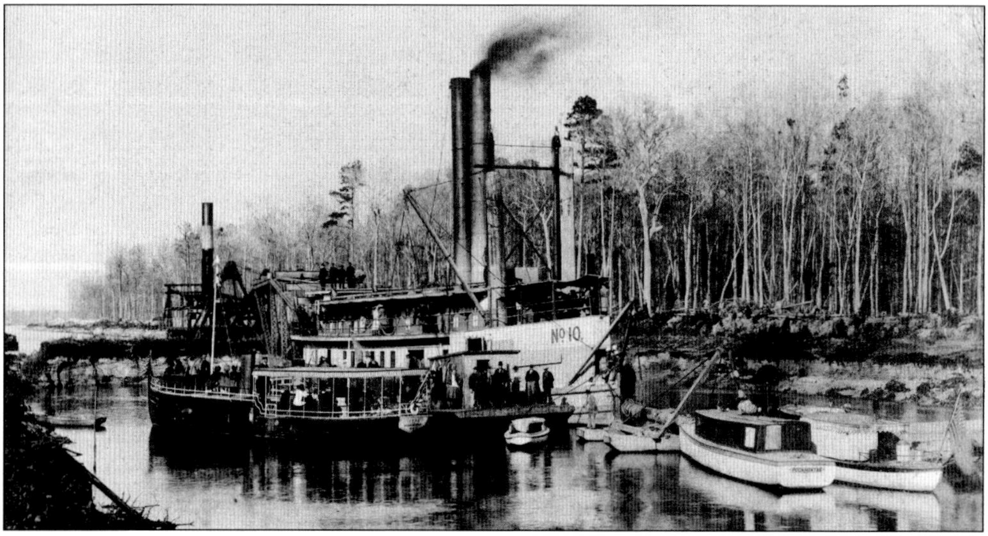

The No. 10 dredge is at work on the Minim Canal, which connected Winyah Bay with the North Santee River basin. It was an important part of the Intracoastal Waterway, which connected the port of Georgetown to Charleston. The undertaking of the dredging was time-consuming and tedious, as some of the dredge work was dredging through cypress swamps. The white boat in the right foreground is the *Pocahontas* from Georgetown, and the larger black hull vessel alongside the dredge is the excursion boat *Iola* from Wilmington, North Carolina.

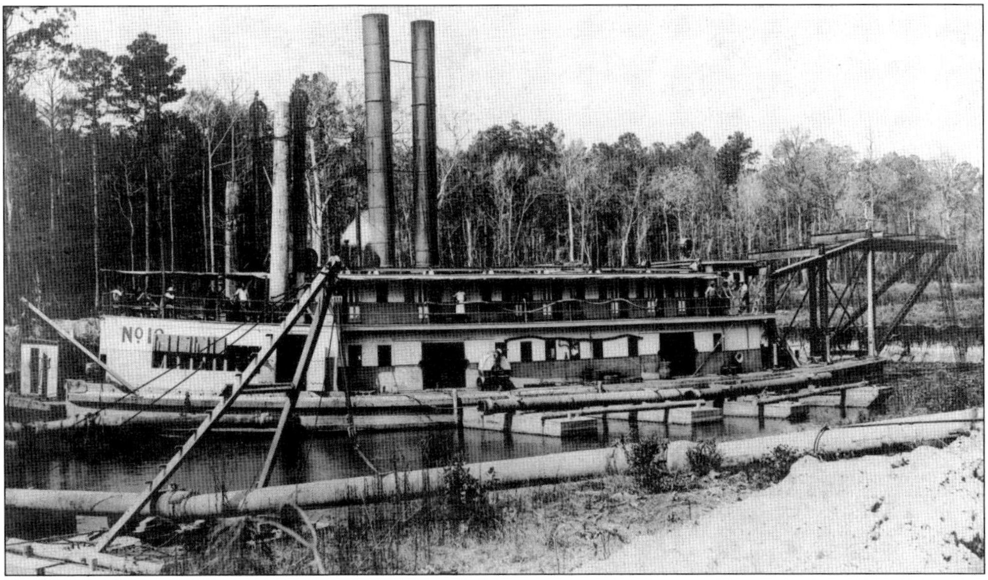

This is the No. 10 dredge at work behind South Island. In the foreground is the dredge pipe, pumping spoil into the impounded spoil area. The location of the dredge is probably close to the middle of Minim Canal. The dredging of the Minim Canal took place prior to 1897 and formally opened in May of that year. Smithville was a small village that grew up along the banks of the Minim Canal. This village had cisterns for fresh water collection, a lumber mill, blacksmith shop, and a small shipyard to support the work that was taking place dredging the canal.

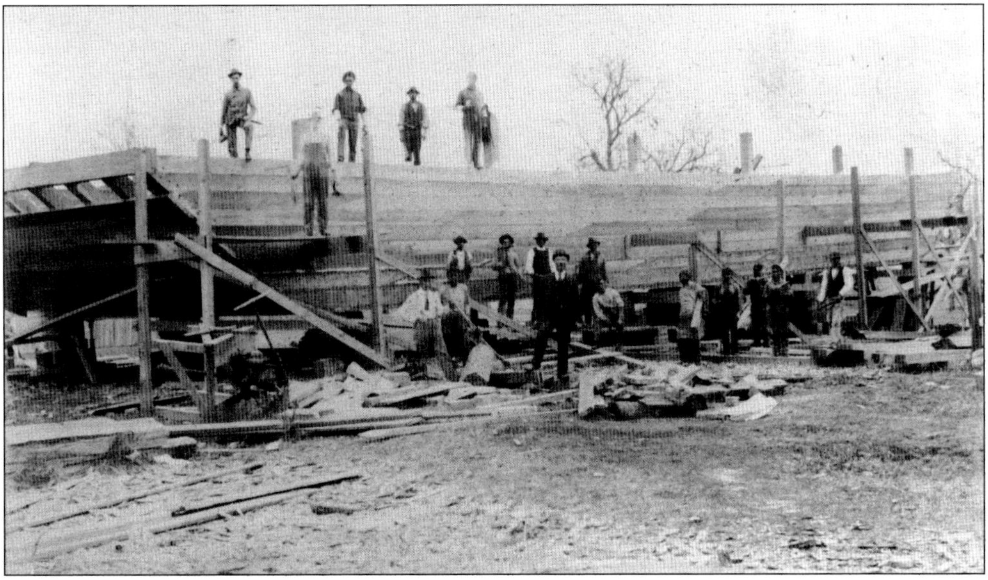

Shipbuilding in Georgetown was a direct link to the shipping capacity of the port and the vast naval stores being manufactured and shipped. Pictured here around 1900 is a shipping barge being built by a large workforce on the Sampit River near the Georgetown city docks. Skilled craftsmen, shipwrights, and foundry workers were in great demand. The large forested areas around Georgetown had cypress and juniper swamps, which grew ideal shipbuilding lumber. The local mills cut and sawed trees that would be used to build barges to ship lumber and move rocks to construct the jetty and build vessels for the merchant trade.

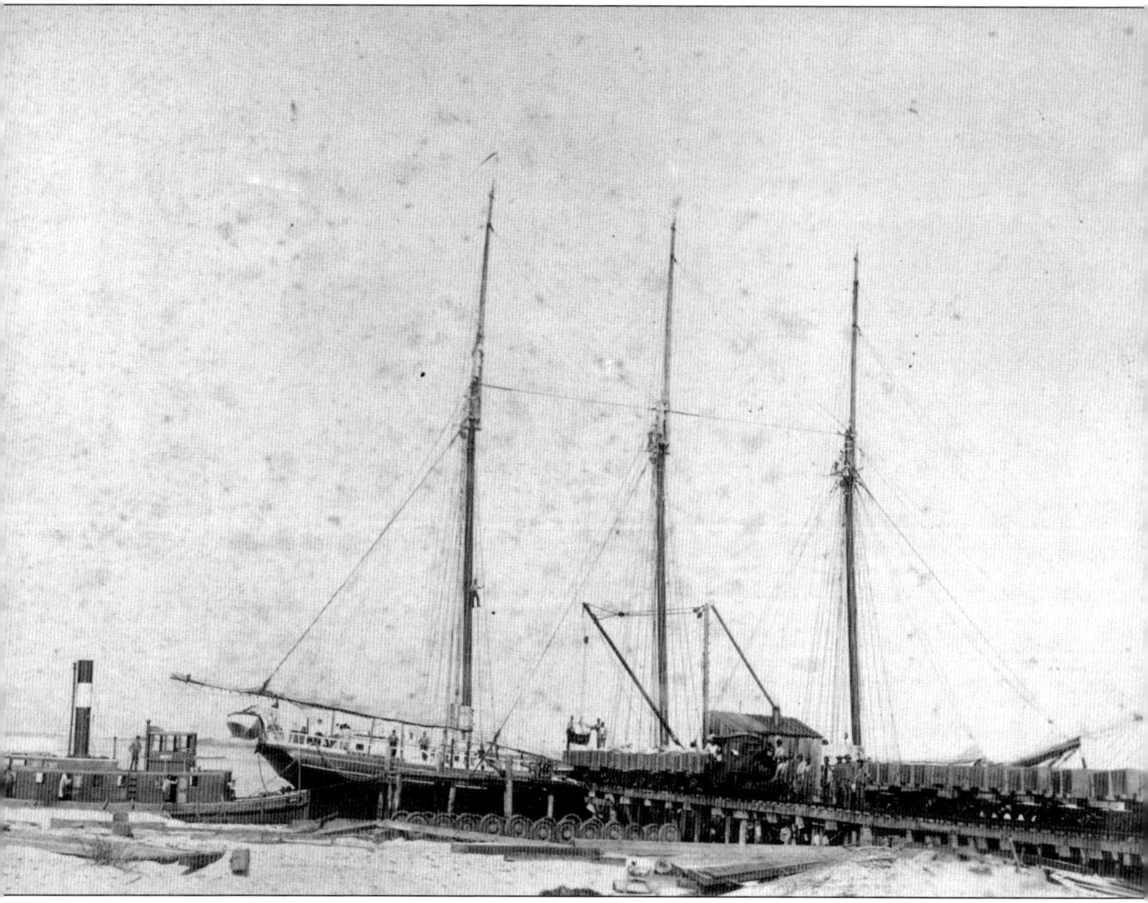

Shown here are large granite boulders being loaded for transport for the construction of the jetties at the entrance to Winyah Bay. A railway was constructed to transport the boulders from land to the ships. The granite boulders were loaded on railroad wheels mounted under dollies. The boulders were loaded onto the ship, and the empty dollies and wheels were lifted off the tracks and set beside the elevated tracks. The empty dollies were then reloaded onto the tracks and railed back.

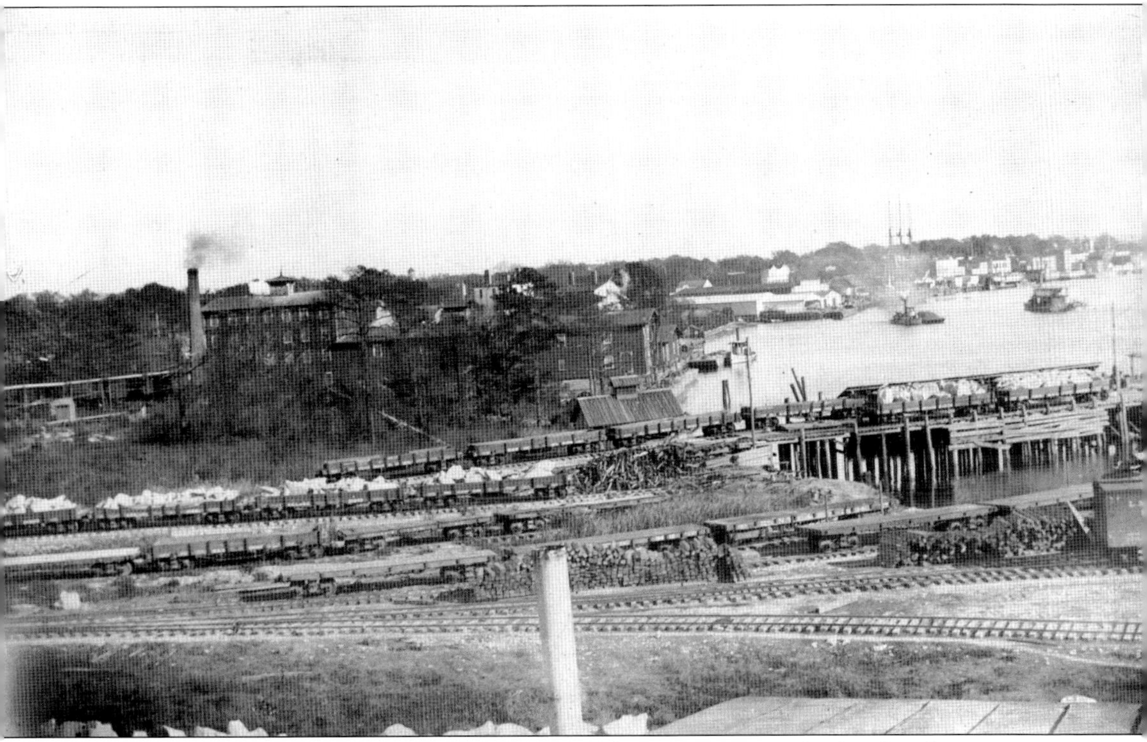

Granite rocks are being unloaded from railcars on the Sampit River. At this distribution point the boulders are being loaded onto small barges called lighters and then transported to the site of the jetty construction at the mouth of Winyah Bay. Railroad transportation was an integral part of the maritime shipping business in Georgetown. Fuel, fertilizer, naval stores, and agricultural products were brought in by rail from the interior of the state for export through the local port.

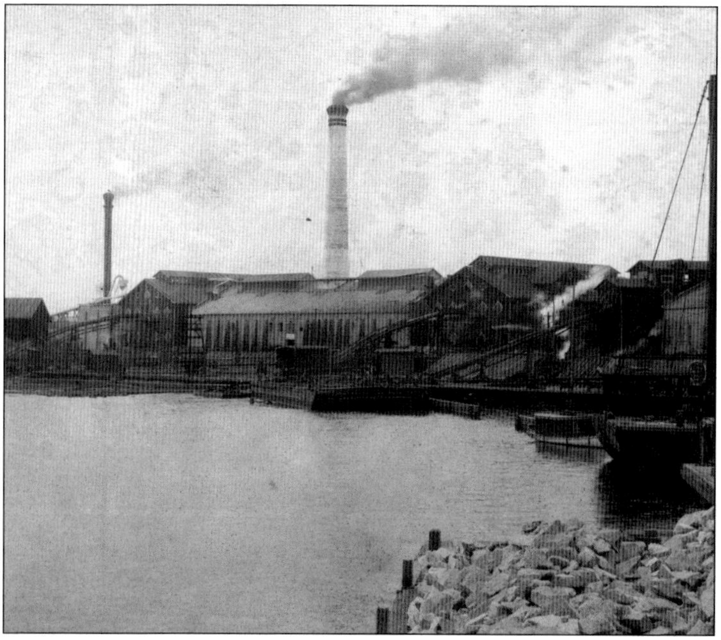

In this *c.* 1902 photograph, the granite boulders for the jetty project are being loaded on barges and then towed out to the entrance of Winyah Bay. The granite boulders came from as far away as New York, and some were shipped from the Columbia, South Carolina, area. The North Island jetty was constructed first, and the South Island side of the jetty project was completed in 1904. The total cost of the jetty project was almost $2.1 million.

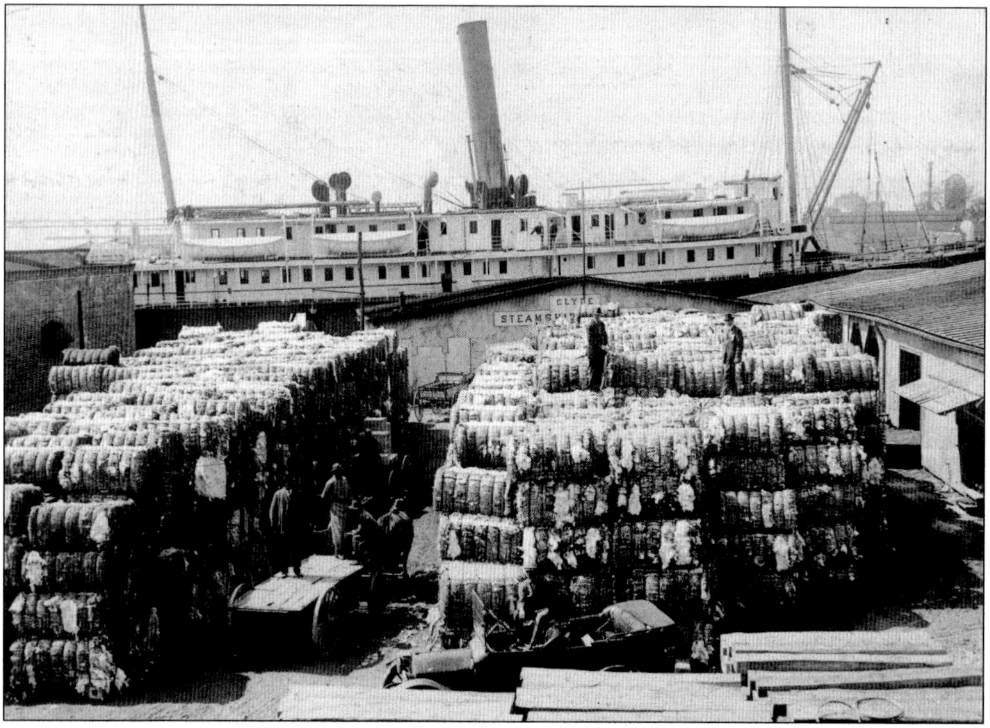

This 1900s image shows cotton stacked at the Clyde Steamship Company loading docks in the 900 block of Front Street. In the foreground is a stack of railroad crossties. Cotton was one of the major exports of the port of Georgetown. A merchant steamer is shown at the docks loading cargo. The Clyde Steamship Company played an important role in shipping, contracting with locally owned merchant vessels to transport cargo up and down the Waccamaw and Pee Dee Rivers, to Wilmington, Charleston, and ports further up the eastern seaboard.

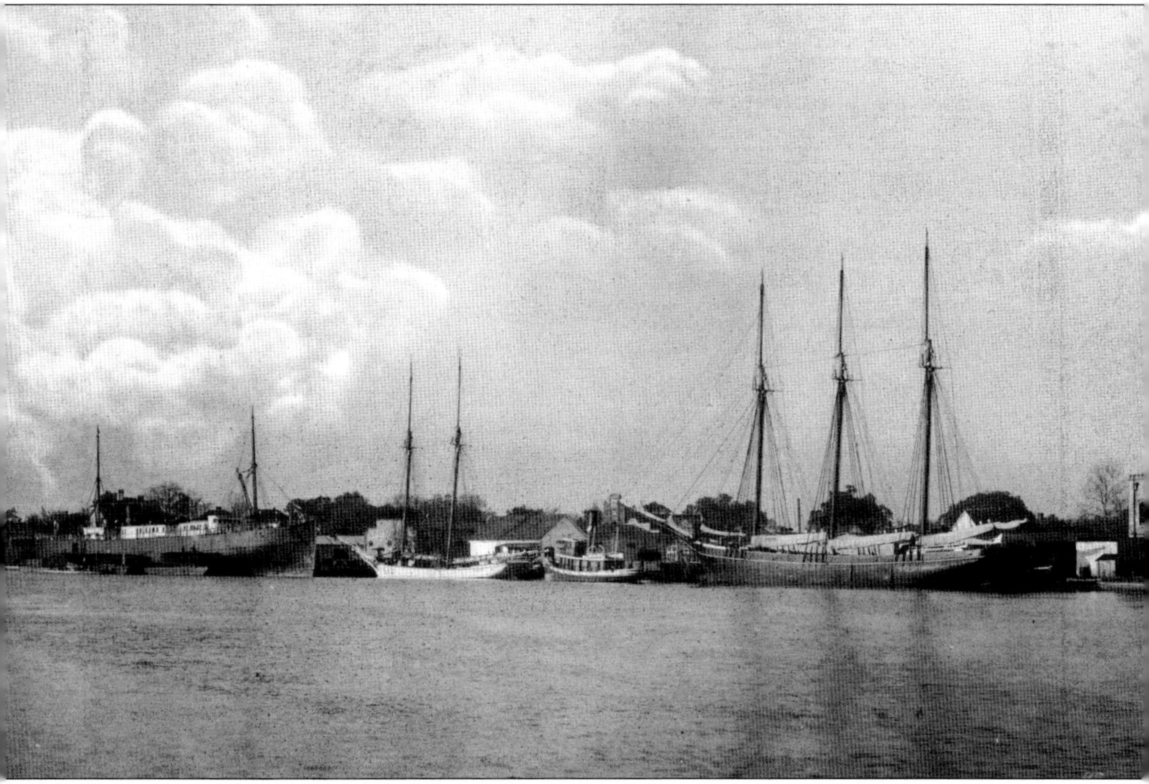

This picture was taken from the north side of Goat Island, looking across the Sampit River at the docks in Georgetown. Moored bow to stern is a three-masted schooner, tug boat, barges, a two-masted schooner, and a steam-powered merchant ship. This 1900s scene was typical of the maritime activity in Georgetown. The vessels represent the past and present, as steam was replacing sail power and wooden barges were being replaced with steel barges.

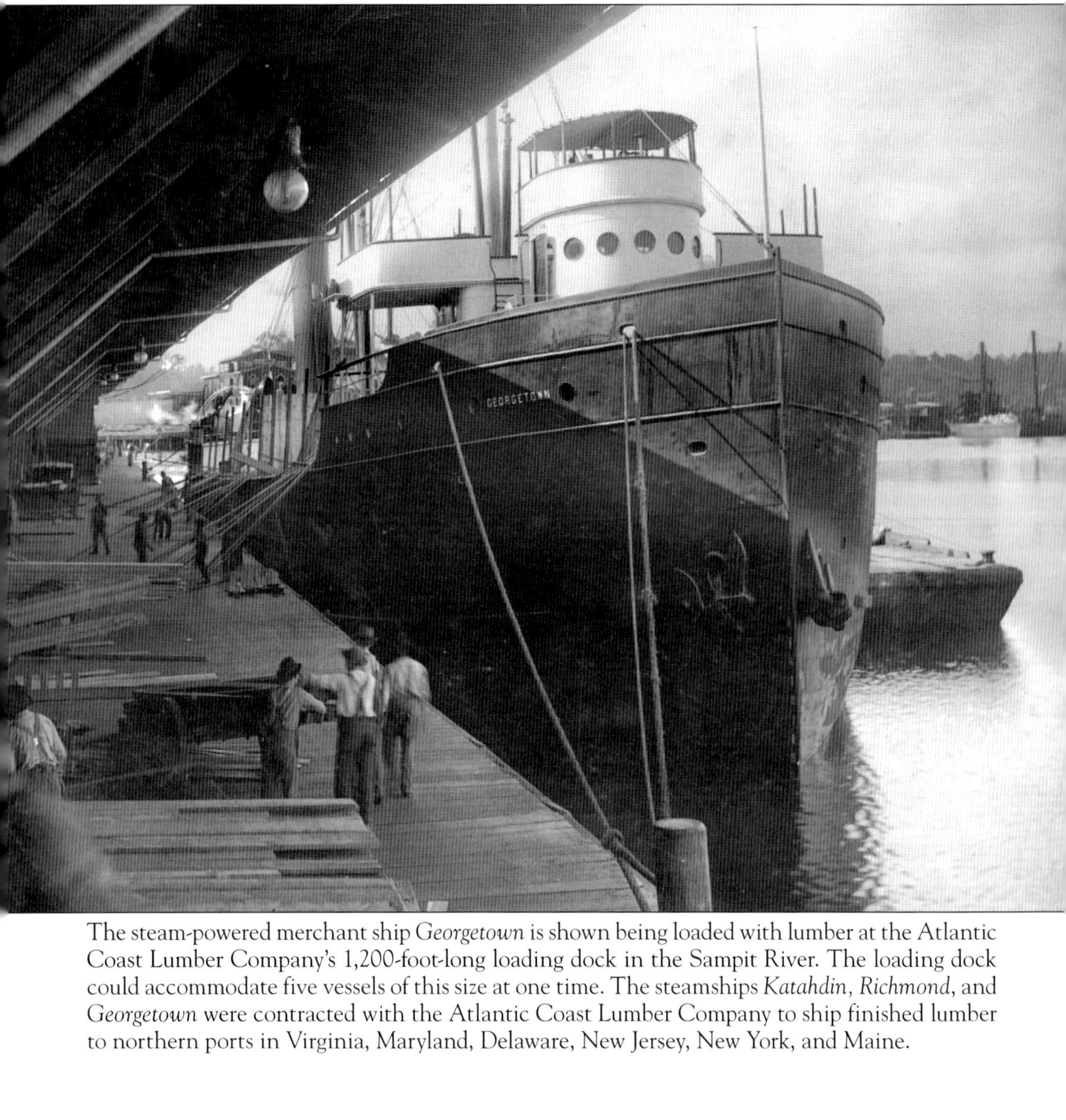

The steam-powered merchant ship *Georgetown* is shown being loaded with lumber at the Atlantic Coast Lumber Company's 1,200-foot-long loading dock in the Sampit River. The loading dock could accommodate five vessels of this size at one time. The steamships *Katahdin*, *Richmond*, and *Georgetown* were contracted with the Atlantic Coast Lumber Company to ship finished lumber to northern ports in Virginia, Maryland, Delaware, New Jersey, New York, and Maine.

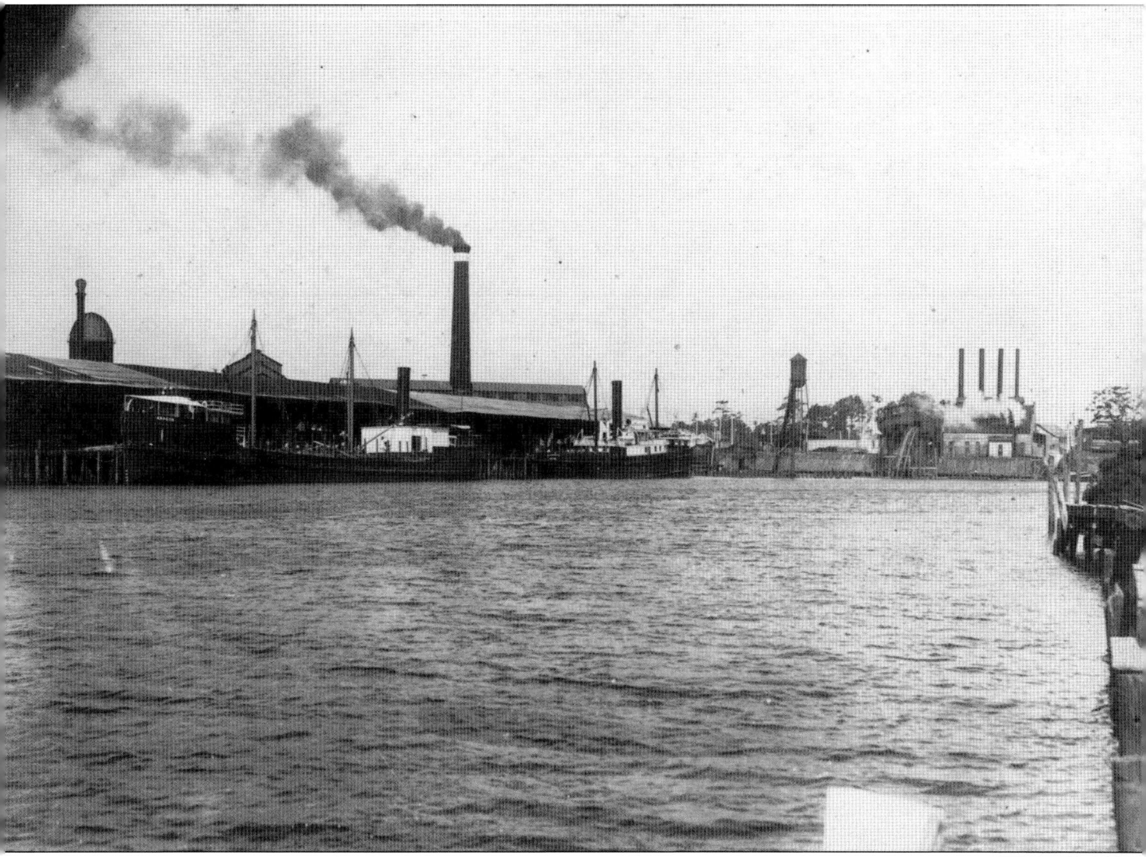

Loading lumber at the Atlantic Coast Lumber Company is the merchant steamer *Waccamaw*. The *Waccamaw* and the *Georgetown* were 256-foot-long twin-screw steel ships with 42 feet of beam at mid-ship and a 14-foot-deep cargo hold. These two ships could carry almost five times the amount of cargo than a sailing schooner and could make the trip from Georgetown to New York in three days.

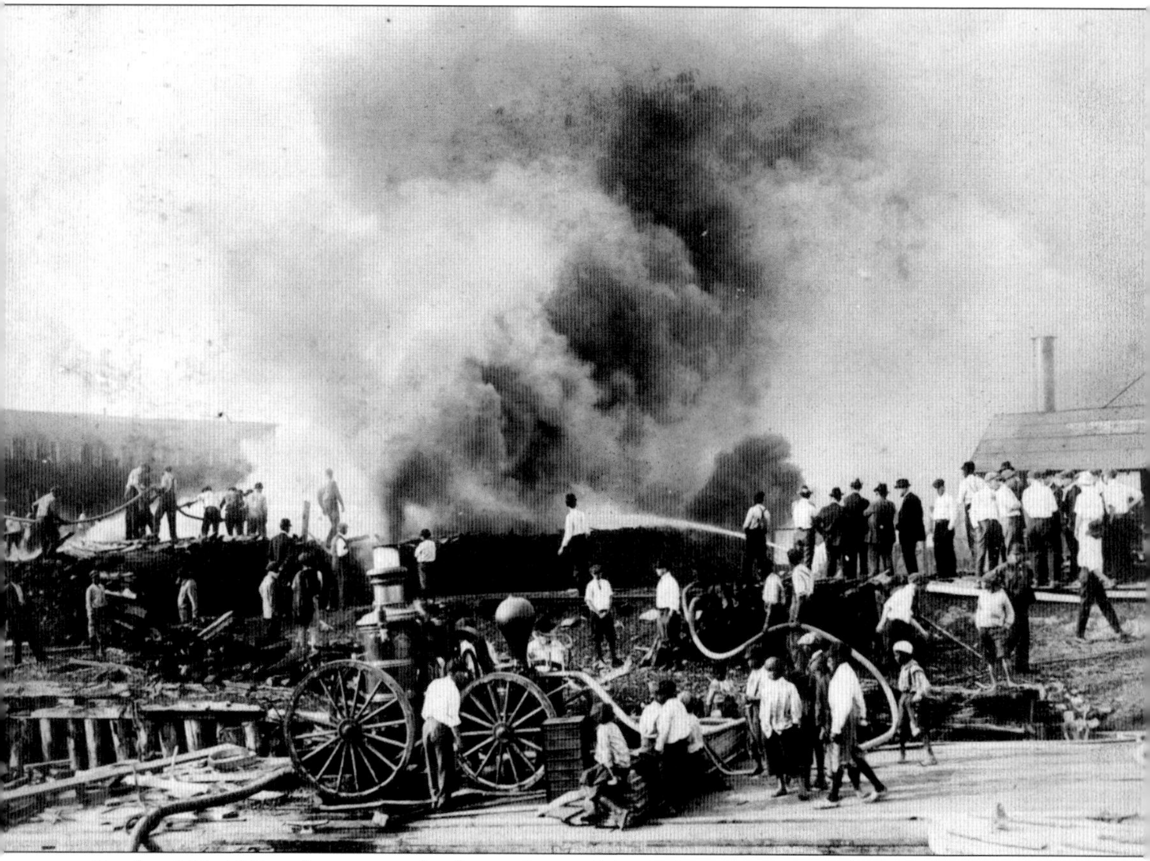

On April 21, 1913, a devastating fire burned two of the Atlantic Coast Lumber Company sawmill complexes. Fanned by strong northerly winds, the fire engulfed the two mills and the adjacent boiler buildings. It was reported that it all burned to the ground in less than three hours. Fire brigades from Georgetown and Atlantic Coast Lumber Company were hampered by the strong north winds and were no match for the fire, which quickly destroyed half the production capability of the mill.

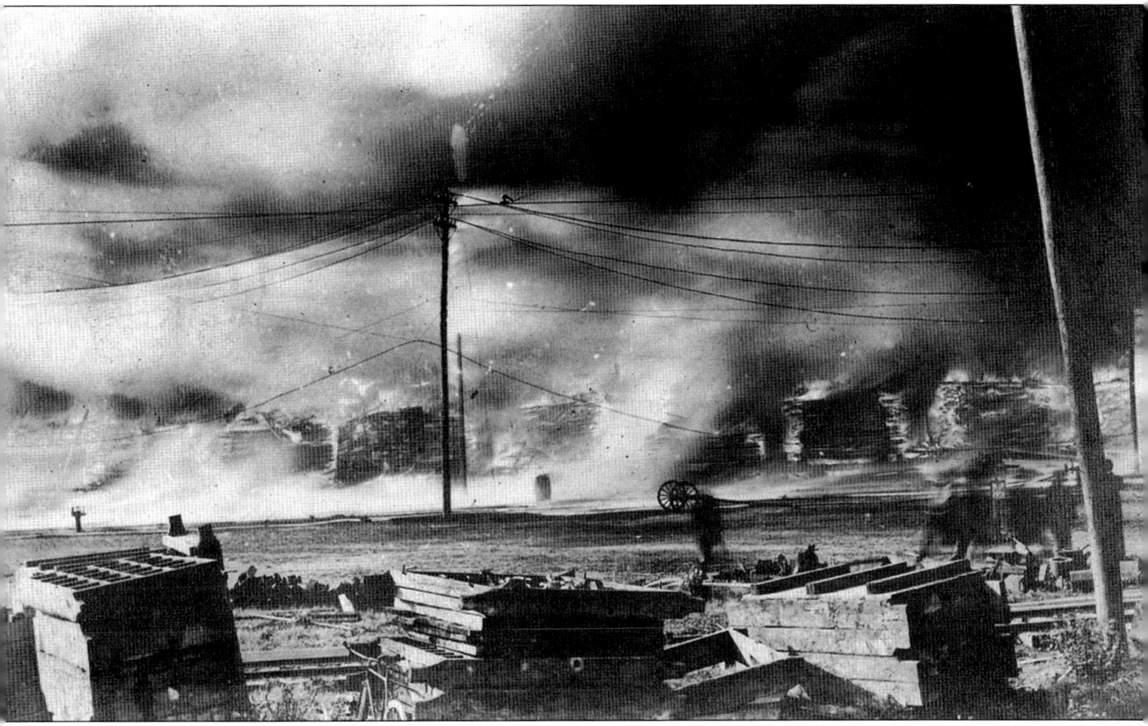

Several men are a blur in the lower right part of this picture as they rush to do what they can in the face of the inferno that consumed the Atlantic Coast Lumber Company mills. Little could be done by human effort as the winds fanned the flames. The mills occupied many acres along both sides of the Sampit River. By 1914, the export of millions of board feet of lumber made the ACL the largest mill on the entire eastern seaboard and perhaps in the United States. Rebuilding the mills took only one year. The ACL continued in operation until the economic effects of the Depression caused it to go under in 1932.

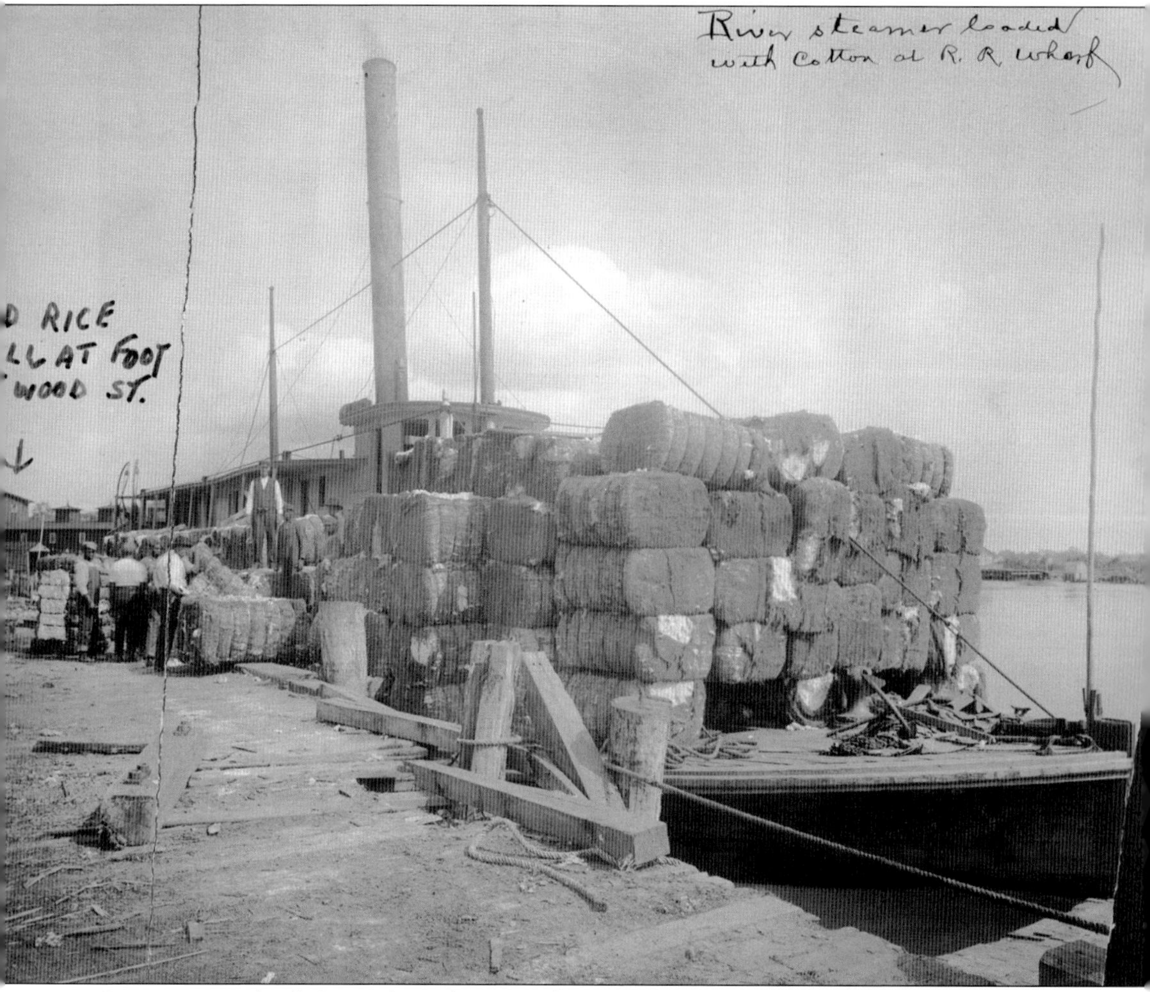

Cotton was indeed "king" from the several pictures showing the vast amount waiting to be shipped from Georgetown docks. The captain of this vessel may be the man wearing a vest and white shirt standing atop the bales of cotton. The old rice mill at the foot of Wood Street is indicated on the left.

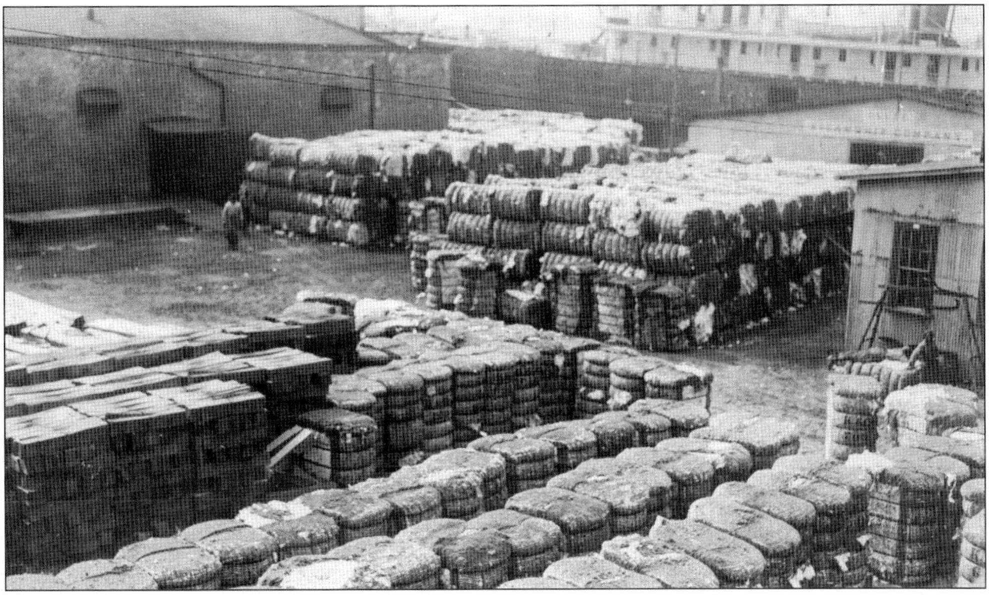

Bales of cotton wait to be shipped from the docks of the Clyde Steamship Company around 1903. In the fall of that year, large inventories of cotton begin to arrive in Georgetown from farms along the Pee Dee River and Waccamaw River basin. Cotton was shipped downriver on shallow draft steam-powered riverboats and then loaded on merchant freighters and railcars to be shipped to North and South Carolina cotton mills.

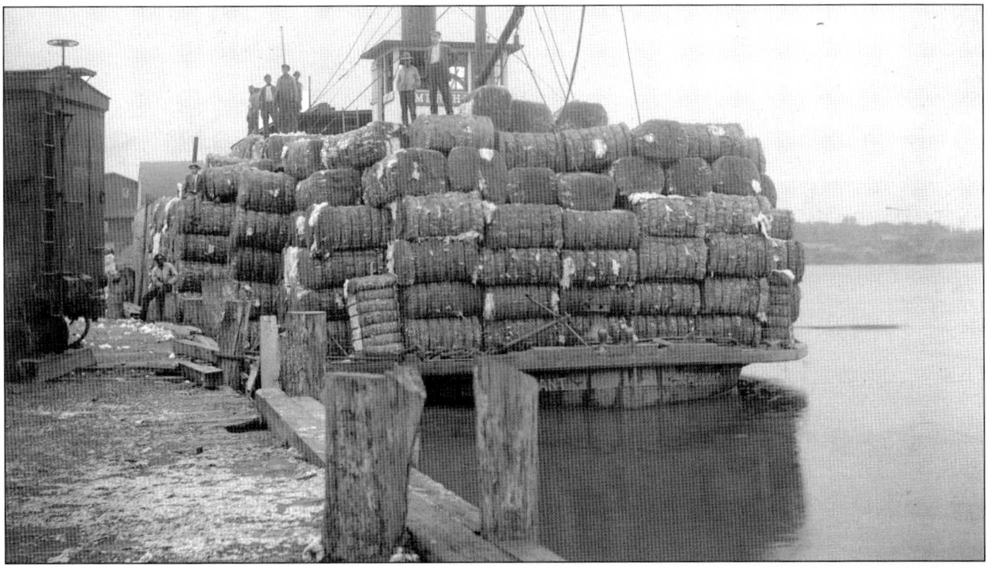

The steamer *Merchant* is shown loaded with cotton, probably picked up from loading docks up the Pee Dee and Waccamaw River. This vessel operated from the South Carolina Steamboat Company's wharf on the Sampit River. Shallow draft steamboats would carry fertilizer and farm supplies to cotton growers upriver and would return downriver with agricultural commodities for shipment. Cotton loaded on these steamboats would then be loaded on the larger seagoing vessels for shipment. Oftentimes cotton grown in South Carolina and shipped from Georgetown would be processed in a South Carolina cotton mill and would return to Georgetown as a finished product.

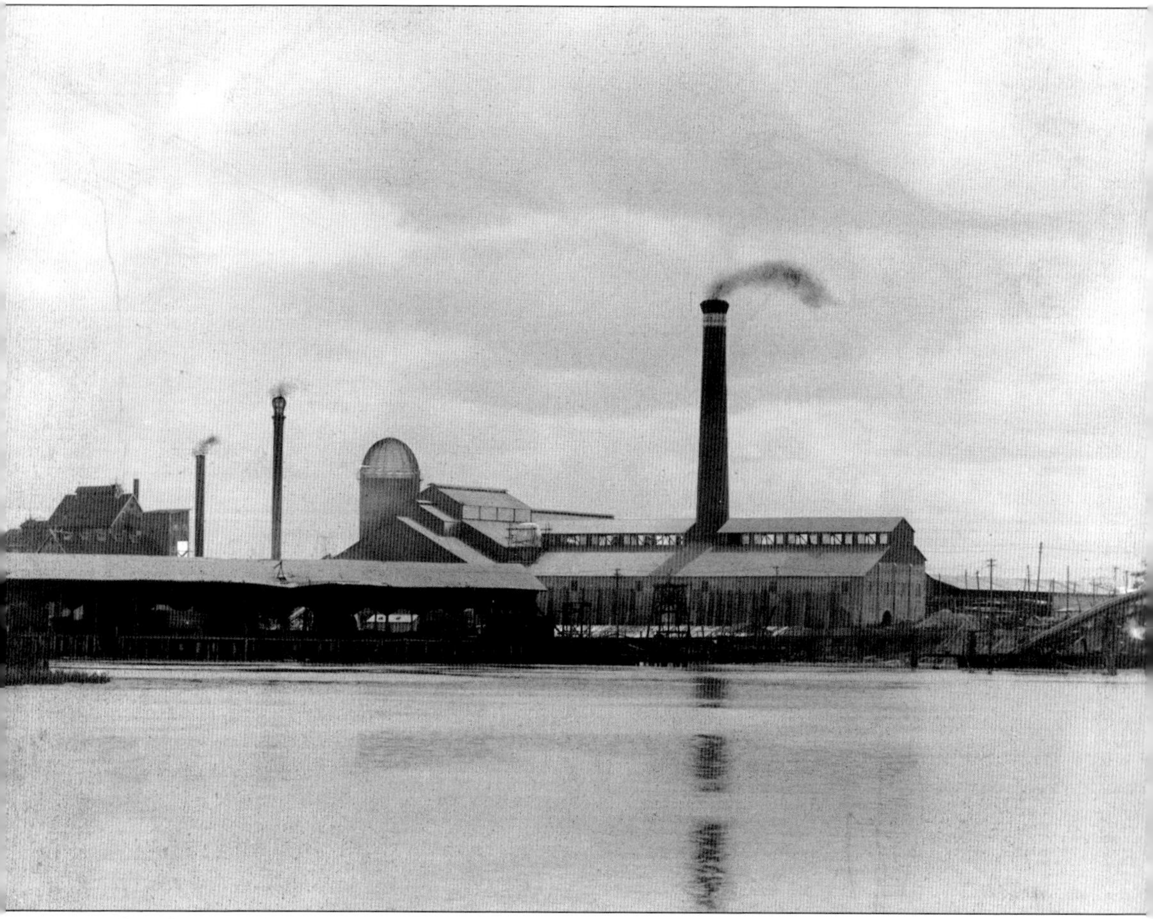

This photograph shows the E. I. Dupont alcohol processing plant located adjacent to the Atlantic Coast Lumber Company. The E. I. Dupont de Nemours Power Company contracted with the lumber company to buy wood waste and sawdust. This unusual industry distilled alcohol from fermented sawdust, which was used in the manufacture of smokeless gunpowder, and produced 2,000 gallons of alcohol a day.

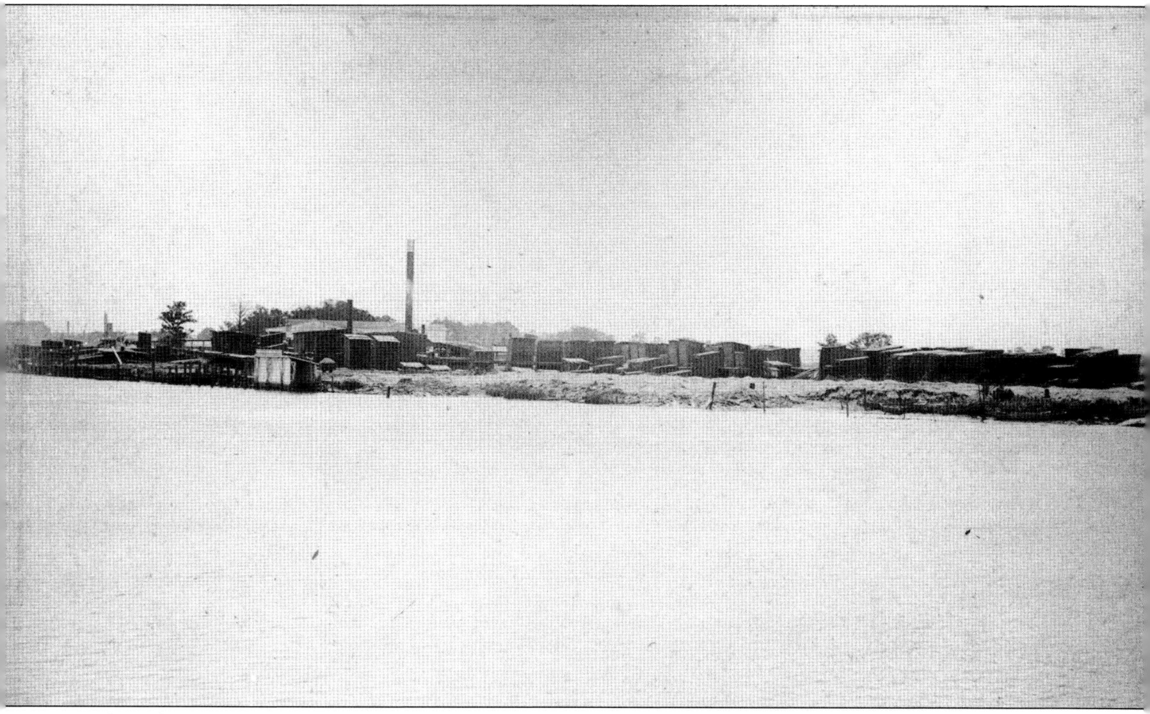

When this photograph was taken sometime after 1899 of the Gardner and Lacy Lumber Company, the peninsula of land in the Sampit River known as Goat Island was attached to the mainland on the southeast end. In July 1951, a channel was cut through the peninsula allowing larger vessels to avoid a hairpin turn in the river. The Gardner and Lacy Lumber Company occupied 15 acres of land and had a production of 45,000 feet of lumber and 70,000 cypress shingles per day.

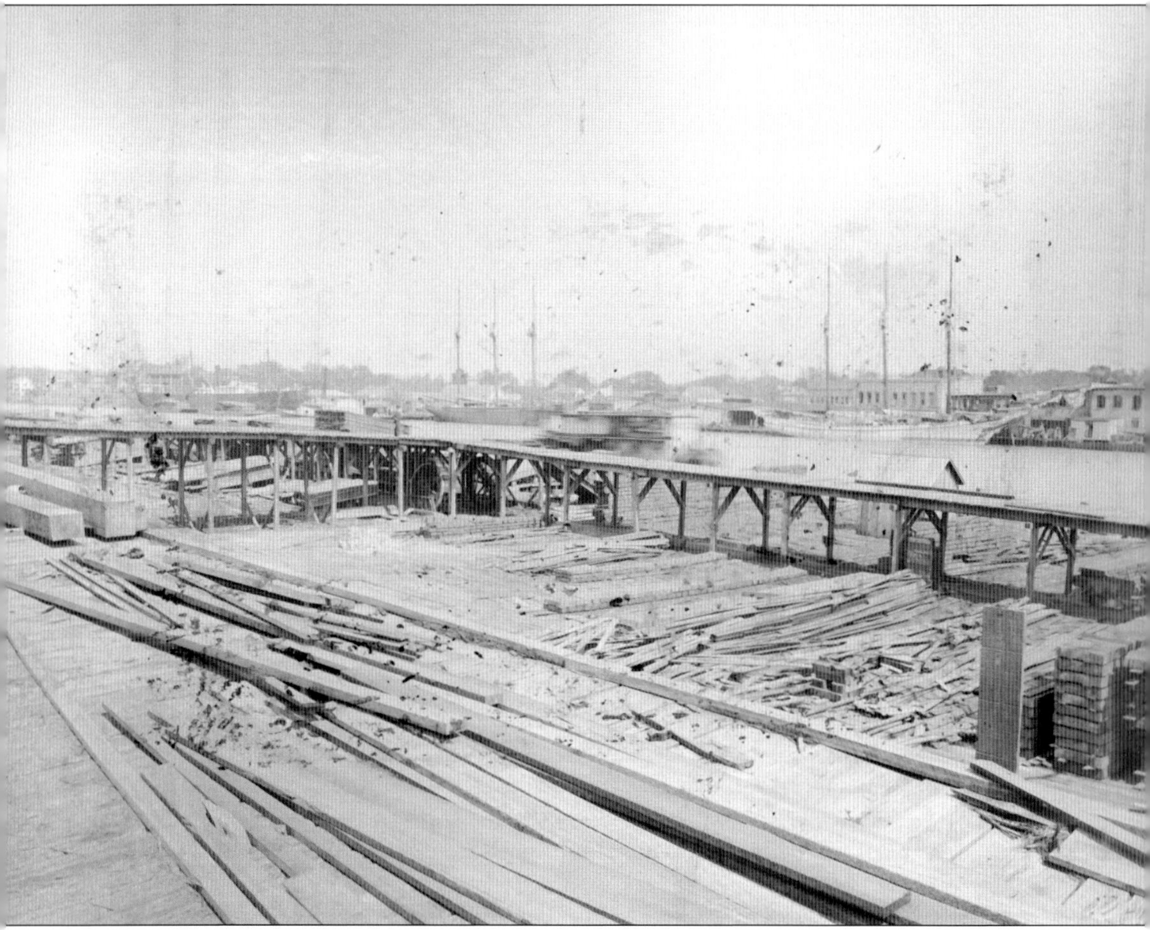

This is a view of the Gardner and Lacy Lumber Company, looking across the Sampit River toward the Georgetown city docks. This extensive lumber operation employed more than 225 men and only sawed cypress lumber. The lumber mill generated its own electrical power and had its own fully equipped fire department.

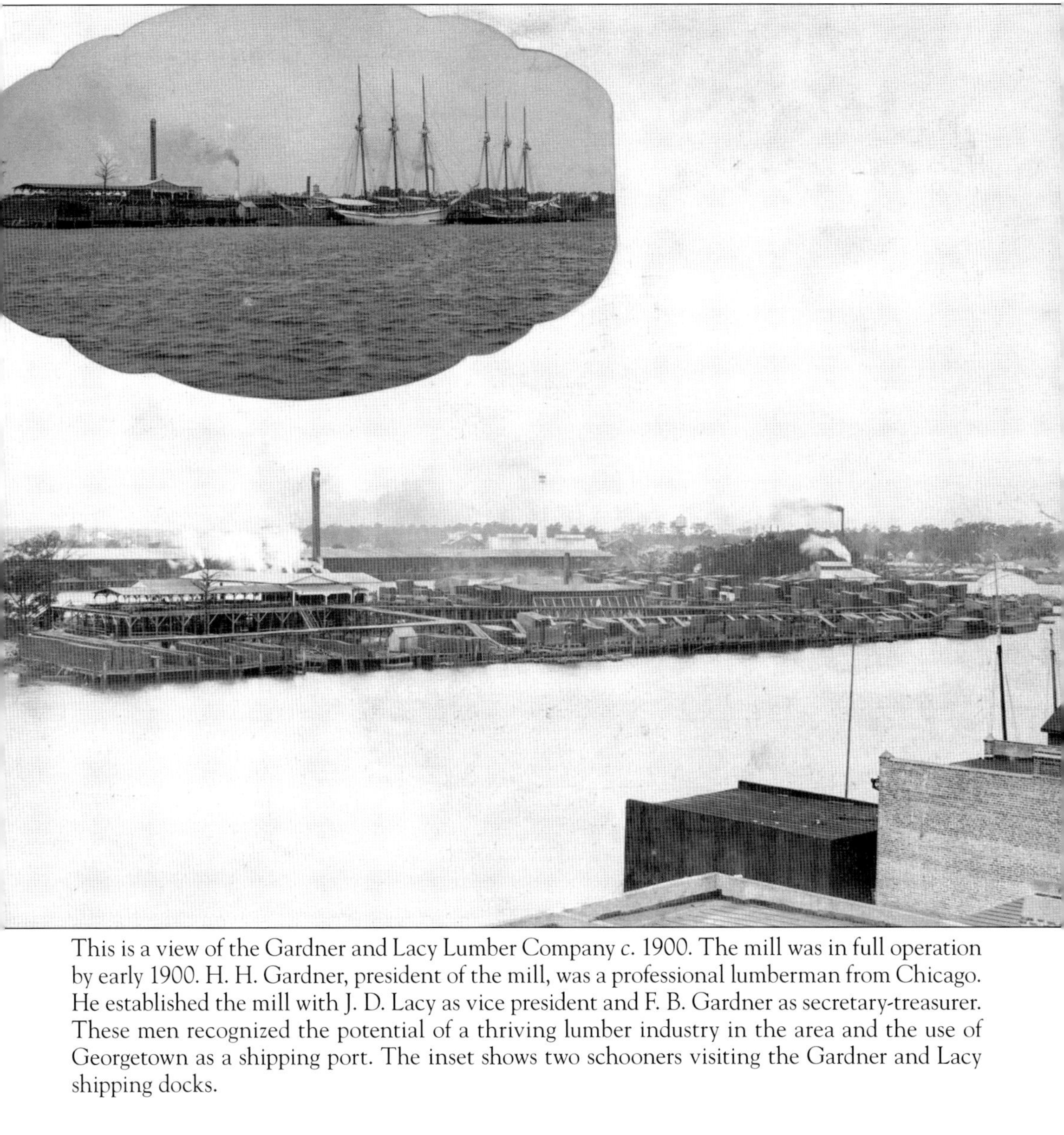

This is a view of the Gardner and Lacy Lumber Company *c.* 1900. The mill was in full operation by early 1900. H. H. Gardner, president of the mill, was a professional lumberman from Chicago. He established the mill with J. D. Lacy as vice president and F. B. Gardner as secretary-treasurer. These men recognized the potential of a thriving lumber industry in the area and the use of Georgetown as a shipping port. The inset shows two schooners visiting the Gardner and Lacy shipping docks.

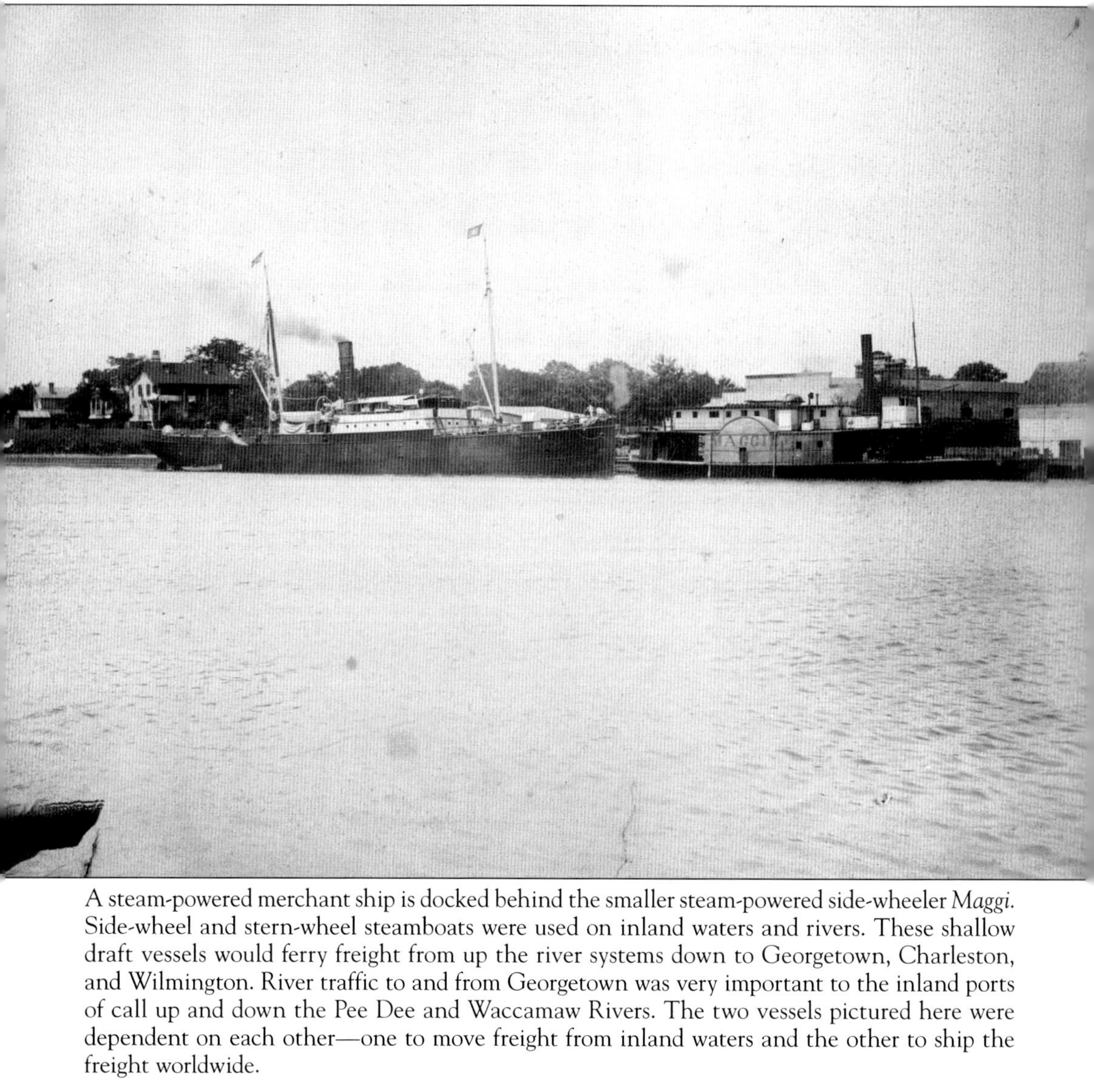

A steam-powered merchant ship is docked behind the smaller steam-powered side-wheeler *Maggi*. Side-wheel and stern-wheel steamboats were used on inland waters and rivers. These shallow draft vessels would ferry freight from up the river systems down to Georgetown, Charleston, and Wilmington. River traffic to and from Georgetown was very important to the inland ports of call up and down the Pee Dee and Waccamaw Rivers. The two vessels pictured here were dependent on each other—one to move freight from inland waters and the other to ship the freight worldwide.

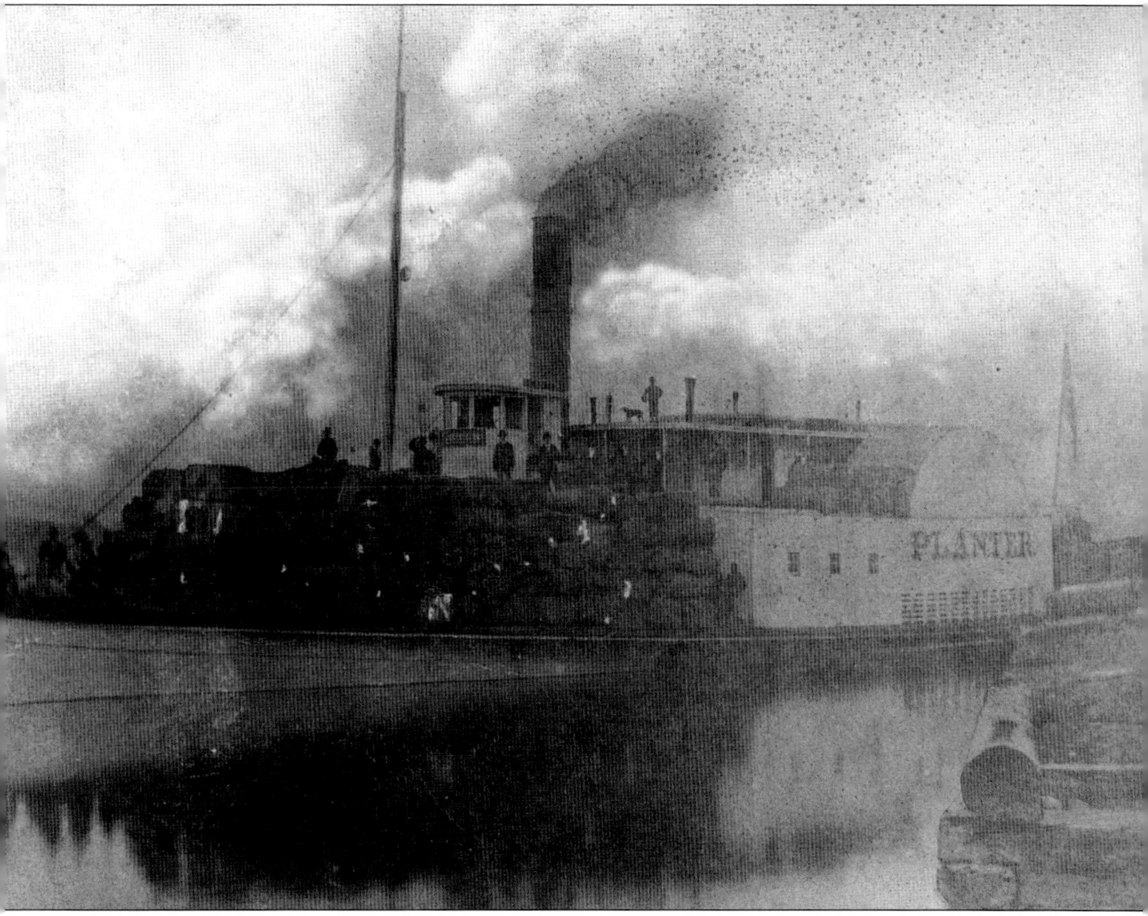

The steam-powered vessel *Planter* sits in Sampit River in Georgetown around 1870, waiting for its bales of cotton to be unloaded. The *Planter* was built in Charleston for inland commerce, and during the early years of the Civil War served as an armed transport vessel for the Confederate army. On May 13, 1862, the ship's African American pilot sailed the *Planter* out of Charleston harbor and turned the vessel over to federal forces. The steamship was part of the navy's South Atlantic blockading squadron. The *Planter* returned to commercial service and called on the port of Georgetown until it was lost at sea in 1876.

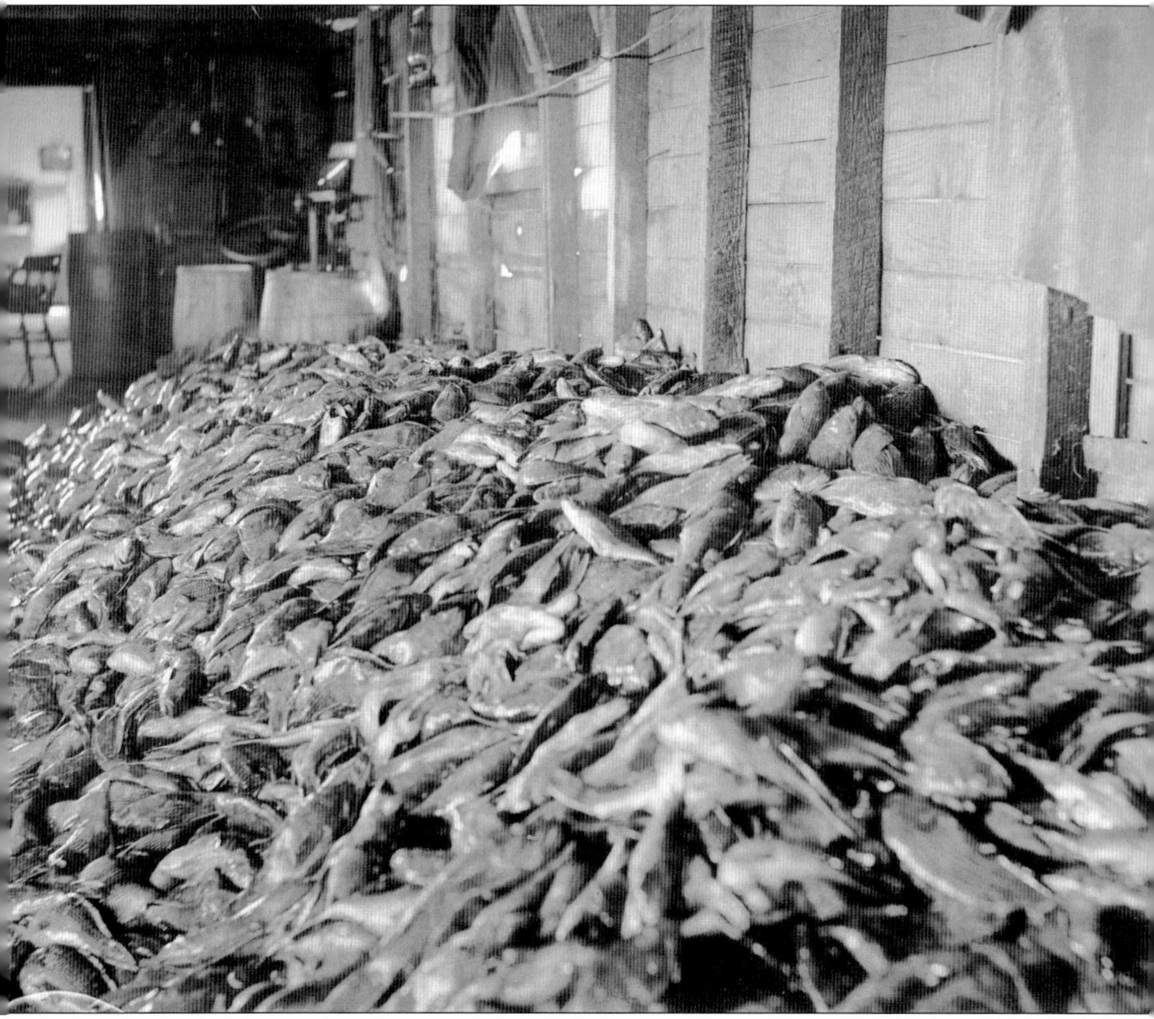

These fish, most likely American shad, were bountiful in Winyah Bay. Commercial fishing in the waters of Winyah Bay and adjoining rivers was a large part of the water-related industry in Georgetown in the 1890s. Large catches of shad were processed, packed, and shipped by railway express to destinations north and south. Shellfish, spots, croakers, mullet, and flounder were valuable commodities harvested in the bay waters and shipped from fish houses along the Georgetown waterfront.

Three

Recreation Heritage of Winyah Bay

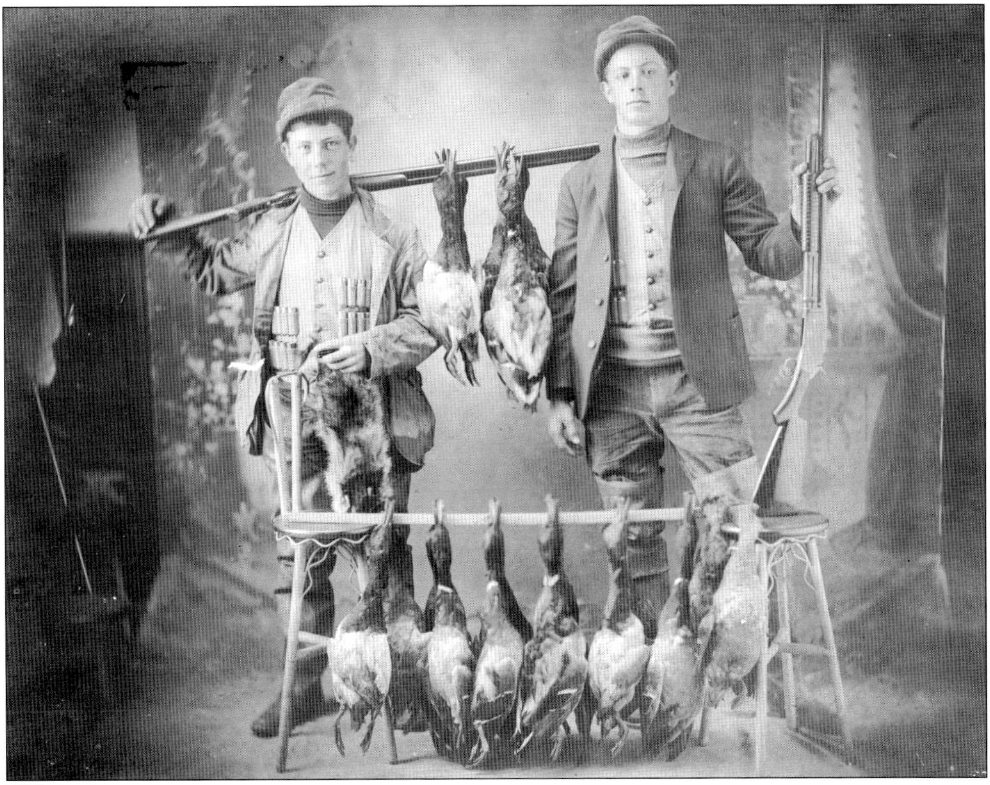

Mariners sailing into Winyah Bay from the Atlantic Ocean are greeted to a large expanse of water and shoreline, which has changed little since the first known mariners ventured into the bay. Other than the lighthouse on North Island and two homesites along shore of Hobcaw Barony, the north side of the bay remains natural. The southern shore has some development but for the most part is unchanged. The watershed of four rivers empty into Winyah Bay—Waccamaw, Pee Dee, Black, and Sampit. These rivers and adjoining tidal marshes are very productive habitat for fish, wintering waterfowl, and migratory shore birds. The waters of Winyah Bay were a destination for Native Americans seeking food for thousands of years. Sport hunting and fishing have been a pastime of citizens of Georgetown since the earliest settlers arrived. These two hunters were probably from out of town and wanted a picture for proof of their successful hunting trip in Georgetown.

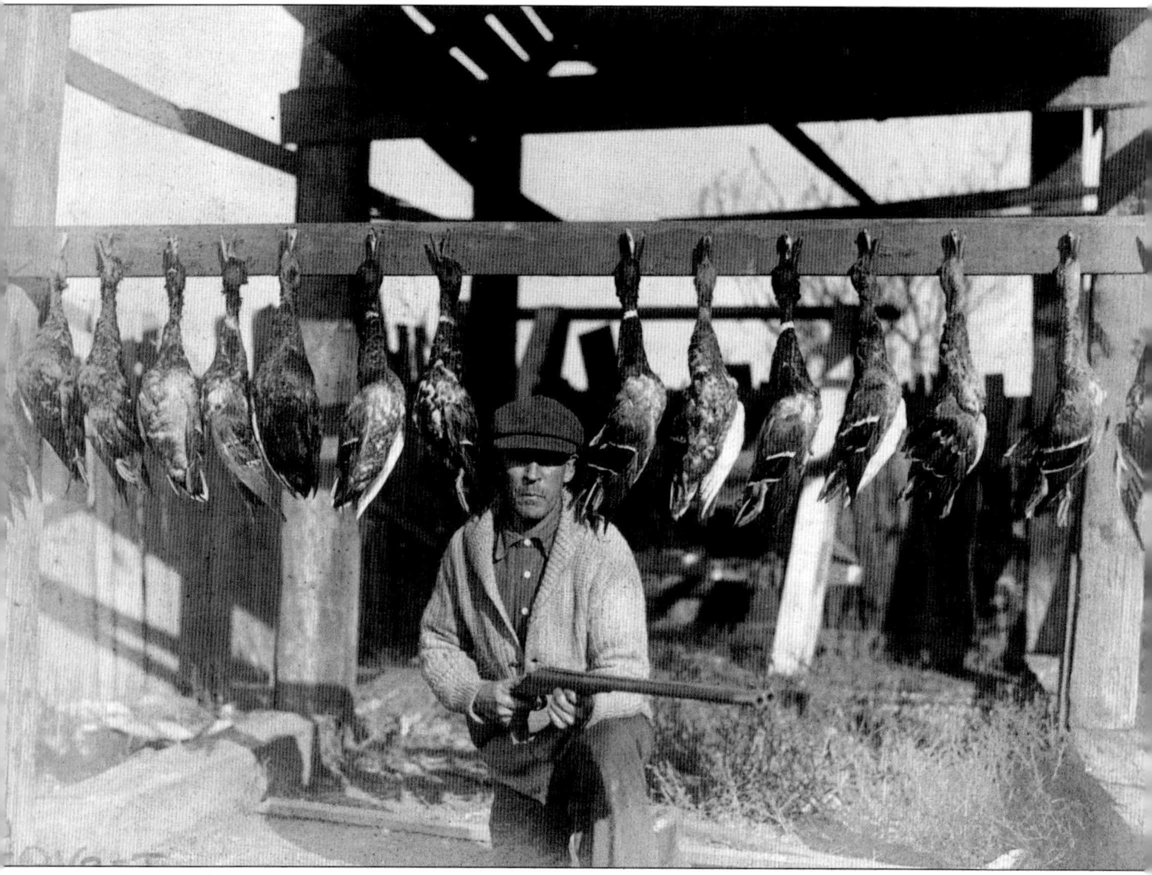

This local hunter had a successful day duck hunting. Area plantations had thousands of acres of abandoned rice fields. These old rice fields were great habitat for wintering waterfowl. Plantation owners prided themselves in having some of the best waterfowl hunting in the United States. Presidents, heads of state, and captains of industry frequented the local area just to hunt the thousands of ducks that wintered in and around Georgetown.

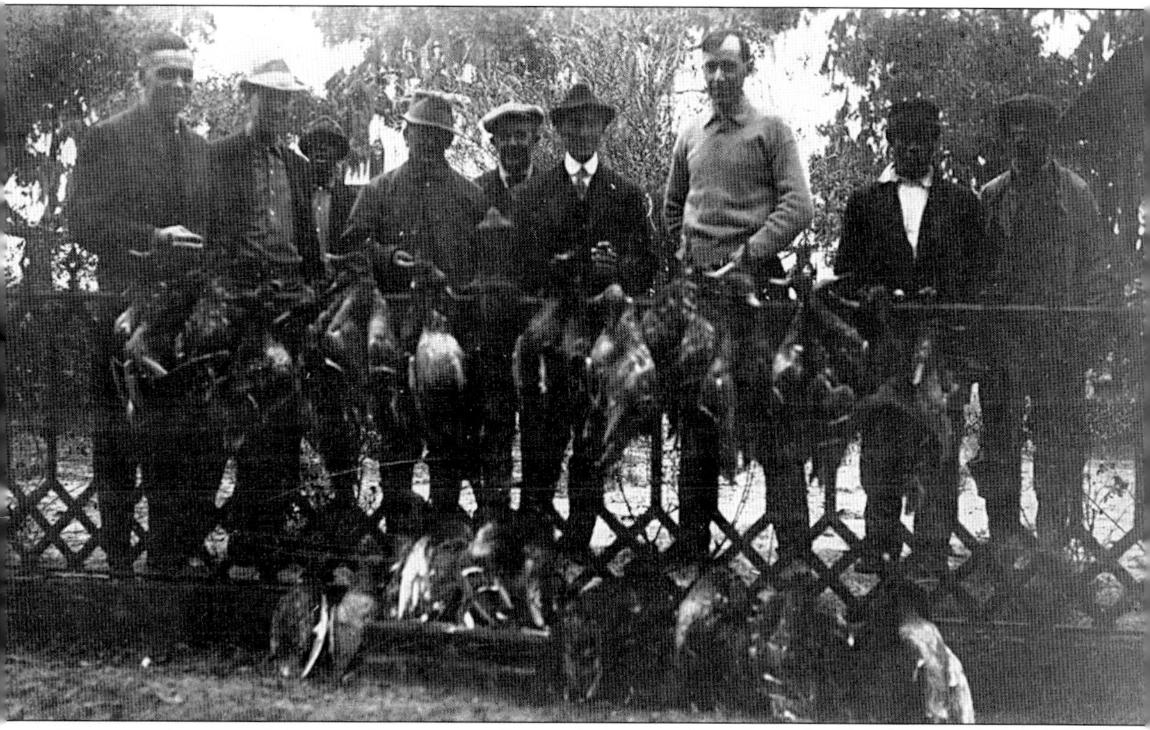

These gentlemen and their guides seem satisfied with their catch at the end of the day. During the wintertime, Georgetown was a very popular destination for wealthy Northerners who were guests at local plantations and gun clubs. Daily bag limits were plentiful during the early 1900s, and the Winyah Bay area wintered all species of waterfowl native to the Atlantic flyway. For decades after the Civil War, many of the former rice plantation houses sat unused, until a visit from Pres. Grover Cleveland in 1894. While hunting ducks as a guest on South Island, the president was tossed from a skiff in a stiff wind. This happy accident drew national attention to the sporting opportunities in the Georgetown area when news of his rescue made national headlines. The ready-made plantations were quickly bought up by rich Northerners, and many of the run down houses were saved.

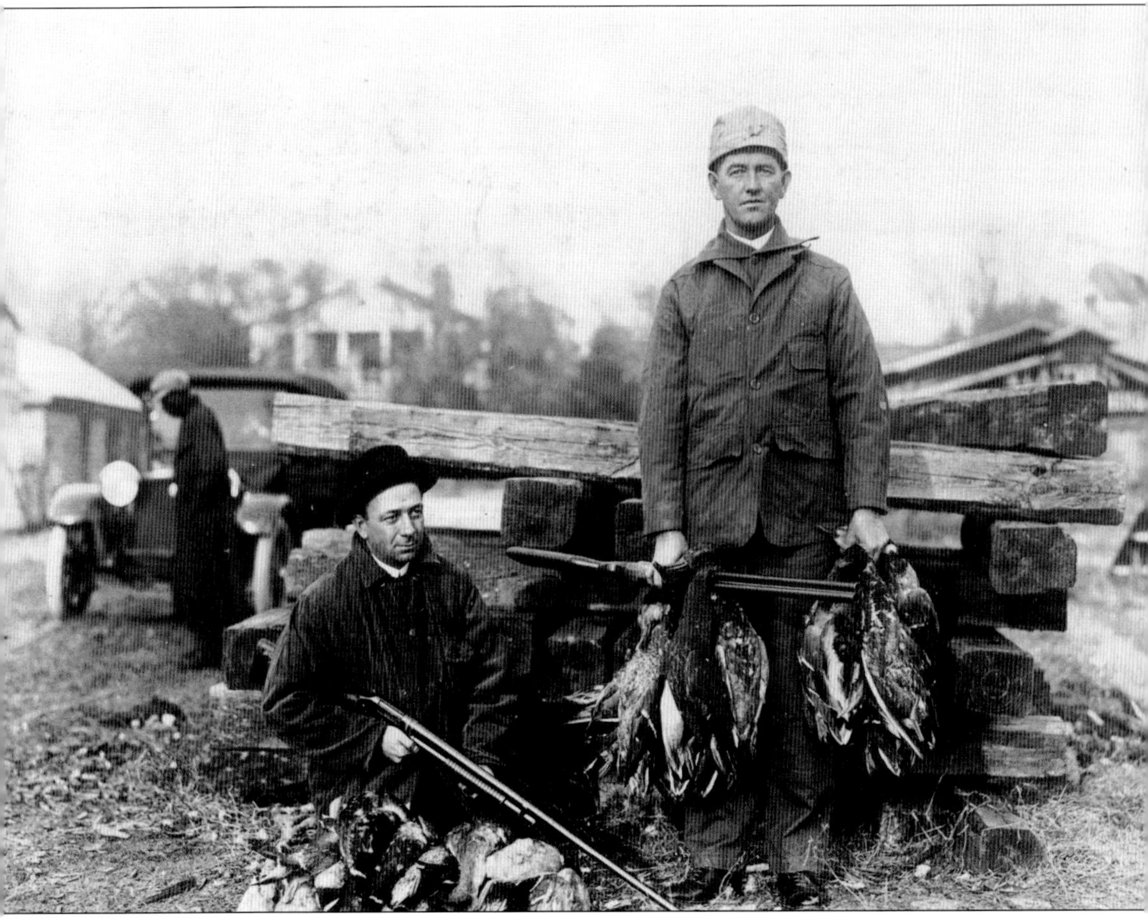

These two hunters pose with their harvest of ducks in front of a stack of railroad crossties. The ducks and the timbers were both commodities shipped from the Georgetown city docks. Railroad crossties manufactured and shipped from Georgetown supported the rails that brought the sportsmen, and then shipped the ducks to northern markets. Note the gun the hunter on the left is holding appears to have an extended magazine, which would enable the hunter to fire multiple shots at the ducks.

Edgar Norton Beaty a well-dressed fisherman of the early 1900s, shows off a large channel bass, probably caught in the waters of Winyah Bay. Sport fishing in Winyah Bay was a favorite pastime around Georgetown for both local and visiting sportsmen. Large catches of channel bass provided sport and food for fishermen and a source of income for local guides and fish houses.

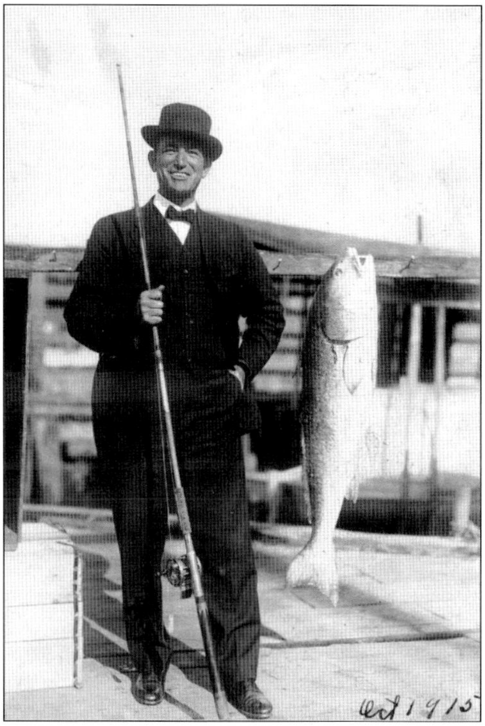

This waterfront scene, taken on the docks of Georgetown, shows a group of men posing with a string of fish. From the looks of the string and the number of fishermen, it seems that each man will go home with a fish. They were probably caught on the sailing vessel pictured, and men were probably the crew that worked on the boat.

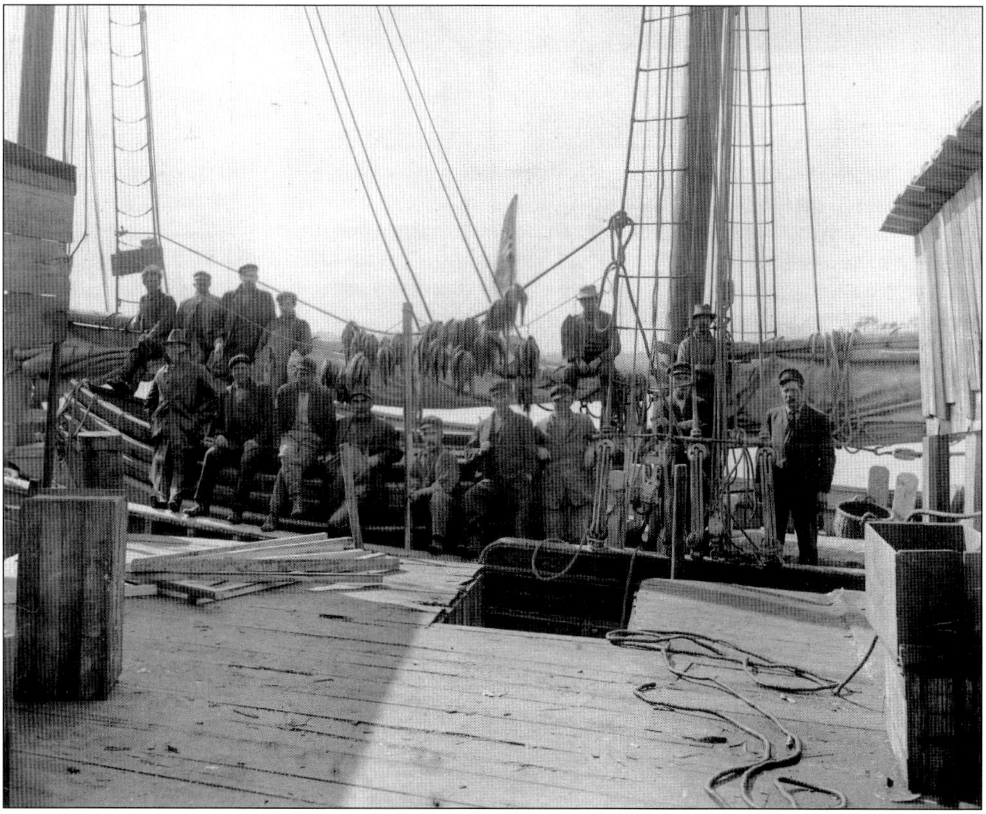

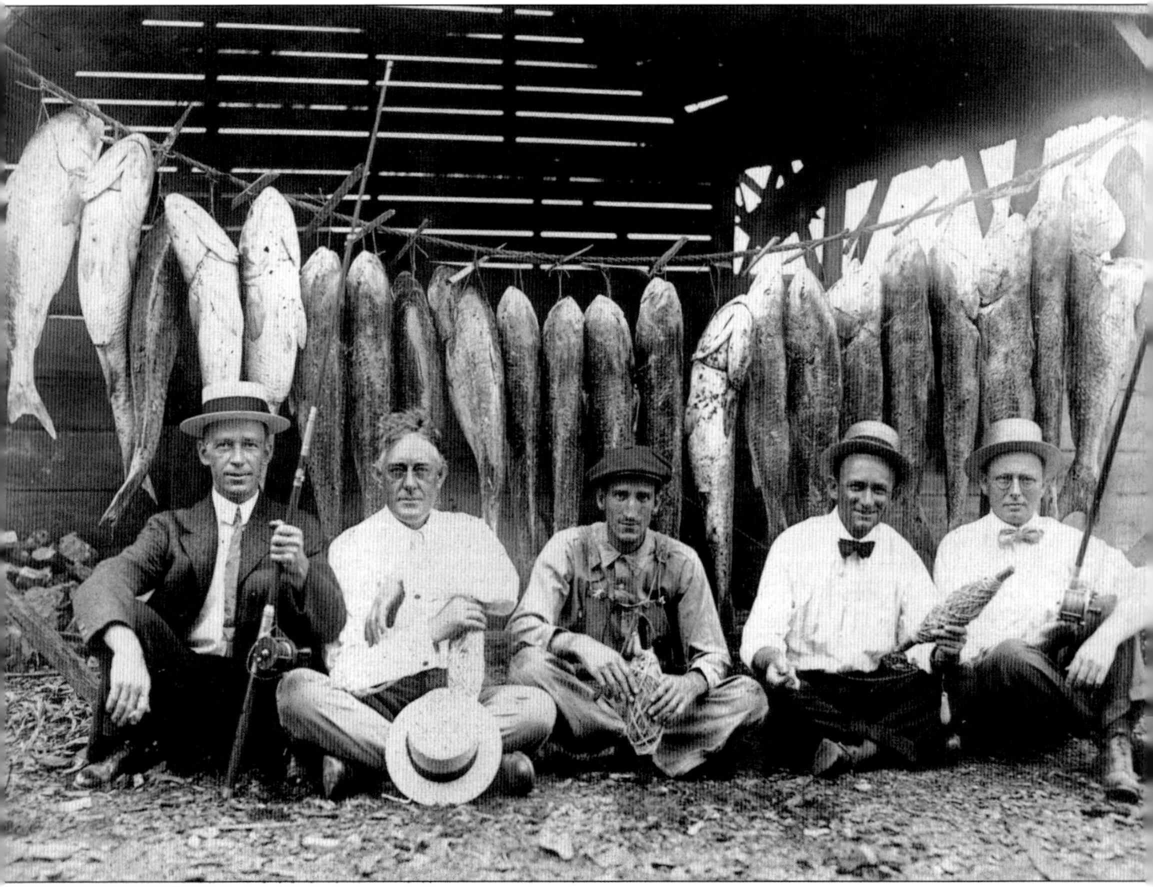

These fishermen appear to have just returned from a successful fishing trip in waters adjacent to Winyah Bay. The man in the middle of the photograph appears to have been the guide for the four well-dressed sportsmen. It has been speculated the man second from the left with his hat off looks very much like Franklin Roosevelt. Georgetown was well known up and down the Atlantic coast as a good place to fish. In 1883, port records show that fish, oysters, and game shipped from Georgetown had a value of $25,000.

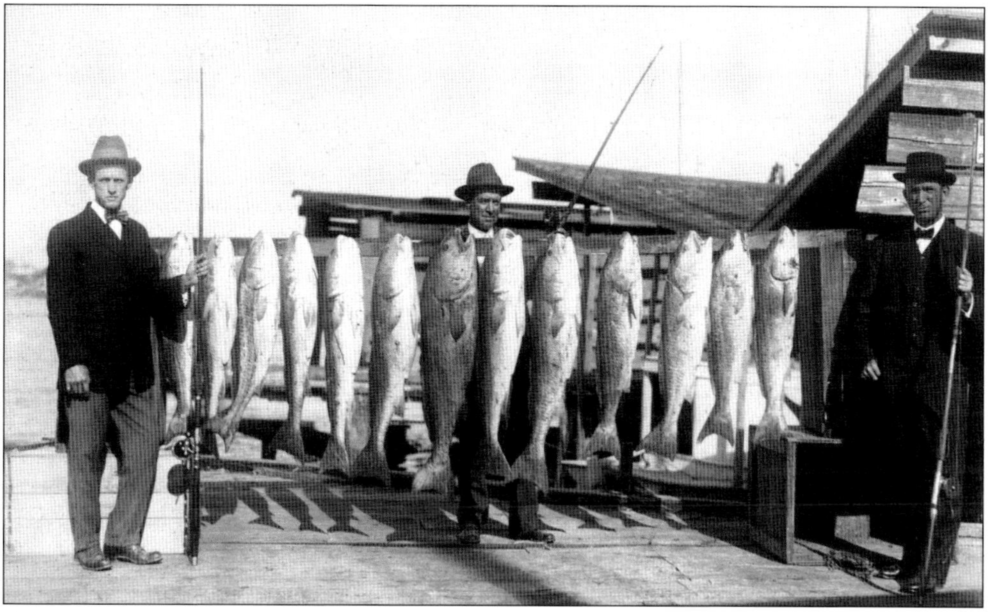

This photograph must have been a posed picture of some Georgetown gentlemen with a large catch of channel bass. These well-dressed men may not have been the anglers that caught this string of fish, but they appear to be proud of the catch. This impressive catch of channel bass was not unusual for the waters of Winyah Bay.

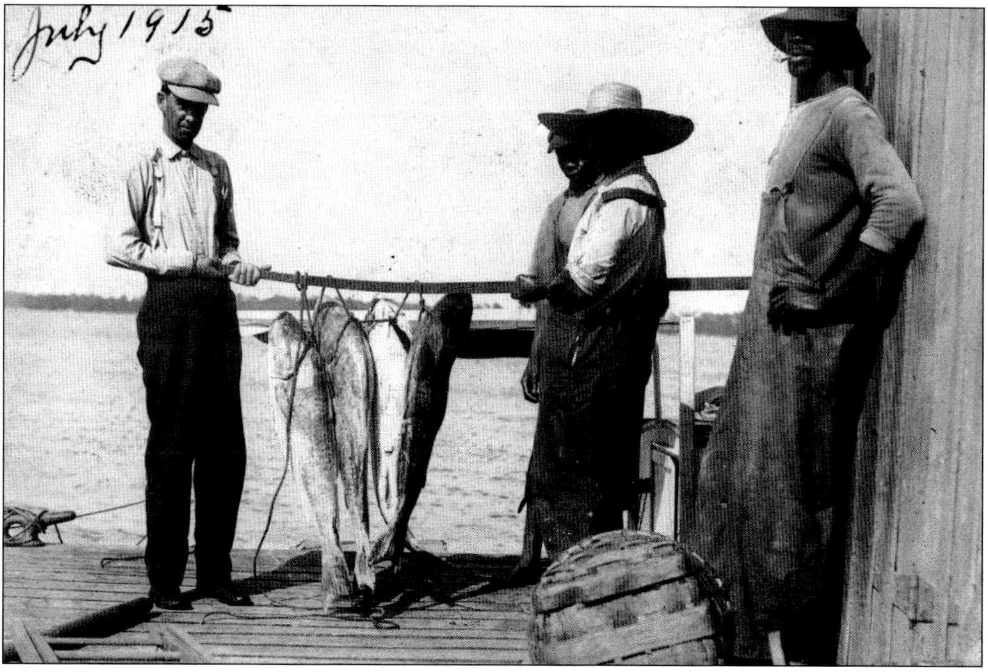

These fishermen have more than enough fish to fry. E. G. Ford and George E. Herriot were two of Georgetown's more prominent black businessmen. They owned and ran the largest fishing operation in Georgetown. These two men owned more than 75 small fishing boats and maintained their own fish-packing and shipping operation. It is likely that this photograph was taken at their loading dock on the Sampit River in the early 1900s.

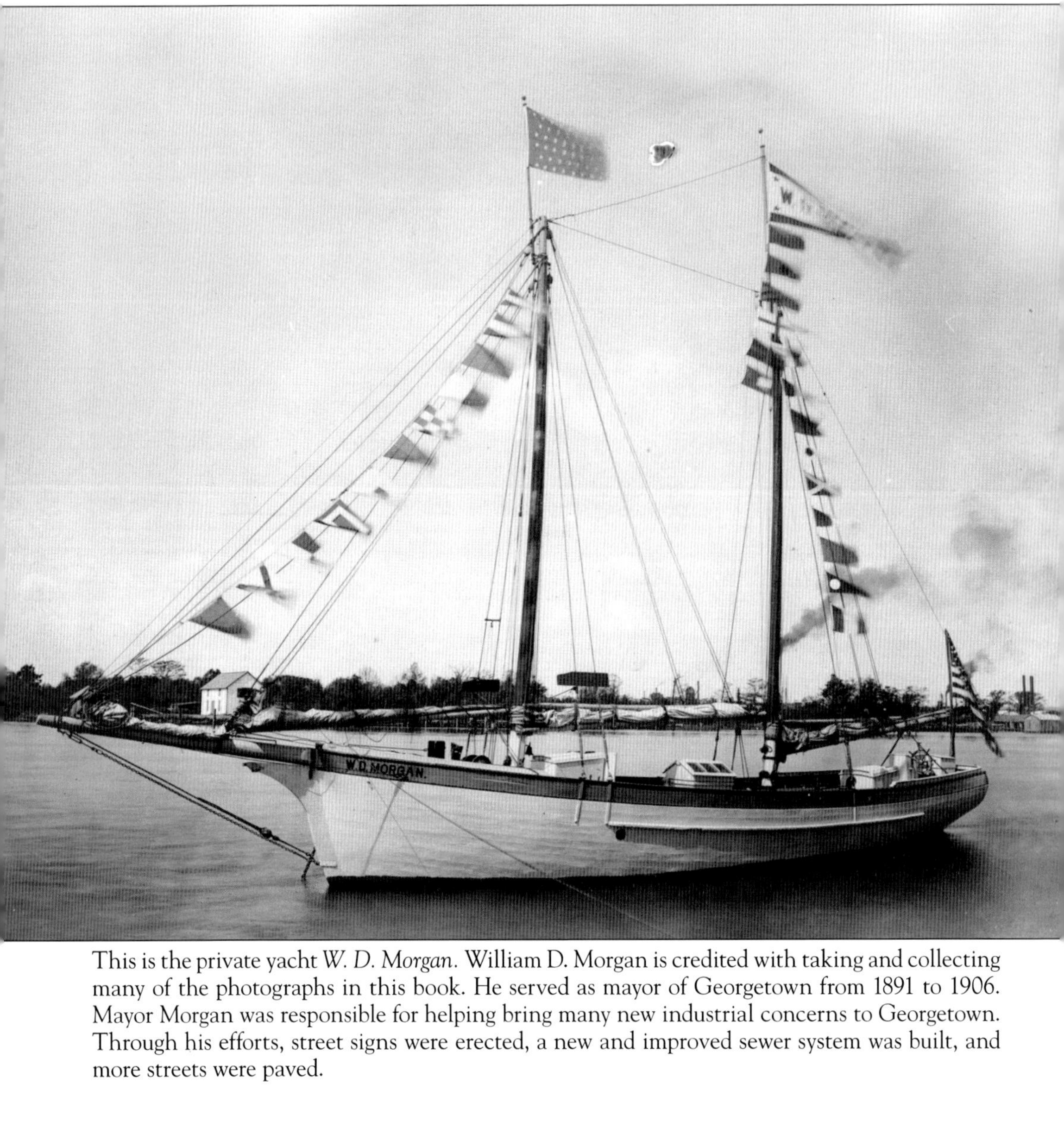

This is the private yacht *W. D. Morgan*. William D. Morgan is credited with taking and collecting many of the photographs in this book. He served as mayor of Georgetown from 1891 to 1906. Mayor Morgan was responsible for helping bring many new industrial concerns to Georgetown. Through his efforts, street signs were erected, a new and improved sewer system was built, and more streets were paved.

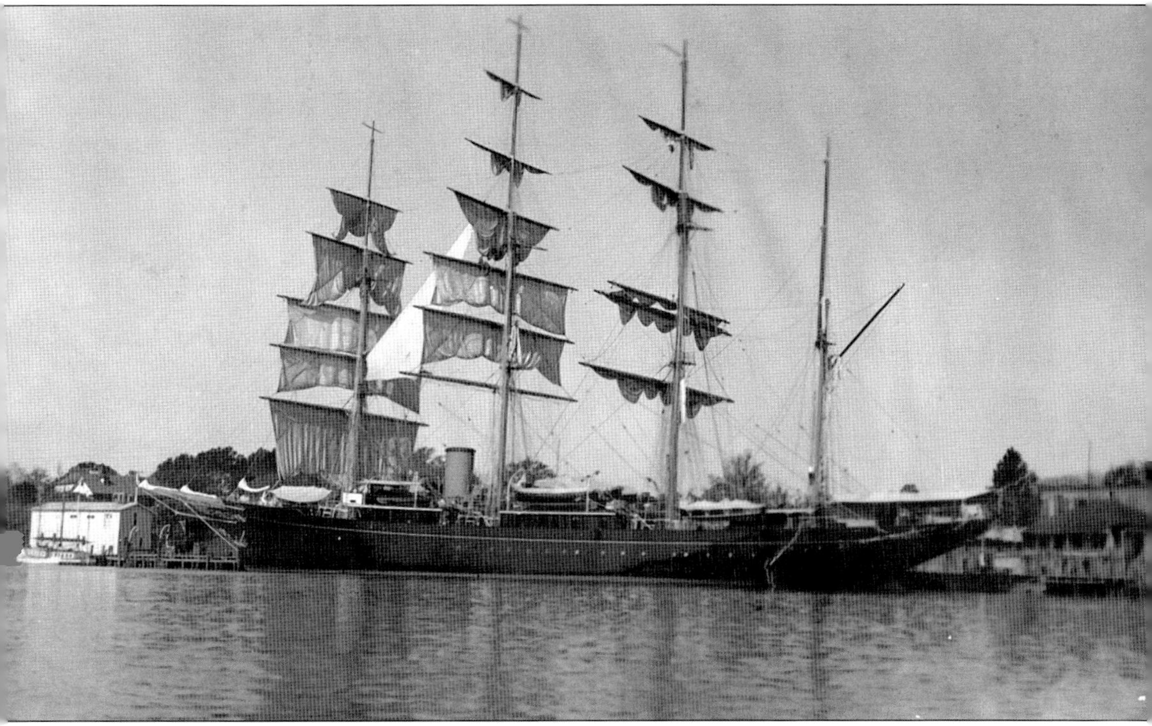

The *Sea Cloud*, one of the largest power-auxiliary yachts ever built, is shown moored in Georgetown. This large four-masted vessel was owned by E. F. Hutton and his wife, Majorie Merriweather Post Hutton. The yacht was 316 feet long and had a beam of 49 feet. The diesel-powered propulsion system and light plant were the most modern of its time (around 1930). Large private yachts often stopped in Georgetown. The owners of these yachts were often guests at local plantations, such as Arcadia Plantation, owned by the Vanderbilt family, and Hobcaw Barony, the home of Bernard Baruch.